ANCIENT IRELAND
LIFE BEFORE THE CELTS

Laurence Flanagan

Gill Books

Published in paperback 2000 by
Gill Books
Hume Avenue
Park West
Dublin 12
www.gillbooks.ie
Gill Books is an imprint of M. H. Gill & Co.
© Laurence Flanagan 1998
978 0 7171 2433 6
First published in hard cover 1998
Design and print origination by Carole Lynch
Printed by SprintPrint, Dublin

This book is typeset in 11/12 pt Garamond

*The paper used in this book is made from the
wood pulp of managed forests. For every
tree felled, at least one tree is planted,
thereby renewing natural resources.*

A CIP catalogue record for this book is available
from the British Library.

16 15 14 13 12

This book is dedicated to my cousin Ruaidhrí de Valera, Professor of Archaeology at University College, Dublin, who died on 28 October 1978.

Tá na daoine greannmhara uilig sa tsíoraíocht.

CONTENTS

PLATES

ACKNOWLEDGMENTS

The author wishes to express his gratitude to the following friends and colleagues, or their representatives, for permission to reproduce illustrations credited to them in the captions:

Arthur ApSimon, Humphrey Case, Seamus Caulfield, David Clarke, Pat Collins*, Caroline Earwood, George Eogan, Estyn Evans*, Peter Harbison, Michael Herity, Ivor Herring, Rhoda Kavanagh, Chris Lynn, Brian O'Kelly, Claire O'Kelly, Seán Ó Nualláin, Brendan Ó Riordáin, Barry Raftery, Michael Ryan, Alison Sheridan, Derek Simpson, John Waddell, Dudley Waterman*, Peter Woodman and to others whom I have been unable to contact or who have been inadvertently overlooked.

The appearance of * after an entry indicates that the drawing/s in questions is 'Crown Copyright Reserved' and is/are reproduced with the permission of the Controller of Her Britannic Majesty's Stationery Office.

The author is particularly grateful to Mrs Deirdre Crone of the Department of Archaeology, Ulster Museum, Belfast, who for many years delightfully embellished his publications with her tasteful and accurate illustrations.

He would also like to record his thanks to the following for assistance with the acquisition of photographs: Miss Sinéad Mac Cartan, Department of Archaeology, Ulster Museum, Belfast; Mr Nick Brannon and Miss Gail Pollock, Historic Monuments and Buildings of the Environment Service for Northern Ireland; Mrs Mary Cahill of the Irish Antiquities Division of the National Museum of Ireland, Dublin; and Mr John Scarry, Dúchas, The Heritage Service, Dublin.

PART 1

THE ARCHAEOLOGY

1

INTRODUCTION

The discipline that helps us to recognise the artefacts, monuments and events in an Ireland that was not merely pre-Christian but was fairly certainly pre-Celtic as well is archaeology.

Many years ago a young, possibly slightly arrogant—certainly self-confident—archaeologist defined archaeology as 'the study of social and economic history through the actual commerciable products of society—or in other words the story of Man's attempts to keep the wolf from the door by means of better doors and better wolf-traps.' Thirty years later I doubt if I would change a word of that definition, except by pointing out that 'commerciable products' includes not only the obvious, such as food, tools, and housing, but also things like tombs and temples, which, even if they have no resale value, have certainly incurred costs in the form of time, labour, and energy.

It is necessary always to remember that although the flint tools, pots, tombs, house plans and decoration so frequently illustrated in archaeological text-books are important, they are important primarily as documents of social history—as clues to how their makers and users eked out a precarious living or enjoyed a lavish life-style. In a photograph of a funerary pot containing the cremated bones of what once was a human being, it is the cremated bones that are vitally important, not the pot: it is primarily important as a sort of fingerprint of the deceased, providing clues about who or what he or she was, how they might have lived, and, finally, how they might have ended up inside it.

ARCHAEOLOGICAL EVIDENCE

Despite the importance of the human being, whether cremated and inside a pot or not—since, as far as we are concerned, prehistoric humans are totally mute and have left no record of their feelings or of their attitudes to life or death or to their fellow-humans—we have to resort to physical evidence that has survived. Essentially this leaves us with the objects they made—the tools, the ornament, the houses, the tombs, reflecting different aspects of their life. In addition, of course, we have the testimony of 'natural history'—the geology, the zoology, the botany, the biology, the pathology, even the physics—that cast light on their environment and their condition.

Genetics

Unlike the inferences drawn from ethno-archaeological parallels, the laws of genetics are normative and inflexible. They determine whether a population is large enough to survive in a healthy condition or whether it is too small to avoid extinction—and they apply both to human beings and to animals, whether domesticated or wild. The influence exerted by genetics on an isolated island colonised by humans for the first time is considerable, even if, in the past, it has not been considered sufficiently or considered deeply enough. Estimates of population sizes have to be considered with regard to the viability of genetic pools—both for humans and for animals, especially the animals that were introduced by humans to form the basis of their nutrition. The endangered species is not a modern invention, though the concept may be.

Genetics, however, is not all bad news for archaeologists. One of the slightly depressing features of prehistory is that we know the names of none of the people whose bones we may be examining, or merely handling, or whose pot—made by them, or merely used by them—we may be examining for any shreds of information about its maker or user. We can never obtain photographs of them, or recordings of their voices. If, however, DNA 'fingerprinting' was applied in the cause of archaeology we could achieve a much closer relationship with them: we could know, for instance, whether we were related to them—or that it is simply impossible for us to be. We could establish whether two people sharing a grave were related, or merely 'good friends'. In a manner of speaking, it would make them into more real human beings.

Unpredictability

One of the quirks of archaeology is its inherent unpredictability. An archaeologist could today make a reasonably confident statement, 'No—copper or bronze nails were definitely not used in the construction of buildings in the Bronze Age in Ireland,' and be proved wrong tomorrow. For many years the lack of evidence of beakers in the southwest of Ireland, where the plenteous supplies of copper are found, has been a dilemma for those who thought that the makers of beaker pottery—the Beaker People—were, notwithstanding this, the most likely people to have introduced metallurgy to Ireland. The recent and unpredicted—though not, in some ways, unpredictable—discovery of the site at Ross Island, County Kerry, with its beaker pottery, its association with copper smelting and its favourable radiocarbon dates has changed all that. Negative evidence is not a very faithful colleague.

In a manner of speaking, the fact that humankind itself is unpredictable is the quintessential stumbling-block for archaeologists. We have to assume that the people whose dwelling-places, artefacts, lives even, we are dealing with were rational, integrated, sane and sensible human beings. Then we look around at our own contemporaries and wonder how this belief can possibly be sustained.

Non-technical and non-practical traits and activities

It is probably inevitable that right from the beginning of the human occupation of Ireland many activities were rife of which we have now no direct—that is, archaeological—evidence. It would seem, from a perspective of modern, and not so modern, society, that sport or games of some sort or other would have been prevalent, even if at Mount Sandel only five-a-side could have competed in the football tournament, kicking the inflated bladder of a pig. Running races would surely have been a popular pastime, right from earliest times—if only because it would have provided

fitness and fleetness for the hunt. Perhaps with the introduction of the horse by Beaker People, horse-racing could
have become established in Ireland. Religion, of course, in
some form or another, was clearly established in the Later
Stone Age or Neolithic Period. Court tombs clearly indicate
a desire to erect monuments to dead ancestors; perhaps we
have not yet discovered a Mesolithic (Middle Stone Age)
precursor. Passage tombs seem not merely to be an expression of some form of religious belief but, much more than
court tombs, of a sort of social supremacy. These innocent-
seeming activities might of course have witnessed the
beginnings of their ultimate opponents: did the matches
between Mount Sandel United and Lough Boora Rovers
attract football hooligans? Did the rival religious groups
burn each other's temples? Fortunately, perhaps, archaeology in Ireland does not (or has so far failed to) reveal this
kind of truth. The true believer, however, is aware that one
of these days it might.

ARTEFACTS INTO ARCHAEOLOGY
The landscape of prehistory is littered with artefacts, as,
indeed, is the landscape of Ireland. There are many kinds of
portable artefact, made of such varied materials as flint,
stone, wood, leather, textiles, bronze, and gold. There are
many kinds of non-portable artefact: monuments of various
kinds, reflecting different needs on the part of the prehistoric inhabitants, showing different sizes, styles and
degrees of complexity and made of materials such as wood
or stone—though it is those made of stone that are most
likely to have survived. At this stage, however, they are
simply dissociated artefacts and reveal little about their
makers and users, except, perhaps, that they had a need for
different types of artefact for different purposes and that
their makers had certain skills in the making of tools or
implements of various materials. How do we persuade them
to tell their stories?

Flint
Artefacts of flint not only constitute the earliest prehistoric
artefacts but also are the most common. Flint itself is
relatively easy to identify (my own eldest daughter could

reliably recognise flint at the age of four). On these grounds, therefore, it seems appropriate to look at them more closely and to see what information they can reveal about our prehistoric predecessors. Even for such a seemingly intractable material they exhibit a wide variety of form and, even superficially, suggest a wide variety of types and functions. A selection of flint artefacts is shown in fig. 1.1.

Flint hollow scrapers
From the array of flint artefacts, we have selected one to follow up (fig. 1.1C). It is a fairly broad flake of flint, thin in

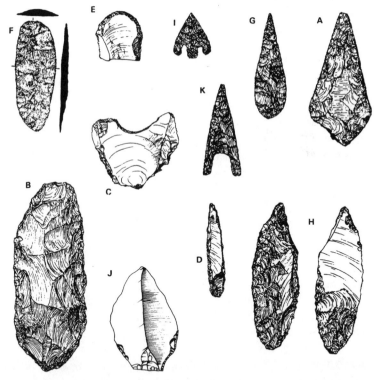

1.1 *A selection of flint artefacts of various forms and functions:* (A) *part-polished javelin-head;* (B) *core tranchet axe;* (C) *hollow scraper;* (D) *double-backed blade;* (E) *convex scraper;* (F) *plano-convex knife;* (G) *leaf-shaped arrow-head;* (H) *perforator;* (I) *barbed-and-tanged arrow-head;* (J) *butt-trimmed 'Bann' flake;* (K) *hollow-based arrow-head (various sources, various scales)*

section, with a pronounced concave feature at one end; because of this pronounced feature, implements of this type are known as hollow scrapers. The shape of the flake varies considerably, and in section it is usually trapezoidal. The 'hollow' varies in outline from a broad shallow arc (of a circle as much as 90 or 100 mm in diameter) to an almost semicircular indentation less than 20 mm in diameter, with almost every conceivable intermediate combination of diameter and depth. The finish of this hollow working edge varies from strongly marked serrations to as smooth an edge as the technique of removing small overlapping flakes will permit. On the main hollow (some specimens display more than one) the working of the edge may be executed from either the upper face or the lower (technically known as the *bulbar* face, from the fact that it is the face that retains the 'bulb of percussion'—a visible relic of the detachment of the flake from the core).

The next stage is to collect together (not necessarily physically) all the known examples of hollow scrapers so that we can see in what parts of the country they occur. Because the flint-bearing outcrop of cretaceous chalk or limestone is restricted to the north-eastern part of the country, it is there that we may expect to find the greatest concentration of flint hollow scrapers (fig. 1.2). And here indeed we find 395 examples, while in the rest of the country we find considerably fewer. (It must be noted that these maps were compiled in 1965 and that the totals both for the north-eastern area and the rest of the country have increased considerably since then, mainly as the result of important excavations in both areas; the overall picture, however, is probably not significantly different.)

The next stage is to establish what other types of object hollow scrapers are found with and in what types of monument, if any. It can fairly quickly and positively be determined that they are frequently found in the burial monuments known as court tombs; in 1965 they had been found in twelve of the twenty-two court tombs that had by then been excavated. They were found with virtually every type and style of Neolithic pottery—except those types specifically confined to the south-west of the country—and with other types of Neolithic flint and stonework, including

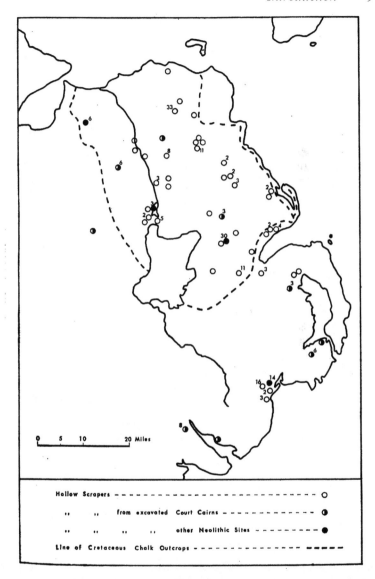

1.2 *The distribution of hollow scrapers in the flint-rich north-east of Ireland (after Flanagan, 1965)*

leaf-shaped and lozenge-shaped flint arrow-heads and ground or polished stone axes. Even more importantly, they were reunited with the people who had made and used

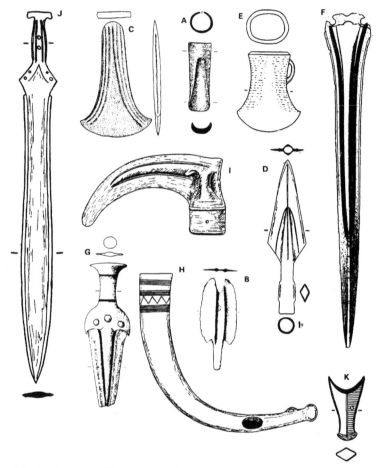

1.3 *A selection of bronze artefacts of various forms and
functions: (A) socketed gouge; (B) razor; (C) flat axe;
(D) socketed spear-head; (E) socketed axe; (F) rapier;
(G) dagger; (H) horn; (I) socketed sickle; (J) leaf-shaped
sword; (K) sword chape (various sources, various scales)*

them and whose remains were also found in the tombs.
Since 1965, of course, hollow scrapers continued to appear
in court tombs. They also occur on domestic sites.

One interesting feature of hollow scrapers is that while
they are found virtually throughout Ireland it is only in
Ireland that they are found, except for one or two examples
from the Isle of Man and a few from the west of Scotland—

two areas to which they were probably introduced with court tombs.

Copper and bronze

While by no means the same ultimate quantity of copper and bronze artefacts exists as of flint ones, there is certainly a greater variation in their forms and functions (fig. 1.3). Obviously the same processes can be applied to copper or bronze artefacts as were applied to flint hollow scrapers. The approved style and description of any particular type can be established by a close and careful study of the potential constituent members of the proposed type; the distribution and the 'catalogue' of associated types of other artefact can be drawn up. Choosing one example, therefore, from the range of artefacts illustrated—an axe of fairly slender ogival form, with a generally rectangular cross-section and a long section that is slender and tapering to a point at each end (fig. 1.3C)—we can establish this as a type that occurs in a hoard from Ballyvalley, County Down (fig. 1.4), and this type of axe is therefore described as the 'Ballyvalley type'.

An additional treatment is available, however, for the study of copper and bronze artefacts, namely the study of the chemical composition of the metals from which the objects were made. We are fortunate that in 1974 some thousand spectrographic analyses of Irish Earlier Bronze

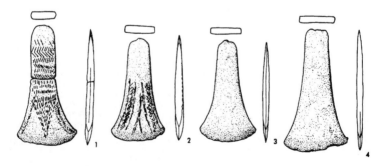

1.4 *Hoard of bronze axes from Ballyvalley, Co. Down (after Harbison, 1969)*

Age artefacts were published. This great mass of analyses includes a number of axes of the Ballyvalley type, including the four axes that compose another hoard, that from Glenalla, County Donegal. The close similarity of composition of these four axes is so striking as to suggest that all four were made from metal derived from a common source and even that, despite slight variations, they may have been made from the same 'mix' of metals.

The analysis of these four axes from Glenalla does lead to another possible lesson to be derived from the 1,000 published analyses. Among these there exist some 29 examples that contain no lead and no arsenic; another 62 examples contain no lead and only a trace of arsenic; a further small group, of only 9 specimens, contains only traces of lead and arsenic. It has been argued that these three groups form a 'family' that derives its metal from outside the area in the south-west where the major source of metal ores is generally thought to lie (fig. 1.5).

CHRONOLOGY

What may be seen by some people as a professional obsession on the part of archaeologists with dating is no such thing: it is essential for archaeologists to know, as accurately as possible, the date of the objects they are dealing with to avoid, in archaeological terms, the same sort of error a historian would be making if he were to consider the role of the CIA in the American War of Independence, or (in terms slightly more compatible with the materials involved) why the de Lorean car never competed in the London to Brighton car race. Dating is important merely so that mistakes of this category are ruled out as far as possible.

Two different styles of dating are used by archaeologists. The first, and in some ways the simplest, is what is known as relative chronology. This simply reveals whether an artefact, structure or event is earlier than, contemporary with or later than another artefact, structure, or event. Of these the indications of contemporaneity are probably the easiest to determine. The four axes in the Glenalla Hoard, for example, were found together, lying on the surface of the ground under a large rock. With the additional evidence that they are all the same type of axe, it would be difficult, even

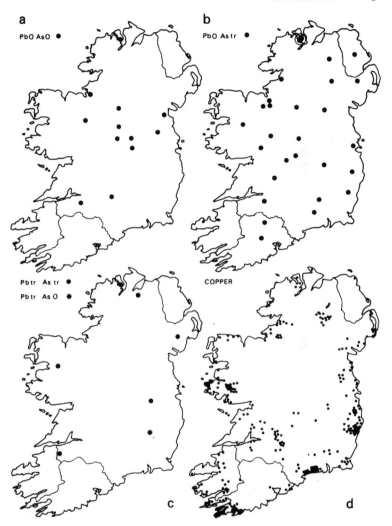

1.5 *The distribution of analysed Earlier Bronze Age artefacts containing no more than traces of lead and arsenic (after Flanagan, 1981)*

perverse, to deny that they were contemporary and constituted an associated find. In the same way a cist at Ballyglass, County Roscommon, contained cremated bone and a bowl; it would be difficult to deny that the cist, the bowl and the cremated bone were contemporary.

That some artefact, structure or event preceded another is best seen in excavation contexts. At Ballyglass, County Mayo, the entire foundation plan of a house was, apart from a portion outside, overlaid by a massive court tomb and so quite clearly predated the construction of the tomb. (That a small portion of the house was outside the kerb of the cairn was fortunate: otherwise it might not have been detected.) The entire 'zoning' system at Newferry, County Antrim, depended on the sections through the site that indicated the vertical sequence of events, and therefore of artefacts, on the site.

Within the last four or five decades natural science came to the assistance of prehistoric archaeologists by opening up avenues to absolute chronology, first by physics, with the development of radiocarbon dating. This technique is based on the fact that all organic materials contain carbon, of which a portion is radioactive carbon; this is known to decay at a given rate, so that by measuring the amount of radioactive carbon that remains in the organic material under examination—for example a tree or an animal—the date at which it ceased to live can be determined.

It all sounds as if the archaeologist was made redundant by the development of the technique, except as a sort of handmaid to the scientist. Unfortunately it wasn't quite like that. Radiocarbon dates were found to differ significantly from known historical dates in parts of the world where these existed, such as Egypt, where the radiocarbon dates were consistently younger than the historical dates. A system had to be developed to overcome this problem, and this was done with the assistance of the bristle-cone pine, which is an immensely long-lived species. Radiocarbon dates were checked against measurements of the radiocarbon activity of samples from this, and the first calibration curves were produced to correct the error inherent in radiocarbon dates.

The other great development in chronology was dendrochronology, a system of dating based on the different widths of annual growth rings in trees as a result of different climatic conditions, which caused different growth patterns. Ireland proved to be an ideal subject for dendrochronology, because timbers of oak were available from all periods. An overlapping chronology was eventually established that stretched back from the present day to nearly 6000 BC, so that substantial pieces of wood from any point in this period could be accurately dated.

This, however, was not the end of the contribution of dendrochronology. It was also used to calibrate Irish radiocarbon dates, which made possible a high-precision radiocarbon dating. Large pieces of wood are suitable for either technique. Dug-out canoes—or log-boats, as they are now more commonly called—have been dated by both techniques, the oldest dated by radiocarbon producing an age of 5,820 years or a date of approximately 3870 BC for a boat from Carrigdirty, County Limerick, and the oldest dated by dendrochronology producing an age of 4,140 years BP or a date of approximately 2771 BC for a boat from Inch Abbey, County Down.

For the great majority of objects or sites for which dates are desired, however, radiocarbon remains the most applicable form of dating, since it is not necessary to have large, intact samples—in fact the samples are most frequently in the form of charcoal. We therefore have quite a number of radiocarbon dates for court tombs and thus for hollow scrapers, for example. We have dates ranging from between 3690 and 2920 BC to between 4230 and 3720 BC for Ballymacaldrack, County Antrim. It is the combination of all these techniques—the pure archaeology of artefact studies, subjected to the various kinds of chronological treatment, sometimes to place an artefact in its place in the pattern, sometimes merely to confirm that it is in its right place in the pattern—that makes archaeology.

2

THE MESOLITHIC PERIOD
8000–4000 BC

Despite the fact that several examples of Palaeolithic flint tools have been found in Ireland, and that a substantial portion of the southernmost part of the country was free of ice during the later part of the Ice Age, it is generally agreed that human occupation is post-glacial, from some time after 8000 BC.

The first settlers to arrive in Ireland were representatives of the hunter-gatherers who lived in Europe after the end of the Ice Age who were, for some reason, motivated to cross the sea to Ireland—possibly simply as a result of seeing the mountains of eastern Ireland and making group decisions to set out to explore this unknown country. The decision to explore might have been spurred on, it is suggested, by the inundation of the areas they occupied.

THE POST-GLACIAL LANDSCAPE
It is hard to visualise an immediate post-glacial Irish landscape, thoroughly ice-scraped and therefore devoid of vegetation and animal life—except, presumably, in the ice-free extreme south. The fact that at this period Ireland was still, ultimately, attached to the land-mass of Europe meant that it was possible, in the rising temperatures, for animals and plants to migrate from there, or from the southernmost area of the island, and colonise the whole landscape of Ireland.

Ireland's natural resources

The animals present in Ireland as potential food sources when it was first colonised by humans included wild pig, red deer—though this appears to have been surprisingly under-represented on the Mesolithic menu—and hare. The only significant predator was the wolf. Birds present, and apparently used as food, included an appetising variety: mallard, teal or garganey, widgeon, red grouse, capercaillie, snipe or woodcock, and wood-pigeon, as well as less notably comestible species such as goshawk and golden eagle, coot, rock-dove, songthrush, and even red-throated diver. In the rivers and the sea several types of fish were available for exploitation: salmon and trout, eels, plaice or flounder, and sea-bass, as well as shellfish of several kinds.

Of the vegetable food sources available, by far the most important was the hazel, whose nuts, weight for weight, contain up to one-and-a-half times more protein, seven times more fat and five times more carbohydrate than eggs. They produce five times as many calories and are four times as rich in calcium and twice as rich in phosphorus as eggs. They also contain ascorbic acid (vitamin C). Surprisingly, acorns were an important source of carbohydrates. Another surprise is the fact that the seeds of water-lilies, which can be boiled to make a sort of gruel, were an available dietary addition, as was goosegrass. To add a little flavour, crab-apples were available, and so were barberries.

Raw materials

Judged by the enormous quantities used in the making of implements, flint—a very hard rock that on fracture gives a durable and sharp cutting edge—was important to Mesolithic colonists. It is equally important to modern students of the Irish Mesolithic Period as the most durable and most frequently found raw material. Because of its structure, a parent lump, or nodule, can readily be struck into flakes of relatively predetermined shape. Fortunately for Mesolithic humans, it occurs abundantly in north-eastern Ireland in the cretaceous limestone or chalk that outcrops conveniently more or less along the borders of modern County Antrim, with a reported small survivor in County Kerry. For those areas where flint was not readily available, substitutes were. The principal substitute for flint that is recorded as having been used by Mesolithic colonists was chert—not quite as satisfactory as flint but fairly widely present in carboniferous limestone. Others included materials such as felsite, a devitrified volcanic glass, and even the rather coarse and unsatisfactory quartz.

For other purposes, including the building of simple huts or shelters and the hafting of tools, wood from such trees and shrubs as hazel, oak, elm and birch was available. The deer would have provided not only skins for clothing and the roofing of huts and shelters but also bone and antler for the manufacture of tools—a contribution that could also have been made by other animals. Even grass could have provided material for the thatching of huts and shelters.

The possible sources of Mesolithic colonists

It is generally agreed among archaeologists that Ireland's Mesolithic settlers came here from some place or places in Britain, from which many features on or near the Irish coast are clearly visible. In the post-glacial period, sea levels in the Irish Sea fluctuated, on the one hand because of the melt-water from the ice-sheets and on the other hand from the lifting of the land as a result of the relief from the weight of the ice-sheets. To complicate matters, the effects of this second factor were not universal, the uplift being greater in the north, where a raised beach at eight to ten metres is still to be observed, than further south.

From the possible routes between the two islands, at least four can be identified, with the northernmost, between the north of Ireland and present-day Scotland, being the most favoured for a variety of reasons, not least its comparatively short distance and the distinct views of each land from the other, with the added advantage for the settlers of easy access to the Antrim flint. It should be remembered that these routes have since been regularly followed not only by small boats but on occasions also by swimmers, so that the practicality of their being covered even by small skin-covered boats of the curach type cannot be ignored.

While these are, for geographical reasons, the most likely routes, there remains the problem that in none of these potential source areas so far has archaeological material been found that is typologically completely compatible with the Mesolithic material found in Ireland. One proffered, and widely accepted, explanation is that the most suitable sites were victims of inundation and, therefore, are no longer accessible. The prospect of the inundation of the colonists' previous homeland would surely have constituted a cogent reason for flight to happier hunting-grounds across the sea.

If it is accepted that the visibility of coastal mountain ranges in Ireland was the initial spur by which the first colonists were attracted, it must follow that easily recognisable profiles would later serve as leading-marks, in both directions, for subsequent settlers, which would help to suggest solutions to some of the many problems associated with the first populating of Ireland.

THE DATING OF THE IRISH MESOLITHIC PERIOD

Until fairly recently, largely because of the concentration of effort on coastal sites associated with the raised beaches, the dating of the Irish Mesolithic Period was derived almost completely from geological and geophysical data. The discovery of the then exceptional site at Mount Sandel, County Derry, and the increasing availability of radiocarbon dates changed the chronological picture drastically, with an observed beginning shockingly early, at around 7000 BC. A total re-evaluation of the Irish Mesolithic Period ensued, showing a division into two distinct technological, if not cultural, phases, with a possible lacuna between, just after 6000 BC, and the second phase continuing to overlap with the arrival of Neolithic cultures around 4000 BC.

THE EXPLOITATION OF NATURAL RESOURCES

As far as raw materials are concerned, we know from Mount Sandel that the Mesolithic settlers there made use of the flint available within a reasonable distance of their homestead, as well as locally available stone, to make axes, hammer-stones, and anvil stones; they also used the timber from the surrounding woods or forests for the construction of their huts and, presumably, for the hafting of flint implements. At Lough Boora, County Offaly, remote from the supplies of cretaceous limestone containing flint so abundant in County Antrim, they used instead chert from the carboniferous limestone.

Most probably, and indeed almost certainly because of their very presence here, they used similar skills to those employed in the construction of huts for the construction of timber-framed and skin-covered boats, similar to those in which they or their ancestors arrived in the first place. For those inhabiting an estuarine site such as that at Mount Sandel it is virtually inconceivable that an art and practice of this nature should be quite forgotten. Even simply for fishing, the use of boats would have continued to serve a useful purpose. Perhaps for those settlers, or their descendants, who penetrated inland, boat-building and boat-using may have fallen into disuse—though even at Lough Boora, so emphatically inland, there was a sufficient expanse of water to generate waves powerful enough to create a sort of 'storm-beach'.

THE EARLY MESOLITHIC PERIOD

The great paradox of the Irish Mesolithic Period is that until the discovery of the important site at Mount Sandel, what was regarded as the total Irish Mesolithic Period was based on the study of material from the raised beaches—material that, with the raising and lowering of sea levels, had been first sorted by the sea and then left high and dry. Small stone tools or microliths were known only from scattered finds along the River Bann. With the discovery of the Mount Sandel site and its radiocarbon dating, all that changed. As the only 'residential' site examined and published, it dominates the period; Lough Boora, County Offaly, some 240 km away, is the only comparable site, though there do exist smaller and less productive sites that are recognised as Earlier Mesolithic because of the similarity of the material they have produced to that from Mount Sandel.

Mount Sandel: the site and the excavations

The Earlier Mesolithic occupation was on a ridge, thirty metres in height, on the eastern side of the River Bann, at that point still estuarine, where flint implements had been found as early as 1888. The threat of housing development, and the finding of further flint artefacts by subsequent ploughing, ultimately led to four seasons of intensive excavation, from 1973 to 1977. The results of the preliminary excavation in 1973 indicated that extensive as well as intensive excavation was required.

Altogether some 700 square metres was excavated. The salient feature was a 'dwelling hollow', with arcs of post-holes surrounding hearths, miscellaneous pits, and considerable quantities of waste flint—the produce of flint-working on the site. There was also considerable evidence of the plant and animal types exploited locally by the inhabitants of the dwelling hollow.

The structures at Mount Sandel
Despite the confusion created by tree-falls and later agricultural activity, it was established that a number of approximately circular huts had been constructed (fig. 2.1), evidently by placing the butt-end of a sapling in a hole and bending it over to meet the upper end of an opposing

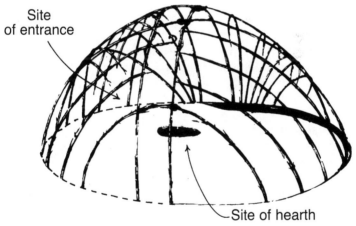

2.1 *Suggested construction of huts at Mount Sandel, Co. Derry (after Woodman, 1985)*

sapling, to which it was secured, until a hemispherical skeleton was created, through the members of which other branches were woven. There is a probability, since there were indications that the sods were stripped off before building began, that a wall of sods was built, perhaps to a height of about a metre, round part at least of the circumference. It is assumed that the roofing may have consisted of a covering of deer-hides. In all, what appear to be the remains of up to seven structures were found. One was a small hut about three metres in diameter, with an external hearth; the others were larger (four may have been more or less successive rebuildings), about six metres in diameter, with internal hearths. Other features included sets of post-holes possibly representing drying-racks for meat or fish. In addition there was a series of pits, which are likely to have been storage pits.

Implications of hut sizes

It has been argued on the grounds of ethno-archaeological evidence that the hut sizes at Mount Sandel, at just under thirty square metres, would indicate an occupying group as small as three people. This figure, based on a formula of ten square metres per person, is probably not applicable either to hunter-gatherer societies or to conditions in Ireland at almost any stage in its history or prehistory. The Irish peasant house of the last century, usually divided into two rooms, enjoyed a fairly standard area of some forty-two square metres. When we recall that the family occupying such a house might consist of as many as fourteen or fifteen people, it seems that the Mount Sandel huts may also have accommodated rather more than a mere three people.

The portable archaeological material from Mount Sandel

The most formidable aspect of the portable archaeological material from Mount Sandel is the enormous quantity of microliths found, amounting to roughly 1,100, many of them burnt and fragmentary. The dominant form was the scalene triangle with two retouched edges (fig. 2.2). These are assumed to have featured as parts of composite implements, set into a shaft to form such pieces as harpoons. Another form of microlith found was the 'needle point', some of which are exceedingly long and narrow, often with abrupt retouch along both edges and with exceedingly sharp points (fig. 2.3). This type of microlith is confined to Ireland and, since it also occurs at Lough Boora, County Offaly, confirms the close relationship of these two widely separated outposts of the Irish Earlier Mesolithic Period. Several other forms of microlith were also found, but heavier tool

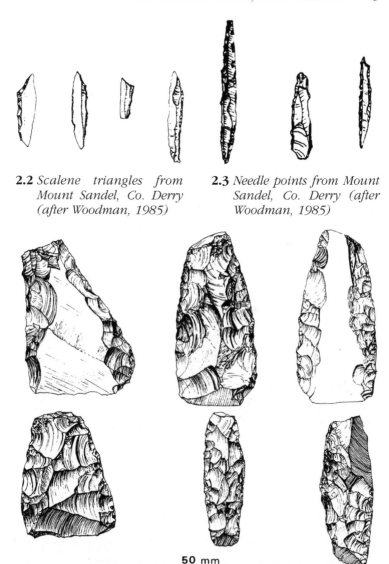

2.2 *Scalene triangles from Mount Sandel, Co. Derry (after Woodman, 1985)*

2.3 *Needle points from Mount Sandel, Co. Derry (after Woodman, 1985)*

50 mm

2.4 *Flake axes from Mount Sandel, Co. Derry (after Woodman, 1985)*

types occurred as well, notably axes of two kinds. One type, the core axe, which, confusingly, can also be made on a flake, is characterised by the removal of one or more transversely struck flakes from the cutting edge. In consequence they are usually associated with numbers of such trimming or sharpening flakes. The other type of axe found was the flake axe, made on a large flat flake, retaining the original sharp edge of the flake as the cutting edge. Often they show a rather trapezoidal outline and have only peripheral retouch on the flat or convex bulbar surface (fig. 2.4). It has been argued, with a certain amount of confirmation from micro-wear analysis, that the core axes were essentially chopping tools, while the flake axes were more probably used as planes or chisels. Other heavier implements included pick-like tools and, of course, scrapers—though scrapers, surprisingly, were very uncommon on the site. Retouched blades, including backed blades, some of which probably served as backed knives, were also found.

In addition to the vigorous flint industry, some implements of other types of stone were recovered, including axes, one of rather soft stone, and a small group of what were evidently hammer-stones.

The use of natural resources

The site of Mount Sandel, on a bluff overlooking the estuary of the River Bann, undoubtedly gave it a number of distinct advantages. Its inhabitants could draw on food supplies from the land: the gourmet menu of desirable game-birds, the acorns, the hazel nuts, the crab-apples even, as well as the wild pig and red deer (even though the evidence at the site for the exploitation of these was minimal). In addition they could exploit the river resource, with its salmon, trout, and eels. From the mouth of the estuary they could exploit the sea-fish, of which there was evidence at the site, the sea-bass and plaice or flounders. No doubt other sea-derived nutrition—shellfish, the occasional seal, and other sea-fish, such as mullet, mackerel, and even cod—came within their ambit.

By and large, the food resources available in spring, summer, autumn and winter, both from the land (including plants, animals and birds) and the river and sea would have been capable of providing enough calories, as well as carbohydrates, protein, mineral traces, and vitamins, to ensure a reasonably healthy life.

Social inferences from Mount Sandel

While Mount Sandel is a mine of information on certain aspects of the Irish Early Mesolithic Period, the evidence it produced cannot be stretched to give complete answers to all the questions we would like to ask. It can be shown at Mount Sandel, for example, that 'roughing-out' activities tended to be performed in the so-called 'industrial areas', and there was evidence of systematic refuse disposal from the hut area. No evidence survives, however, of expected activities such as butchering—possibly in the main because the soil was too acid to permit the preservation of unburnt bone.

Two big problems remain. The first and most obvious is, what size of population is likely to have inhabited the site, with an area preserved and investigated of some 700 square metres? By reference to ethno-archaeological comparative material and sites, the excavator came to the conclusion that the largest resident population that could be envisaged for these 700 square metres was less than fifteen. The other question is whether Mount Sandel was purely a seasonal camp or whether it was occupied the whole year round. On the whole, the advantageous position of the site, with ready access to so many useful resources, the sheer quantity of lithic material produced and the fact that locally accessible food supplies virtually guaranteed year-round provender, would suggest that it was occupied the whole year round.

Other Early Mesolithic sites

While caches of microliths have been quite common, particularly in the northern part of Ireland and especially along the valley of the River Bann, the only site really remotely comparable to Mount Sandel is that at Lough Boora, County Offaly, unfortunately not yet fully published. The lithic industry here is closely comparable to that at Mount Sandel—even allowing for the fact that in the absence of local flint they had to use chert, a rather less tractable material, from the local limestone. They also made ground axe-heads of slate. Apart from the fact that sea-fish was naturally not available, food debris was similar to that at Mount Sandel, but in addition to wild pig they made more observable use of red deer and hare. Apart from microliths found along the River Blackwater, but without the identification of possible residential sites, Lough Boora is the most southerly site of the Early Mesolithic Period in Ireland (fig. 2.5).

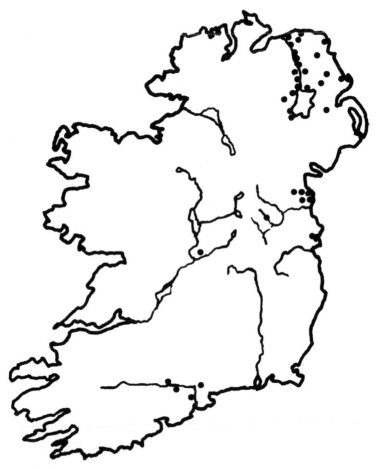

2.5 *The distribution of Earlier Mesolithic material (after Woodman, 1985)*

THE LATER MESOLITHIC PERIOD

The great irony about the Irish Late Mesolithic Period is that its material consists of that which, before the excavation and dating of the site at Mount Sandel, was considered to constitute the entire Irish Mesolithic Period. It existed mainly in raised beach deposits along the Antrim coast; because one of these was on Curran Point, at Larne, the entire Irish Mesolithic Period was dubbed the 'Larnian'. Many of these sites, including that at Larne itself, had been discovered by the flint collectors who had been such a feature of pre-historic studies in the north of Ireland. Some of the rather heavy implements, so typical of the deposits in the raised beaches and of the Late Mesolithic Period, as now defined, are shown here (fig. 2.6).

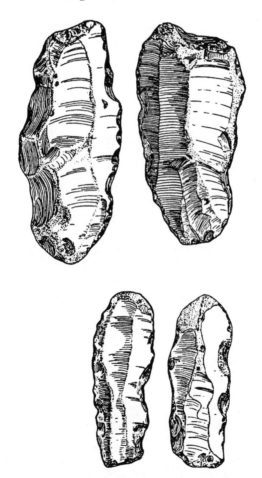

2.6 *Heavy forms of flint implement found by collectors at Curran Point, Larne, Co. Antrim (after Movius, 1953)*

Newferry, County Antrim

As Mount Sandel is the dominant site of the Early Mesolithic Period, so a site at Newferry, also on the River Bann, was to become the dominant site of the Late Mesolithic. While Mount Sandel was important 'horizontally', Newferry was important 'vertically'. It was the recognition of the hut sites and the contemporary microlith-rich industry, as well as the surviving evidence of food resources, that made Mount Sandel so important. At Newferry it was the sequence and development shown in the sections of the cuttings that made it important. Viewing the exposed sections at Newferry was like a lesson in basic archaeology, with a succession of black occupation deposits neatly dividing the sequence into zones. While it had the great advantage of showing fairly clearly the sequence of the industries, it had the disadvantage that much of the site was waterladen. It had also the disadvantage that because of the excessive acidity of the soil, little organic material survived.

In the event, the archaeology of the site was divided into nine zones. The first of these (the lowest), named zone 9, produced just enough material to suggest that humans had arrived on the basal orange sand at the site; several large stones appeared to have been arranged in a slight arc, and two small struck flakes were found. This was followed by zone 8, consisting of a layer of peat and a lens of diatomite, which produced a small scatter of material. Apart from a number of blades and flakes and a few cores, there was a borer, slightly rolled, with extensive traces of use along both edges; an axe of chlorite schist and fragments of two others. Zone 7 consisted mainly of occupation debris and produced quite a body of archaeological material: fifty-four implements of various types, quite large numbers of blades and flakes, and a number of stone axes and polishing-stones.

Above the main part of zone 7 was what might have represented a discrete single occupation phase, termed zone 7 upper; among the items it produced was an end scraper with little sign of use. In zone 6, a layer of silt, were found quite a number of flint implements, including tanged flakes (fig. 2.7) as well as flint axes, a backed knife, blade points, and a heavy borer. The succeeding zone 5 produced

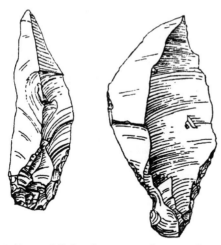

2.7 *Tanged flakes from zone 6 at Newferry, Co. Antrim (after Woodman, 1977)*

large quantities of material, including blade points, spoke-shaves, and backed knives, as well as stone axes. Interestingly, three fragments of bone points survived in this layer—probably the remains of fish-gorges, which were used to snare fish, which would swallow the baited bone point and, when it was twisted, be unable to eject it.

Zone 4 contained several washed-out remains of hearths and produced quite large numbers of flint implements, including scrapers, fabricators, and a backed flake. In zones 3 and 2 erosion channels had destroyed what stratigraphy there might have been, but in zone 2 Neolithic material occurred, including a diagnostic flint hollow scraper and a broken leaf-shaped arrow-head, as well as a mass of pottery.

The significance of Newferry
The Newferry sequence of dates is the key to the dating of the Irish Later Mesolithic Period. Although there was so much free charcoal on the site as to make it virtually impossible to guarantee that any individual sample was completely free of contamination, it is still possible to see to what extent industries changed over a period of nearly two thousand years, from the starting point, in effect in zone 8, of nearly 6000 BC. In sum, as far as the industry is concerned, a weak time progression can be discerned towards broader types of flake, but with the almost total disappearance of microlithic forms.

Other Late Mesolithic sites
While Late Mesolithic material had been discovered in the raised beach sites along the Antrim coast, other northern

coastal sites, such as Ballylumford, County Antrim, have produced material similar to that from zone 8 at Newferry. The most distant site is at Ferriter's Cove, County Kerry, where a rock platform was used as a campsite; hearths, with charcoal, bone, shells, and implements, were scattered over the platform, to be preserved under wind-blown sand. Most of the sites for which radiocarbon dates have been established, such as Lough Derravaragh, County Westmeath, and Sutton, County Dublin, occupy niches towards the end of the Newferry phenomenon—very nearly encroaching on the earliest Neolithic Period.

3

THE NEOLITHIC PERIOD
4000–2000 BC

In many ways the problems of the Irish Mesolithic Period are almost negligible in comparison with those pertaining to the introduction of a total farming economy to Ireland. There is no agreement about the probable source of the earliest Neolithic settlers. There are considerable archaeological difficulties about drawing them from Britain; there are greater practical problems about drawing them directly from continental Europe. There was also the problem of transporting sufficient numbers of men and women to establish a genetically viable population (though this could have been solved, or at least alleviated, by the presence of 'natives', both male and female); the change of economy and life-style would seem to require, and be able to support, a rather larger population.

LIVESTOCK
There was also, however, the less tractable problem of transporting livestock in adequate quantities. Dogs, already present in the Mesolithic Period, are represented at Neolithic sites such as the court tombs at Ballyalton and Audleystown, County Down, and would undoubtedly have been of great assistance with such farming tasks as managing the flocks and herds and protecting them from predators. The other types of domesticated animals present in Irish Neolithic times include cattle, attested at such varied sites as the court tomb at Annaghmare, County

Armagh, and the passage tomb at Knowth, County Meath. Sheep or goats (indistinguishable in fragmentary skeletal form) are attested in court tombs such as Audleystown; while pigs are represented by a complete jaw in the court tomb of Audleystown—though it is possible that these could have been derived from the native wild pigs, or the stock genetically assisted by the presence of the native wild pigs. At a time when doubts are cast on the continuing viability of the Portland sheep because only three hundred breeding ewes exist, some idea of the scale of the problem becomes obvious. That this threat applies to only one modern breed is irrelevant: it suggests that if the level of the breeding stock falls below this rather small number, the future of the local breed, or the species locally, is at risk. One must assume, therefore, that from the beginnings of Neolithic farming settlement . the national flock must have considerably exceeded in size the three hundred breeding ewes, and the national cattle herd must have been of similar size.

It is usually suggested that a version of the circumpolar *umiak*—a skin-covered, timber-framed boat rather more capacious than the curach—was used, with the cattle, for example, being transported in the prone position. It is likely that even this solution severely restricted the range of the colonising fleets. The volume of animal transport apparently required suggests strongly that anywhere other than Britain, with sea crossings varying from as little as twenty-four kilometres, becomes more and more unlikely as the source of at least the livestock involved in the introduction of a farming economy into Ireland. This is supported by the 'contra-rotating' tidal regime held to have been operating in the Irish Sea since shortly after 4000 BC.

The creation of enclosures to prevent the straying of stock, and also to protect them from predators such as the wolf, would have been necessary. Such enclosures, formed by the construction of a complex of dry-stone walls, are evidenced not only at the Céide Fields at Behy and Glenulra, near Ballycastle, County Mayo, but at many other sites throughout the country.

CROPS

Two main cereal crops were introduced to Ireland by the Neolithic farming colonists: wheat and barley, both in several varieties and both of which have been detected at numbers of Neolithic sites. The main evidence for their presence consists of impressions on pottery, where a cereal grain became embedded in the surface of a pot before it was fired. While the grain itself was destroyed by the firing, it left an impression on the surface of the pot, which could be studied by botanists. In such a manner, wheat—both emmer (*Triticum dicoccum*) and bread wheat (*Triticum aestivum*)—has been identified on pottery from such sites as the court tombs at Ballymacaldrack, County Antrim, and Ballyreagh, County Fermanagh, while charred grains have been identified from sites such as Baltinglass Hill, County Wicklow, and Townley Hall, County Meath. A third variety of wheat, einkorn (*Triticum monococcum*), was identified at the Ballymacaldrack court tomb, but this is thought to be a casual 'weed' in an emmer crop.

Barley has so far been identified on only two Neolithic sites, the court tomb at Creggandevesky, County Tyrone, and on Donegore Hill, County Antrim. The planting of cereal crops would have entailed in the first instance the clearing of the forest to create an open space and of course the breaking of the ground by ploughing. Usefully, the stone blade of a plough was discovered during the excavation of the Céide Fields in County Mayo. The body of the plough would have been of wood and could have been drawn either by humans or by cattle.

It would have been desirable to enclose the areas devoted to the growing of grain to protect them, possibly by the construction of stone walls, as at the Céide Fields, or even by the construction of simple wooden fences. Wheat enjoys the particular advantage of self-fertilisation. These cereals provided a useful and more normal source of carbohydrates than was available to the Mesolithic settlers.

It appears that cats, whose earliest attested appearance is in the passage tomb of Fourknocks, County Meath, accompanied the farming settlers, providing a useful means of protecting the stored grain from the activities of rodents.

LIFE-STYLE

The cultivation of crops and the husbandry of livestock brought about necessary changes in the life-style of the people, apart from the need to establish more long-term dwelling-sites. To provide space for the crops and the herds and flocks it was necessary to clear areas of forest, which entailed the use of stone axes far superior to those of the Mesolithic hunter-gatherers. The Neolithic stone axes were usually of igneous rock—much harder and more enduring than the mudstones and schists formerly used.

Axes and axe factories

Sources of suitable stone were found and systematically exploited. A number of these 'axe factories'—more properly quarries rather than factories, as the manufacture of the axes was not regularly performed on the quarry site—have been distinguished and even specifically identified. The most notable of these is at Tievebulliagh, County Antrim, where an outcrop of hard, fine-grained porcellanite occurs and the scree of the mountainside contains abundant waste flakes of the hard blue-grey speckled rock. Other outcrops of porcellanite occur at Brockley on Rathlin Island and, possibly, near Limavady, County Derry. Since the finishing stages, after the axe has been chipped into shape—at this stage known as a rough-out—require abundant supplies of both water and sharp sand, to make a slurry in which the final grinding and polishing were effected, an elevated mountainside, largely devoid of these, was not appropriate. This stage of the manufacture was therefore carried out where these necessary ingredients were to be found in abundance. A seaside situation was ideal; and at coastal sites such as Cushendall and White Park Bay, County Antrim, there is ample evidence that porcellanite axes were indeed finished here. Other known sources of stone for axes include Feltrim Hill, County Dublin, while in County Limerick there occurs a group of axes of a distinctive straight-sided form, in a greenish rock, suggesting a local source and even a local style.

Since the main thrust of petrological (rock study) examinations has been directed at Tievebulliagh and its products, it can be seen that they have been transported all over

Ireland, occurring on Neolithic sites as far away as County Limerick, as well as being exported to the islands of Scotland, to the Scottish mainland, and even to the south of England. Recent work on their distribution, greatly increasing their recorded numbers (fig. 3.1), tends to suggest that journeys from Ireland to the neighbouring island were much more frequent than some authors have allowed. It is perhaps not altogether surprising that axes from 'axe factories' in England, such as Great Langdale, and in Wales, such as Craig Llwyd, have been found in Ireland. Whether such imported finds could be construed as evidence of the source of the Neolithic colonists of Ireland is, perhaps, irrelevant;

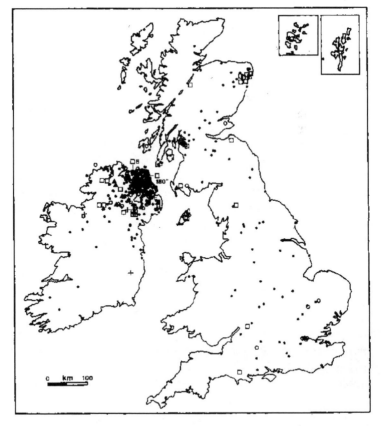

3.1 *The distribution of porcellanite axes from Tievebulliagh or Brockley throughout Ireland and Britain (after Sheridan, 1986)*

certainly the exports of Irish axes indicate that contacts between the two islands were extensive and continuous.

Several examples of hafted polished or ground stone axes have survived, presumably preserved in bogs, including one from Carrickfergus, County Antrim (which was preserved in a bog), which shows a straight haft, thickening towards the top to permit the excavation of a slot to receive the narrower end of the axe. It is quite likely that a leather thong was used to lash the blade more firmly into place, though this, understandably, has not survived. It should be noted that the manner of felling a tree with a stone axe differs from that with a metal axe. With a stone axe it is necessary to chop almost along the grain, prising off portions of wood; this should be done both from above and below the point at which the tree is to be severed— almost like sharpening an enormous pencil.

Other novel tool and implement types

A whole range of new tool and implement types arrived with the colonists: flint scrapers, an armoury of flint arrow-heads, flint knives, even polished or ground axes of flint. The main types of scrapers that appeared include 'hollow' scrapers, where the scraping edge is the inside of a more or less semicircular indentation on the end of a broad flake (occasionally on the side, either instead or additionally). Very enlarged forms have been recorded. These scrapers, while appearing for the first time in the Neolithic Period, are not recorded from places other than Ireland, except in circumstances where they are manifestly exports from Ireland, either ancient or recent. They appear, therefore, to be a peculiarly Irish development, not introduced from out-side. Their presence in the sandhills at Glenluce, Scotland, and in the Isle of Man certainly reinforces the concept of frequent contact between Ireland and Britain. They may have been used for shaping and smoothing the shafts of arrows, rather like a spokeshave—though they occur in such quantities as to make this seem rather an overkill. They may have been used as small saws; they may even have been used as sickles, for only one example of the kind of flint sickle common in the English Neolithic Period has been found in Ireland. The scraping edges of all the used examples bear the gloss characteristic of organic silica, making any of these uses possible. All have been shown by experiment to be feasible.

The most numerous scrapers are steep or end scrapers, which had been known in the Mesolithic Period; they occur in great abundance on Neolithic sites of all types. These are generally assumed to be woodworking or leatherworking tools, in woodworking used as small planes, in leather-working to scrape the inner sides of skins or pelts.

Another introduced tool type was the flint knife, occur-ring in two slightly different forms. Both are described as plano-convex knives, simply meaning that the underside is flat, in practice being the original or bulbar surface of the flake from which the knife was formed, while the upper sur-face has been carefully chipped into shape, giving a round-ed or convex section. In one form, one side ends in a slight tang—presumably for greater comfort in use rather than as an assistance to hafting. The other form bears no tang but is generally more perfectly finished on the upper sur-face; sometimes even the under-surface has been worked (though it is still, perhaps incorrectly, known as a 'plano-convex' knife). From the fact that calcined or thoroughly burnt examples of these knives have been found in tombs among the material of cremations, it has been suggested that they may have been used in the dissection of bodies to facilitate cremation and then found their way into the pyre along with the disarticulated body.

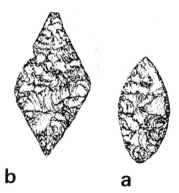

b   **a**

3.2 (a) *Leaf-shaped flint arrow-head from Tullykittagh, Co. Antrim;* (b) *lozenge-shaped flint arrow-head from Glenarm, Co. Antrim (after Flanagan, 1970)*

Of the several types of flint arrow-head that occur in Irish Neolithic contexts, one, and probably the earliest, is the leaf or lozenge form (fig. 3.2). Arrow-heads of this form are found throughout Britain and Ireland at Neolithic sites.

While this is the type predominantly found in the type of tomb known as a court tomb, it occurs in situations not so culturally identifiable. From the simplest truly 'leaf-shaped' form, carefully, even meticulously, flaked on both surfaces to produce a very slender and sharp projectile tip, a wide and subtle range of forms occurs: elongated forms resembling the leaves of willow and ones with straight edges but rounded junctions, to the ultimate truly lozenge form, with straight edges and angular junctions. (The truly lozenge form is generally considered to be the latest, both in the English and the Irish Neolithic Period.)

Joining the leaf or lozenge arrow-head is a form that in

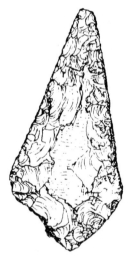

some ways looks more like an 'ideal' arrow-head. This type seems more characteristic of the type of tomb known as the portal tomb—though leaf or lozenge forms occur in them as well. Essentially these are triangular pieces of flint, worked on both faces with a good sharp point and often with a semicircular hollow at the base, giving two barbs, between which the shaft would be fixed, possibly by means of a mastic such as resin. Lashing with sinew, such as is attested for leaf and lozenge forms, would have been ineffective. Larger forms, sometimes polished thoroughly after flaking, known as javelins, also occur (fig. 3.3).

3.3 *Part-polished flint javelin from Drumadonnell, Co. Down (after Flanagan, 1970)*

Pottery

One of the most useful innovations of the Neolithic colonisation was pottery, the making of which was quite unknown to the Mesolithic hunter-gatherers. This pottery was hand-made, not thrown on a wheel, and after being allowed to dry it was probably fired in primitive kilns, of a type that has in fact been found on sites in Scotland, consisting of shallow trenches terminating in small chambers.

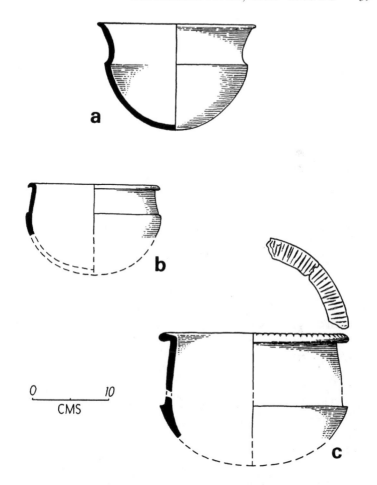

3.4 (a) *Plain Western Neolithic bowl from Lyles Hill, Co. Antrim;* (b) *shouldered Western Neolithic bowl from Ballyutoag, Co. Antrim;* (c) *rim-decorated Western Neolithic bowl from Knockadoon, Co. Limerick (after Case, 1961)*

The manner in which this pottery broke suggests that it was made by taking a ball of clay and shaping it into a hollow hemisphere, smoothing and modelling it by hand until the walls of the pot were of the desired thickness. Sometimes a straight neck was added, the junction between the neck and the body creating an angular shoulder (fig. 3.4). Often the outside was polished or burnished, which would have had the effect, in the absence of glazes, of making the pot more watertight. It has been shown that the clay used was normally from a nearby local source, suggesting that the manufacture was on a fairly small scale—despite the many thousands of fragments of pottery commonly found on excavated sites.

These simple, round-bottomed, undecorated pots are common throughout Britain and Ireland and indeed much of the Continent: they are generally, and generically, described as 'Western Neolithic'.

In the course of time, decoration began to appear on these pots, simple stitch patterns appearing, for example, on the shoulder, perhaps suggesting a recollection of a vessel of leather stitched to a wooden former. Eventually pots with decoration all over appeared. Often this decoration con-sisted of what is known as 'imitation whipped cord', where a sharply cut stick has been pressed into the clay serially, creating a decorative motif that is indeed reminiscent of whipped cord. Pots of this type are so typical of the Irish Neolithic Period that they are known as 'Ballyalton bowls', from one of the court tombs at which they have been found. Similar pots are known from western Scotland, where they are known as 'Beacharra ware' and are found in tombs simi-lar to the Irish court tombs, adding fuel to the controversy about the direction of the influence; though most authorities would now agree that these pots were introduced to Scotland from Ireland.

While both the plain and the decorated vessels are typical of the Irish court tombs, occurring on numerous sites, and the related portal tombs, they occur not only on settlement sites obviously inhabited by their builders but also on sites associated with passage tombs, as if they assumed the role of ordinary domestic pottery throughout the Neolithic Period. The fact that the hollow scrapers and other items of the flint repertoire so frequently found with this style of pottery are also found on sites with passage tomb affinities has led to a suspicion that a fairly uniform domestic Neolithic assemblage existed and was maintained throughout the period, almost regardless of religious affiliations, as reflected by the type of tomb preferred.

SETTLEMENT SITES

Neolithic settlement sites are known from virtually all over the country. In County Limerick the complex of sites at Lough Gur, including Knockadoon, contains many indications of Neolithic settlement. In addition to abundant supplies of round-bottomed pots there also occur flat-bottomed, rather coarse vessels known here as 'class II ware'. Here was discovered a rectangular Neolithic house, measuring over twelve metres long, constructed with a row of posts on each side of a wall-footing of stone. A circular one was found as well. Conjectural reconstructions of both types have been made (fig. 3.5). The flint tools and

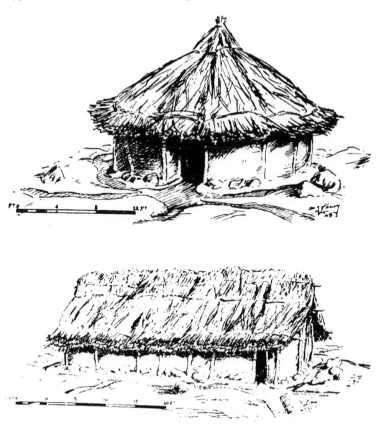

3.5 *Reconstructions of round and rectangular houses at Lough Gur, Co. Limerick (after Ó Ríordáin, 1954)*

weapons described above are also present. At Ballynagilly, County Tyrone, there was a considerable amount of evidence not only of Neolithic activity in the form of pottery and flint but of a rectangular house as well, with walls of split oak planks. A similarly constructed house was found at Tankardstown, County Limerick.

Enclosures and field systems
Sometimes these Neolithic houses have been associated with field systems or enclosures. Several of the Lough Gur houses were situated in stone-walled enclosures, and evidence of stone walls beneath the peat has been observed in various places, including Malinmore, County Donegal, an area rich in Neolithic tombs. It is on the other side of Donegal Bay, however, that the most spectacular field systems have been found. Near Ballycastle, County Mayo, in an area of bleak bogland overlooking the bay at Behy and Glenulra, preserved under the peat, there is an extensive and impressive system of fields, now known as the Céide Fields (fig 3.6). The fields are defined by stone walls, with the occasional use of banks of earth. About a square kilometre has been uncovered—a tiny proportion of what is known to exist.

The use of the fields appears to have been predominantly pastoral, with a small provision for arable agriculture. The system consists of long parallel walls running down towards the sea, with offset subsidiary walls dividing the long enclosures into individual fields. All in all, the system gives the impression of being planned and laid out as an entity.

The excavator is convinced that the system was designed for the management of cattle. There is now a grass-growth season in Mayo of nine to ten months, depending on winter temperatures. In the slightly warmer temperatures at the time of the establishment of these fields, between 4000 and 3000 BC, it may well have been even longer, making the provision of winter fodder by hay-making unnecessary. It has been estimated than a tract of fifty square kilometres would have supported 200 to 250 families, each family occupying a farm of about twenty-five to thirty hectares, each hectare yielding the equivalent of 100 kg of beef every year. It is assumed that there would have been extensive co-operation—as indeed is implied by the very existence of the field system—with neighbours participating in the

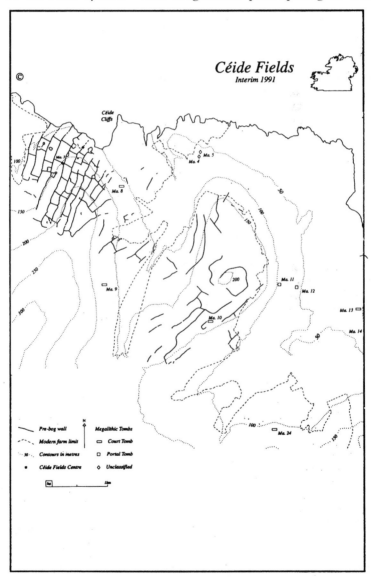

3.6 *The field system known as the Céide Fields, near Ballycastle, Co. Mayo (after Caulfield)*

slaughter and conducting an agreed programme of stag-
gered slaughter to ensure a continuity of supply.

Neolithic hoards

A slightly surprising feature of the Irish Neolithic Period is
the number of hoards of flint implements that have been
found. Understandably, the greatest concentration is in
County Antrim, where the flint to make them from was also
to be found. Whether they were the stock of a flintsmith or
the tool-kit of a craftsman is not easy to determine. The
largest known, with a massive total of 138 scrapers, from
Glenhead, County Antrim, is quite likely to have belonged
to the former category, while the hoard from the Three
Towns, in the Braid Valley, County Antrim, consisting of fourteen varied hollow scrapers, each with a different breadth
and diameter of hollow, and seven end or convex scrapers,
is more likely to have belonged to the latter.

BURIAL SITES

The two dominant, and most numerous, types of burial
monuments in Ireland during the Neolithic period were the
court and portal tombs, represented by some 470 sites, and
the passage tombs, represented by over 200 sites of greatly
varying size and importance. Each of these monument types
has been accorded a separate chapter below.

4

THE COURT TOMBS

The Neolithic Period or Later Stone Age was the time when the first megalithic monuments were constructed in the Irish landscape. They are 'monuments' not merely in the sense that they were later to become 'ancient monuments' but in the sense that they were clearly constructed to commemorate, to identify, to glorify even, something or someone. Being made, as the word *megalithic* indicates, of large stones—sometimes very large stones—they are, by definition, impressive. Since they were burial monuments, it is not perhaps too rash an assumption that they were intended to commemorate those dead whose mortal remains were contained in them.

There is, inevitably, some controversy about which particular monuments were the first to be erected. There has been controversy about which main group—the court tombs or the passage tombs—was the first, mainly as a result of radiocarbon-induced confusion in the early eighties. Most authorities would now agree that chronological primacy belongs to the court tombs.

DISTRIBUTION

With over three hundred examples known, court tombs are the most numerous examples of Neolithic monuments in Ireland. They are not distributed evenly throughout the country but instead are most densely concentrated in the area north of a line from Galway to Dundalk, with a handful of survivors to the south, even the extreme south

(fig. 4.1). The reasons for this apparently restricted distribution we cannot even begin to guess at, though several
factors may have contributed to the present picture: the
growth of bog in the midlands, and intense agricultural
activity in the south (that is, intense agricultural activity after
their building, which has led to a faster rate of destruction).
It is very unlikely that the examples in the extreme south
could, in reality, have enjoyed such splendid iso-lation.
While a number of court tombs may be sited near one
another, as with those of Bavan, Shalwy and Croaghbeg,
County Donegal, they do not appear as 'cemeteries'.

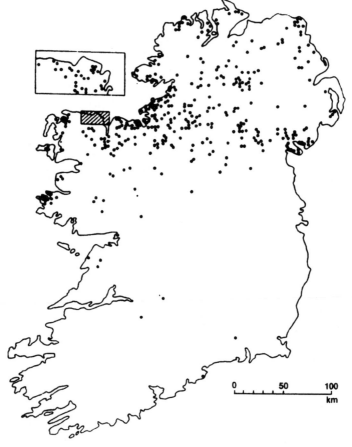

4.1 *The distribution of court tombs (after Ó Nualláin, 1989)*

There are unmistakable court tombs in Scotland—indeed at one period it was thought that Scotland was the source of the Irish tombs and their accompanying material. It is now, however, apparent that the Scottish tombs have their greatest affinity with tombs that typologically are rather late in the Irish series and whose accompanying ceramic and lithic material is also late in the Irish series.

LAYOUT

Essentially, a court tomb consists of a series of chambers, which can be arranged in an almost infinite variety of patterns. In practice they may have two, as at Bavan,

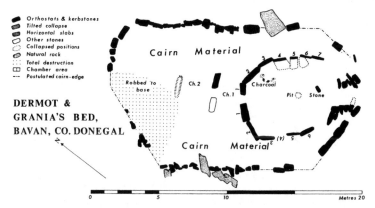

4.2 *Plan of court tomb at Bavan, Co. Donegal (after Flanagan, 1966)*

County Donegal (fig. 4.2), three, as at Annaghmare, County Armagh (with two subsidiary chambers) (fig. 4.3), or four, as at Audleystown, County Down (in each of two burial galleries) (fig. 4.4). They are constructed of orthostats or upright stones set end to end to form a burial gallery; to the front entrance of this gallery, normally erected to face the rising sun or at least the point on the local horizon where the rising sun was first to be seen, was added a court or forecourt, ranging from a number of stones set on the arc of a circle, as at Ballintaggart, County Armagh, through more or less semicircular forms, as at Ballyalton, County Down, to fully circular or oval forms, as at Creevykeel, County Sligo.

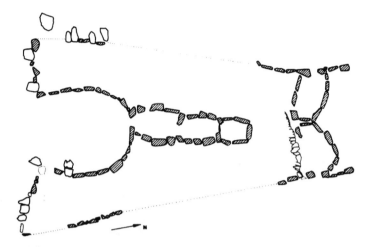

4.3 *Plan of court tomb at Annaghmare, Co. Armagh (after Waterman, 1965)*

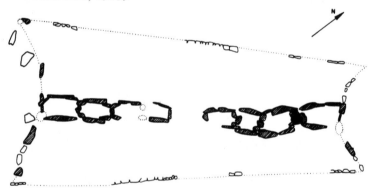

4.4 *Plan of court tomb at Audleystown, Co. Down (after Collins, 1954)*

In some instances the available burial space was increased by setting two galleries side by side, as at Malinmore, County Donegal, or setting two galleries end to end, either sharing a common back-stone, as at Aghanaglack, County Fermanagh, or separated, as at Audleystown, County Down. The additional gallery could be set facing the primary one, sharing a common central court, as at Ballyglass, County Mayo (fig. 4.5). The burial gallery or galleries were then enclosed in a mound or cairn

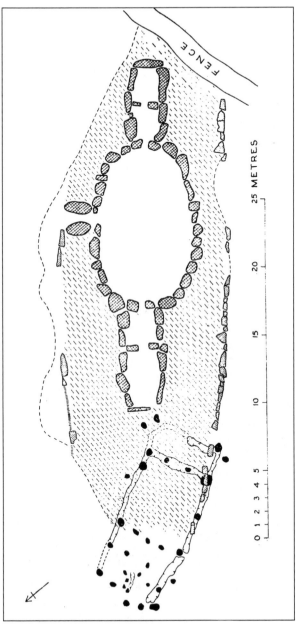

4.5 *Plan of court tomb at Ballyglass, Co. Mayo (after Ó Nualláin, 1972)*

of stones, usually trapezoidal, with the wider end at the front, or east. In the dual-galleried example at Ballyglass, the covering cairn was lozenge-shaped.

Another way of increasing the capacity was to insert additional subsidiary chambers into the cairn, into one or both sides of the court, as at Croaghbeg, County Donegal, or into the sides of the cairn, as at Annaghmare, County Armagh (fig. 4.3), or even into the back of the cairn, as at Barnes Lower, County Tyrone. At Tamnyrankin, County Derry, a subsidiary two-chambered gallery has patently been built onto the end of the cairn, which was then extended. In some places, such as Behy, County Mayo, additional chambers were added to the rear of the gallery as transepts, forming a sort of cruciform gallery.

SIZES

Obviously the overall size of the cairn depended ultimately on the number of chambers to be accommodated, and their size; on whether the court or courts were full or less than so; on the restrictions imposed by the site; and, of course, on the local stone supply. (There is no evidence that stone was transported over long distances to fill the needs of the builders.) At Ballintaggart, County Armagh, a four-chambered gallery, with a very shallow forecourt, was accommodated in a cairn a mere 13 m long; a two-chambered gallery at Knockoneill, County Derry, with a broad open forecourt, is in a cairn 16 m long; a two-chambered gallery with a full forecourt at Croaghbeg, County Donegal, is in a cairn 36 m long; while the original 29 m cairn at Creevykeel, County Sligo, accommodating a two-chambered gallery with a full oval court, was lengthened to 46 m to accommodate two subsidiary chambers.

It is worth recording that the chambers of tombs in the west tend to be much more spacious than those in the east: the chambers at Tamnyrankin, County Derry, are even big enough for a grown man standing in one of the chambers to be completely invisible from outside, while he would be visible even kneeling at Audleystown, County Down. In many ways this trait is a direct result of the local availability of stone: quartzite tends to come in more generous slab sizes than schist.

SITING

It has long been observed that court tombs are to be found for the most part at altitudes that are neither too little nor too great; in practice most are to be found at a height between thirty and two hundred metres. The received explanation has been that, for agricultural purposes, their builders preferred to avoid the heavier soils of the lowlands and, at the other extreme, the scant soils of the higher ground.

While this is a grand statistical truth, prone to grand universal interpretation, it manages to conceal the actuality of the diversity of sites occupied by court tombs and the diversity of land types on which they occur. In a small valley in south County Donegal with a small stream flowing into Donegal Bay are grouped three court tombs; in ascending order of altitude they are Croaghbeg, at 38 to 69 m, Shalwy, at 38 to 69 m, and Bavan, at 102 to 138 m. All are of two chambers, with full, rather oval courts. Croaghbeg and Shalwy are in a part of the valley that is not now, and probably never was, likely to achieve any great fertility. It is only at Bavan that the adjoining land could ever have boasted any depth of soil and any consequent pretence at fertility; the hill slope to the south and east of the sites, however, claims a much more hospitable aspect.

The message seems to be that good land was too valuable to be cluttered with monuments, especially when the stone necessary to construct them was concentrated in the valley bottom. Even in this situation the selection of sites was not easy. The monument in Shalwy was constructed on a narrow ridge, facing upstream. Unfortunately the ridge proved a little narrow for the cairn of the tomb, and on the northern side both revetment and cairn must have started collapsing almost while construction was proceeding. On the other hand, at a much higher altitude, the tomb at Knockoneill, County Derry (again two-chambered but with a broad, fairly open court), at 200 to 233 m, was sited on a pleasant, fairly level expanse of parkland.

CONSTRUCTION

Obviously the first stage in the construction of a court tomb was to set up the orthostats of the chambers, frequently in prepared sockets, with packing-stones if necessary, but always ensuring that the intended primary gallery was correctly aligned on the rising sun. If sills between the chambers were to be used, as was normally the case, they would be set at this early stage of construction; and if a monstrous internal closing slab was to be installed, as at Shalwy, County Donegal, chipped into shape like an enormous flint implement, it would necessarily be installed at this stage also.

For convenience of construction, the next stage should be the placing in position of the roof. This could consist of a large slab to completely cover the interior, as at Shalwy, or a combination of a large slab with corbel slabs (slabs set at an angle and held in place by the superimposed weight of cairn material built up over their lower ends), or even corbelling alone, as appears to have been the case (over a fairly small span) at Audleystown, County Down.

There is evidence from Shalwy and Croaghbeg, County Donegal, in the form of small chock-stones, that the raising of lintels and roof stones into place was not achieved by building inclined ramps and using rollers but by a system of 'jacking'. One end of, say, the lintel was raised with the aid of a lever, and stones were set under that end while the other was raised, and so on until the lintel could be positioned over the supporting orthostats. The chock-stone, of course, stayed in place, so that the lever could be removed. The raising of the orthostats of the forecourt could then be effected and the covering cairn amassed. This was held in place along the edges either by rows of orthostats forming a kerb, as at Bavan, County Donegal, or by dry-stone walling, as at Audleystown, County Down, or by a combination of the two, as at Shalwy, County Donegal.

A notable feature of court tombs is the lintels that are placed over the entrance; indeed at Shalwy there is an impressive double lintel, almost suggesting architectural pretensions.

At Shanballyedmond, County Tipperary, a most unusual structural feature was discovered. Here a two-chambered gallery set in a rather U-shaped cairn, revetted with a combination of non-contiguous orthostats and dry-stone walling, was further embellished by a series of thirty-four posts set to echo the outline of the revetment but slightly more than two metres outside it. It has been remarked that similar features have not been observed in connection with any other Irish megalithic monument. (At Shalwy and Croaghbeg, indeed, such a feature would have been quite impossible.)

PURPOSE

The natural assumption that court tombs, as the name given to them implies, were burial monuments has in fact been challenged, the submission being that they were rather 'temples' of some sort—a focus for some religious activity or other. To deny this is not at all to deny that they enjoyed a ritualistic role as far as their builders were concerned. The courts and forecourts often contain features suggestive of ritual: pits containing food remains in the form of animal bone, for example, as if it had been tidied away in the wake of a wake.

Possibly this 'temple' notion was inspired by the fact that human remains in the tombs are remarkably scanty for the effort involved in their construction. In many tombs where traces of cremated human bone have been recovered, examination has resulted in only one or two individuals being identified. These, of course, are minimum figures, based on the existence of certain diagnostic bones, suggesting in fact that at least one or two individuals were present. To make matters apparently worse, many of the tombs have produced no evidence at all of burials and certainly no evidence of how many people might have been buried in the monument. Even in these cases, however, there are often traces of ash or charcoal, accompanied by heat-shattered flint implements.

The problem, particularly in the west, lies in the fact that the soil is too acidic for the preservation of even cremated bone. In the less acidic soils of County Down, however, the tomb at Audleystown, consisting of two four-chambered galleries, produced evidence of at least thirty-four individuals, not evenly distributed. The tomb at Creggandevesky, County Tyrone, produced, surprisingly, evidence of at least twenty-nine individuals.

When the evidence is summed up, it appears that from a total of twenty-seven court tombs that have produced any bone at all, the cremated bone discovered has amounted to no more than (a minimum of) eighty-one individuals, of whom thirty-five have been classed as adults and of whom at least ten were males and eleven were females. Only four could be classed as adolescents, while seven were estimated to have been under ten years of age at death. All in all, it seems a remarkably small total for the expending of so much effort in their burial.

GRAVE-GOODS AND OTHER FINDS

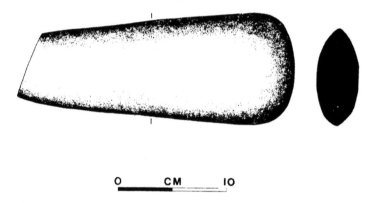

0   CM   10

4.6 *Ground stone axe from Belfast (after Sheridan, 1986)*

The Irish court tombs have produced, by and large, a remarkably consistent range of material (the term grave-goods should be restricted to those items found inside the burial galleries), though not all the items in this repertoire are necessarily to be found in any single site. The pottery recovered from court tombs is mainly of the type known as Western Neolithic, either simple plain bowls or more complex forms with shoulders (fig. 3.4); decorated examples occur, including the ware known as Ballyalton bowls (originally known as Beacharra ware, because of an assumed source in Scotland) and a coarser ware known as Sandhills ware. The typical flintwork includes hollow scrapers, plano-convex knives, end scrapers, and leaf or lozenge-shaped arrow-heads (fig. 3.2) and javelin-heads (fig. 3.3). Beads of various forms are represented too, ranging from simple little disc-shaped ones to globular and even very sophisticated lozenge-shaped ones.

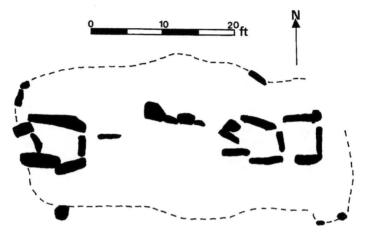

4.7 *Plan of portal tomb at Ballyrenan, Co. Tyrone (after Davies, 1937)*

Occasionally ground stone axes appear. Some sites, such as Audleystown, County Down, and Bavan, County Donegal, have produced almost ideal mixtures of the typical grave-goods or finds.

While the pottery found is, not unexpectedly, usually in fragments, occasionally complete pots—or at least pots that were complete when deposited—are recovered. This was the case at Knockoneill, County Derry, where a lintel that had collapsed onto the rear of the first chamber had protected a complete Western Neolithic bowl, and at Ballintaggart, County Armagh, where deliberate blocking of the entrance to the gallery enclosed several pots that had clearly been complete when they were incorporated in the blocking.

PORTAL TOMBS

It is generally agreed that portal tombs are derived from court tombs, and particularly from the subsidiary chambers, or galleries, inserted in the cairns of court tombs, presumably to provide additional space for burials at a more economic price (in terms of labour) than would be entailed in building additional, and separate, court tombs. Two-chambered portal tombs exist, as at Ballyrenan, County Tyrone (fig. 4.7), reflecting the fact that two-chambered subsidiary galleries exist, as at Tamnyrankin, County Derry.

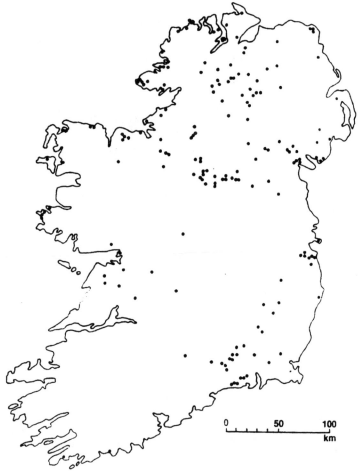

4.8 *The distribution of portal tombs (after Ó Nualláin, 1985)*

The distribution of portal tombs in Ireland extends the area covered by the court tombs further into the south and east (fig. 4.8); some are even present in Wales, suggesting again that the movement of people was not always into Ireland.

Grave-goods and other finds
For the most part, the finds from portal tombs are strikingly similar to those from court tombs. At Ballyrenan, County Tyrone, in addition to normal Western Neolithic pottery, some

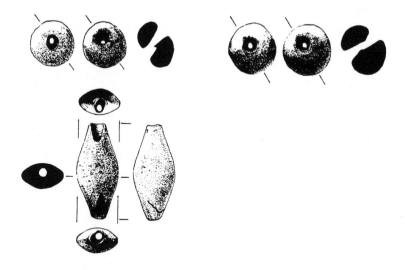

4.9 *Stone beads from the court tomb at Bavan, Co. Donegal (after Flanagan, 1966)*

decorated, as well as a flint leaf-shaped arrow-head, were found stone beads, both globular and lozenge-shaped, identical to those from the court tomb at Bavan, County Donegal (fig. 4.9). At Ballykeel, County Armagh, a most ornate pottery vessel was discovered. This almost total identity of finds certainly reinforces the notion of their relationship.

STONE CIRCLES
Although stone circles will be considered further under the subject of Beaker culture, because they have proved to be a very fruitful source of Beaker pottery, there is no doubt that many of them first saw the light in the Neolithic Period; even those that have also produced Beaker pottery have usually produced greater quantities of Neolithic pottery, such as those in the Lough Gur complex. There are, however, a number that have been excavated, or examined for some other reason, that seemed devoid of Beaker attributes. That at Drumskinny, County Fermanagh, produced a small fragment of Neolithic pottery, while the stone circle at Cuilbane, County Derry, produced a large cache of flint flakes and implements of unmistakable Neolithic character.

LINKARDSTOWN CISTS

There exist in Ireland, particularly in the south-east (fig. 4.10), a number of burial monuments that have been described as 'Linkardstown cists'. Essentially they consist of a rather 'megalithic' cist, or burial chamber, set inside what could be described as a stone circle, or a double stone circle, and then covered with a cairn or mound of stone. A typical example is at Baunogenasraid, County Carlow (fig. 4.11). What is most notable about them is that in addition to containing normal Western Neolithic pottery they also contain very ornate decorated pots (fig. 4.12), which

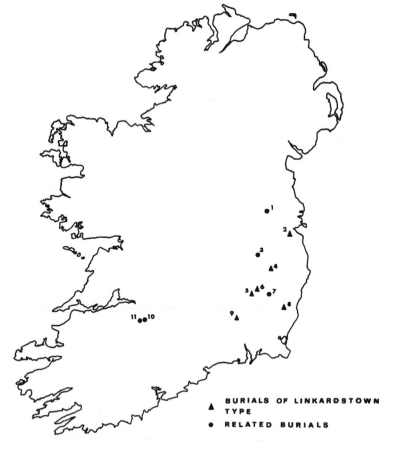

4.10 *The distribution of Linkardstown cists (after Raftery, 1974)*

strikingly resemble the equally ornate vessel from the portal tomb at Ballykeel, County Armagh (fig. 4.13).

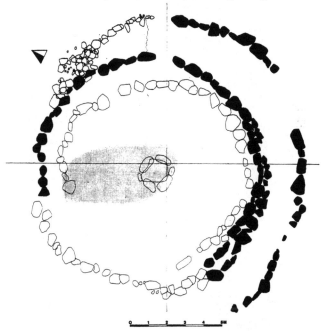

4.11 *Plan of Baunogenasraid, Co. Carlow (after Raftery, 1974)*

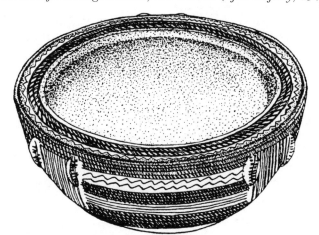

4.12 *Decorated vessel from Linkardstown cist at Jerpoint West, Co. Kilkenny (after Ryan, 1973)*

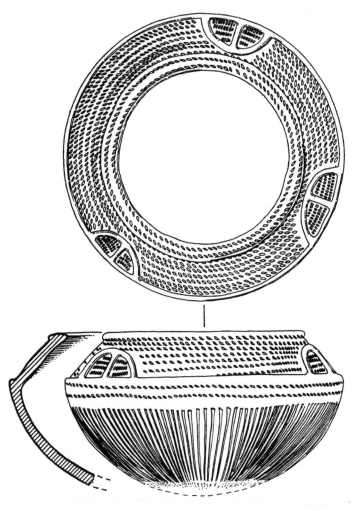

4.13 *Ornate pottery vessel from portal tomb at Ballykeel, Co. Armagh (after Collins, 1965)*

5

THE PASSAGE TOMBS

The other main type of megalithic tomb present in Ireland is the passage tomb, of which over three hundred examples are known (fig. 5.1). Unlike the court tombs and portal tombs, they have a strong tendency to cluster together to create what has been called a 'cemetery' but which might more properly be called a necropolis. Several of these clusters have been identified, including the most famous of all, that in the valley of the River Boyne, which contains some of the best-known sites, such as Knowth and Newgrange. Other great clusters occur at Loughcrew, County Meath, and Carrowmore, County Sligo.

Another way in which the passage tombs differ from the other main types of tomb is in their liking for sites on high ground—often the very summits of hills or small mountains. Perhaps the most spectacularly sited is the so-called Méabh's Carn, topping the 300 m Knocknarea in County Sligo and plainly visible over an enormous stretch of countryside.

Another great difference between the passage tombs and the other two main types is that passage tombs universally prefer to be covered with round cairns rather than long cairns. The final great difference is the presence in so many passage tombs of decorated stones, often in profusion.

DIVERSITY
While the 'ideal' passage tomb might appear to be Newgrange, County Meath—where a definite passage, some thirty metres long, penetrates a huge circular cairn some eighty-

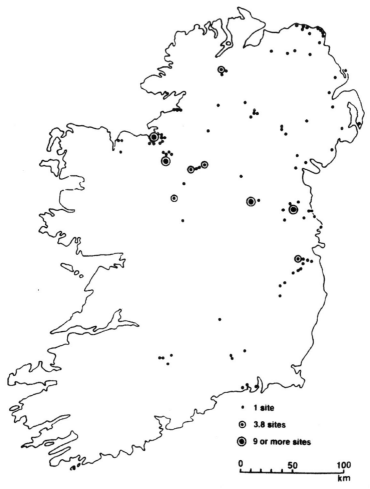

5.1 *The distribution of passage tombs (after Ó Nualláin, 1989)*

five metres in diameter and terminates in a cruciform chamber with a great 'vaulted' (in fact corbelled) roof—there is a surprising diversity to be seen among the range of Irish passage tombs (fig. 5.2). For a start, not all the cairns, or covering mounds of stone, are on such an impressive scale. Some of the cairns, among them some in the Loughcrew cluster, can be as small as eight metres in diameter. Some, known as undifferentiated passage tombs, appear not even to have a passage but only a slight widening of the entrance

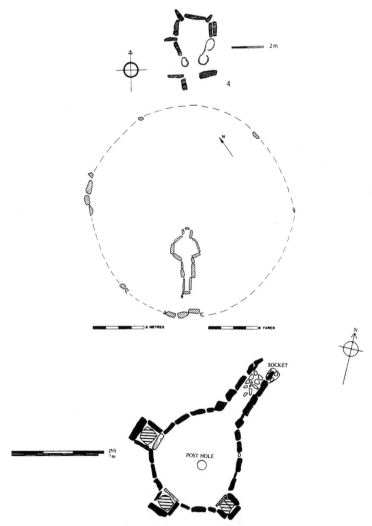

5.2 *Ground plans of passage tombs as an indication of the diversity that occurs in their layout:* (a) *Knockmany, Co. Tyrone;* (b) *Slieve Gullion, Co. Armagh;* (c) *Fourknocks, Co. Meath (after Herity and Eogan, 1977)*

as it merges with the chamber, with perhaps a sill-stone to mark the junction between the two elements (fig. 5.3).

Another common, but not universal, trait of passage tombs is the existence of a number of satellite tombs

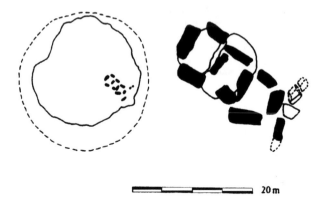

20 m

5.3 *Plan of undifferentiated passage tomb at Tara, Co. Meath (after Herity, 1974)*

grouped round the skirt of a larger tomb, even when that tomb is part of a major cluster, as at Knowth, County Meath. As Mount Sandel dominates the Irish Earlier Mesolithic Period, so do two of the excavated passage tombs in the Boyne Valley dominate the story of passage tombs in Ireland: Newgrange, which has three satellites, and Knowth, with seventeen.

NEWGRANGE

Even before the extensive and systematic excavation of Newgrange began in 1962 it had been well known and admired for several centuries—although the old belief that it had been raided by the Vikings in 861 or 862 has been competently dismissed. There is a letter by the Welsh antiquary Edward Lhwyd, dated to 1699, shortly after its discovery, describing, among other things, the celebrated entrance-stone, 'rudely carved,' the chamber and its 'three apartments,' and the 'barbarous sculpture' of the side-stones of the passage. Newgrange was long regarded as 'one of the most important ancient places in Europe.'

The monument itself is on the highest point of a low ridge overlooking the River Boyne, with several other passage tombs in the immediate vicinity. The mound, which still stood to a height of between 10.9 and 13.4 m, was not perfectly circular, having a diameter from north-west to south-east of 78.6 m and from north-east to south-west of

85.3 m (fig. 5.4). At the base of the cairn, ninety-seven massive contiguous slabs laid on their long edges form a kerb; many of them bear characteristic decoration. The cairn itself is surrounded by a non-concentric circle of standing stones, of which twelve survive out of a possible thirty-five or so.

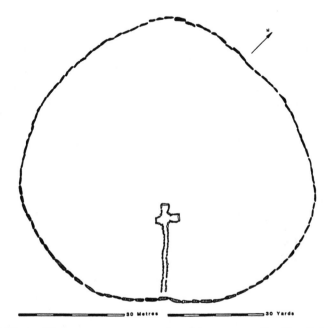

5.4 *Plan of the great passage tomb at Newgrange, Co. Meath (after O'Kelly, 1982)*

The passage, with its celebrated decorated entrance-stone, has been accessible since Lhwyd's time. It runs south-east to north-west for a distance of 18.95 m. Its sides are lined with large orthostatic slabs, many of them decorated and increasing in height towards the chamber; on these the slabs used for the roof rest, either directly or on corbels laid on them.

The chamber at the end of the passage is cruciform, each 'apartment' having some decorated side-stones. The corbelled roof rises to a level some six metres above the floor and is sealed with a single cap-stone. Two of the apartments contained a so-called 'basin-stone', while the third, the largest, contained two, one inside the other.

The excavation

Excavation of the material that had slipped from the cairn after its completion showed that originally there had been a covering of white quartz, forming a nearly vertical revetment, between two and three metres above the level of the kerb. It was also demonstrated that the belief that an ancient 'bank-and-ditch' feature had surrounded the cairn was erroneous.

Beneath the cairn-slip a hut foundation was found, slightly oval, with an external diameter of between three and four metres, marked by a partial trench and a number of post-holes, which was thought to be either contemporary with the mound or very slightly later. Finds associated with this included a flint axe fragment, a flint hollow scraper, and a fragment of a stone bowl.

The stone circle surrounding the cairn was shown to be probably either contemporary with, or earlier than, the cairn. Excavation in the material of the cairn itself showed that the mound had a layered structure: the stones that formed the main cairn mass were interspersed with layers of turves or sods, and turves had been used to help hold the cairn material in place.

Excavation and examination of the top of the passage and chamber revealed many interesting aspects of the tomb's construction—as well as resulting in the discovery of a number of additional decorated stones. It was discovered that grooves had been made on slabs to lead water percolating through the cairn away from the passage; and in the gaps between roof-stones a filler of burnt soil and sea sand had been used as a caulking material.

The most spectacular discovery, in many ways, was that of the 'roof-box'. A decorated stone that had long been visible and had even been termed a 'false lintel' proved to form the roof of a small box or chamber. It is through this chamber that the rising sun penetrates at the winter solstice (21 December) and illuminates the rear of the chamber.

A great deal of disturbance had taken place in the passage and chamber, for a variety of reasons, ranging from ill-judged and ill-recorded 'excavation' and attempts at conservation to the activities of burrowing animals. Despite this, a surprising amount of archaeological material and information was recovered. In addition to a quantity of human bones, seven stone 'marbles', four pendants, two beads, a used flint flake, a bone chisel and fragments of several bone pins were recovered from the passage and chamber, all of them very compatible with the passage tomb tradition.

Structural skills

When all is said and done, the main contribution of Newgrange to the archaeological record, apart from the 'gallery' of decorated stones, is its demonstration of the architectural and engineering skills employed by its builders. The correct alignment of the roof-box to achieve the penetration of the rising sun at the winter solstice and so the illumination of the rear of the chamber is, clearly, a spectacular feat that entailed considerable observational, recording and architectural skills. No less remarkable, however, was the skilful use of turves to act as a buffer against the slippage of cairn material during construction.

The engineering and organisational skills required to create such an immense and enduring monument were clearly considerable. It has been calculated that in addition to the 97 slabs forming the kerb (none weighing less than a tonne) and a further 450 large structural stones used to form the passage, chamber, and roof, the monument consists of some 200,000 tonnes of stone. Fortunately, most of the rock of which the structural stones are composed is greywacke, available within a reasonable distance of the site—not from a quarry, since they were weathered at the time of the tomb's construction, but gathered from the land surface more or less where they had been left by the ice. The great mass of cairn material also was available within a reasonable distance, in the river terraces of the Boyne.

It has been estimated that the entire monument could have been constructed by a well-organised work force of some four hundred people, abandoning their agricultural activities for two months after the spring sowing over a period of at least sixteen years. During those sixteen years too the work of executing the decoration would have been carried out, possibly by specialist craftsmen.

The art

Whether we regard the decoration on the stones at Newgrange and the other passage tombs as 'art' or merely 'decoration' is a moot point, its outcome totally dependent on modern perceptions and definitions (fig. 5.5). Whichever term we choose, the display at Newgrange—on the kerb-stones, the side-stones of the passage, and even in places where the decoration became invisible immediately after the placing of the stone—is both prodigious and spectacular.

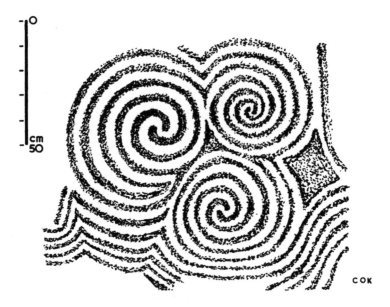

5.5 *The decorated 'entrance-stone' at Newgrange, Co. Meath (after O'Kelly, 1982)*

In all, there are 75 stones bearing decorations, some of these on more than one face, so that the total number of decorated faces at present recorded is 84. (Since the entire perimeter of the mound was not excavated, there are certain to be additional decorated stones—indeed tantalising snatches of decoration can be discerned on the upper portions of stones whose greater part is still buried.) Of the motifs in the repertoire of passage tomb art (fig. 5.6), lozenges and zigzags are the most commonly used at Newgrange. Circles are the next most common motif but are

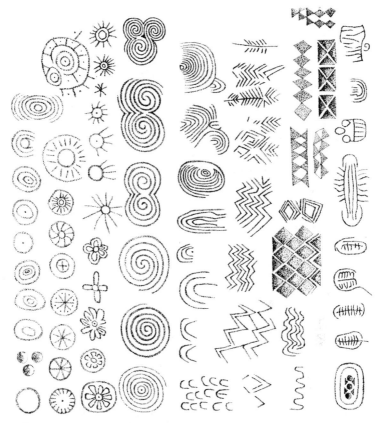

5.6 *Some examples of motifs that constitute the repertoire of passage tomb art (after Herity, 1974)*

often relegated to rather inconspicuous positions. While spirals of differing types are less common, their frequently prominent positions seem to imbue them with an importance at odds with their numerical frequency.

All the decoration at Newgrange is geometrical, curvilinear or rectilinear, and aniconic: no attempts at representational art can convincingly be detected. It is difficult, therefore, to interpret any originally intended symbolism.

KNOWTH
While Newgrange, particularly now, with its partially reinstated white quartzite facing, is at first sight the most

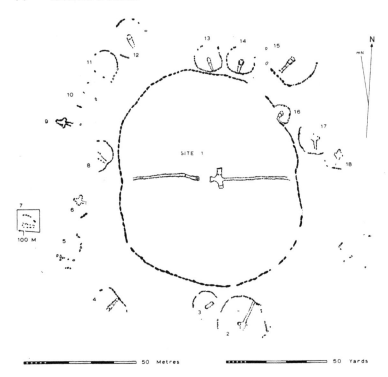

5.7 *Plan of the great passage tomb at Knowth with its subsidiaries (after Eogan, 1986)*

spectacular of the passage tombs, Knowth, County Meath (fig. 5.7)—of slightly smaller size, in a rather oval cairn, with a diameter of eighty metres from east to west and ninety metres from south to north—presented such a number of surprises that it rivals or even exceeds Newgrange in importance.

It had long been known that there was one passage; the discovery of a second, entering from the other side of the mound, was not altogether to be expected. One passage, 34.2 m long, penetrates from the west and terminates in a simple squarish chamber, while another penetrates from the east, 40 m long, terminating in a cruciform chamber. The two chambers are very nearly back-to-back.

Grave-goods and other finds

The great cruciform tomb—the eastern tomb—at Knowth terminates in a 'vaulted' (actually corbelled) central chamber, off which open three 'recesses', in which the burials were placed. One burial deposit, evidently properly belonging to the right-hand recess, was in fact just outside its entrance. Inside this recess, and of a size to preclude its having been inserted in the recess after the building of the passage or even after the erection of the jambs flanking the entrance to the recess, was a large decorated basin-stone. There were six deposits of cremated bone, which, after insertion, had been covered with a thin layer of earth or small flat stones.

The associated finds included pieces of antler pins, stone beads, and various forms of pendant. In addition, however, was a flint mace-head, superbly fashioned and decorated. In the left-hand recess, although it was divided into ten 'compartments' by a number of smallish stones, there was a general blanket of cremation. Grave-goods in this recess consisted of two pestle pendants, parts of two mushroom-headed pins, and parts of five other pins. On a layer of dark earth covering the burials was an overturned basin of sand-stone, from which a portion had been broken. The end recess contained the remains of a cremation.

The western tomb also contained a sandstone basin, apparently displaced. It also produced part of a stone pestle or mace-head and part of the stem of a large antler pin.

The satellite tombs
Superficially there was little or no indication that the main tomb at Knowth was more or less ringed with smaller satellite tombs; all of these had been damaged, in some instances extensively. Five of these satellite tombs have cruciform chambers (fig. 5.8); ten are simple tombs, with no differentiation between passage and chamber (fig. 5.9); while the other two are almost completely destroyed. They are grouped around the hilltop, close to the main tomb; some adjoin it, others are a few metres away. Only one tomb is some distance from it.

The tombs with cruciform chambers are housed in cairns between twelve and twenty metres in diameter, of low surviving height, with many orthostats missing. All five contained remains of cremated burials. Site 2 had remains of both adults and children, though the numbers could not

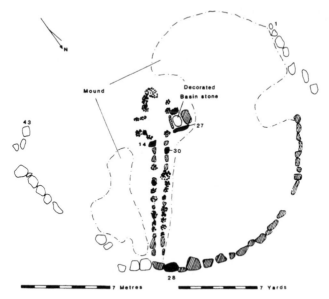

5.8 *Plan of one of the cruciform satellite tombs at Knowth (site 2); decorated stones are shown in solid black (after Eogan, 1986)*

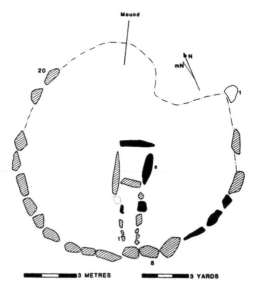

5.9 *Plan of one of the undifferentiated satellite tombs at Knowth (site 14); decorated stones are shown in solid black (after Eogan, 1986)*

be calculated; site 6 had several adults and at least one child about three years old; site 9 had two adults and two children; site 17 had an adult and two children; while site 18 had a single adult. Small finds from these smaller tombs included stone basins, Carrowkeel ware, chalk balls, flint flakes, and bone pendants.

The undifferentiated tombs had diameters between ten and twenty metres. Sites 10, 4, 13 and 14 contained spreads of cremated bone, too meagre or damaged to identify. Site 12 contained the cremated remains of at least one infant and one adult; site 15 contained three adults and three or more children; site 16 contained the cremated remains of four adults, six children, and a baby. Finds from these sites included bone pins and flint fragments, including hollow scrapers and Carrowkeel ware.

Of the destroyed sites, site 3 produced the cremated remains of a person aged nearly twenty, a decorated bone or antler object, and Carrowkeel ware. The other two, sites 5 and 11, produced neither burials nor small finds. Decorated stones, 41 of them, employing 57 surfaces, occurred in twelve of the smaller tombs.

The art or decoration
Another surprise at Knowth was the richness of the decoration. At least 250 of the stones of the kerb and of the passages are decorated, some on more than one face. (This is the equivalent of some 45 per cent of all the examples of Megalithic art from all the sites in Ireland that contain decorated stones.) The predominant technique was picking, with either a chisel or a punch; incision was used as well, involving drawing a pointed implement across the surface of the stone. The motifs employed include rectilinear styles consisting of chevrons, triangles, and lozenges, and curvilinear styles, including spirals, grouped arcs, meander-patterns, and grouped and dispersed circles.

This bald list, however, does little credit to the glories of the decoration. Perhaps, however, the *chef d'oeuvre* of the art or decoration at Knowth is that on the ceremonial flint mace-head found in the right-hand recess of the chamber of the eastern tomb. It is difficult to reconcile the splendour of the decorated stones with the crudeness and coarseness of the pottery that is such a characteristic of passage tombs, the so-called Carrowkeel ware (fig. 5.10).

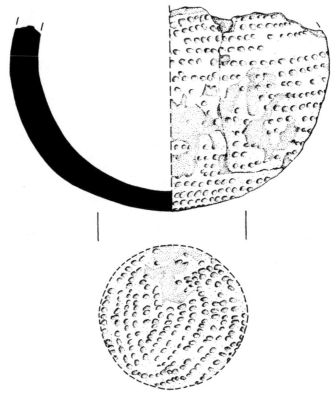

5.10 *Carrowkeel ware vessel found under peat at Bracklin, Co. Westmeath (after Herity, 1974)*

Neolithic occupation at Knowth

To the west of the great tomb at Knowth and overlaid by five of the satellite tombs was an area of Neolithic domestic activity. Features include a sub-rectangular structure, which may have been a house, pits, hearths, palisade trenches, and rough paving. The sub-rectangular structure, directly under one of the satellites (tomb 8) and therefore considerably disturbed by its construction, measures some ten by twelve metres, delimited by a trench dug into the sub-soil but with an undug stretch in the north-eastern corner.

The trench is deepest on the western side, with a row of eleven circular post-holes, each about 150 mm in diameter. On the other three sides the ditch was much slighter. Inside the enclosed area were several features, including an area of rough paving, with a hearth between it and the entrance. Two smaller hearths were also found. Also inside the enclosed area were seven pits, one of which predated the ditches, as part of it was cut away when the southern ditch was dug. All were filled with soft, dark earth.

The finds from this structure included pottery, all Western Neolithic but with a rather surprising trait: many of the sherds have cavities, usually on the outside, caused by the original presence of large grits, which subsequently became detached. This, it is suggested, would have made the fabric porous and therefore unsuitable for containing liquids, for which only the better-finished and burnished vessels would have been suitable. The flintwork found was not very extensive: it included two scrapers and a leaf-shaped blade.

There were two curved and roughly concentric palisade trenches, between fifty-eight and fifty-nine metres long. The eastern trench was better preserved than the western and showed evidence of more post-holes, not at regular intervals. No really satisfactory purpose could be established for the palisades. In the area between them considerable activity took place: there were two areas with pebble floors, which may have constituted a living area, though no indications of a house were discovered. There was a small area in which flint fragments were particularly concentrated and which was deemed to be a flint-knapping area, where the predominant raw material appears to have been pebble flint.

In general, the finds were of Western Neolithic pottery, in considerable quantity: the butt end of a basalt axe-head, and three arrow-heads, two of which were leaf-shaped. Interestingly, no hollow scrapers were present, despite the fact that in the absence of Carrowkeel ware (which does occur in the tombs) the assemblage bears more resemblance to material from court tombs.

GENERAL FINDS

In addition to the stones bearing art or decoration and the contrastingly plain Carrowkeel ware, there is a distinctive repertoire of items that occur and recur in passage tombs. One of the two most common is bone pendants (fig. 5.11), which have been found not only at Newgrange but at sites

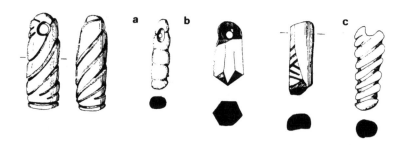

5.11 *Pendants from passage tombs:* (a) *from Tara, Co. Meath;* (b) *from Loughcrew, Co. Meath;* (c) *from Carrowmore, Co. Sligo (after Herity, 1974)*

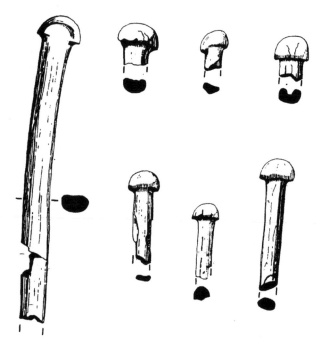

5.12 *Antler pins from the passage tomb at Fourknocks, Co. Meath (after Herity, 1974)*

all over the country: in the tomb on top of Belmore Mountain, County Fermanagh, in the Carrowmore cemetery in County Sligo, and in several of the tombs at Carrowkeel in County Sligo. The next most common item is beads, again often of bone, which are represented again in the tombs in the Boyne Valley and in tombs at Carrowkeel and Carrowmore. Bone or antler pins are another common component, featuring in tombs in all the major cemeteries (fig. 5.12).

SITES RELATED TO PASSAGE TOMBS

A few sites exist that, while exhibiting features in common with passage tombs, are not obviously themselves passage tombs. At Ballynoe, County Down, a large stone circle exists. There may formerly have been a passage tomb on the site, for among the finds were sherds of Carrowkeel ware.

Not far away, at Millin Bay, County Down, is an oval cairn over a long stone-lined burial gallery; quite a number of the stones bore decoration, but not in precise passage tomb style. Again Carrowkeel ware was present. The most interesting feature of this site is that underneath it were the remains of a dry-stone wall, presumably indicating land division.

6

BEAKERS AND THE BRONZE AGE

The nature of the beaker presence in Ireland is peculiar, to say the least. Beakers are present in considerable quantity (fig. 6.1), and since their construction introduced a technical novelty, in that they are not only flat-bottomed but also ring-built (the flat, circular base being turned up with a chamfered edge, to which the first ring, with a chamfered edge on the inside, is added, until the whole pot is constructed), there is a very strong suggestion that the makers were also present.

'Beaker-compatible material' (that is, other tools and weapons that are associated with beakers in other parts of Europe but have seldom, if ever, been found in such association in Ireland) is also well represented. The tanged but rivetless copper dagger is present, although not in great quantities (fig. 6.2); flint arrow-heads with barbs and with tangs scarcely protruding beyond them, which seems a type particularly similar to those found with beakers in Britain and the Continent, are common enough (fig. 6.3). Bracers or archers' wristguards are reasonably common, including some of a type that would not seem out of place in beaker assemblages elsewhere (fig. 6.4).

The main problem with all these types of beaker-compatible material is that they tend to have a greater concentration in the northern part of the country, which traditionally is regarded as the part of Ireland least blessed with sources of copper. It is this fact that has led many authorities to question the role of Beaker People in the

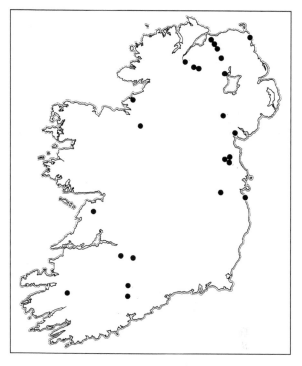

6.1 *The distribution of Beaker pottery (after Case, 1995)*

introduction of metallurgy to Ireland. (The recent discovery of Beaker pottery, apparently connected with copper-mining and other metalworking techniques, at Ross Island, County Kerry, may help to solve this problem.) In the light of the apparent separation of the bulk of the beaker material from the copper sources, it was only the evidence from the stream sediment analyses in northern Ireland that provided an escape from this conclusion. While one problem with the results of the stream sediment analyses in northern Ireland is that it is by no means clear what other elements may have been associated with the copper in the parent ore, the published analyses of specimens of native copper ore from County Antrim showed that they consisted of virtually pure copper (99.4 per cent, as against 98.9 per cent), with only minor quantities of other metals.

Importantly, three groups of metals, also remarkable for their purity, in that they contain no more than a trace of lead

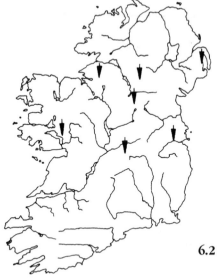

6.2 *The distribution of rivet-less tanged copper daggers (after Harbison, 1978)*

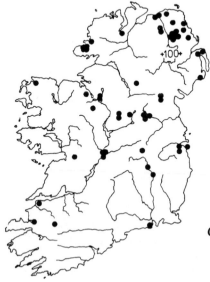

6.3 *The distribution of flint barbed-and-tanged arrow-heads (after Harbison, 1978)*

or arsenic, have been shown statistically to have an origin other than either County Antrim or Counties Kerry or Cork.

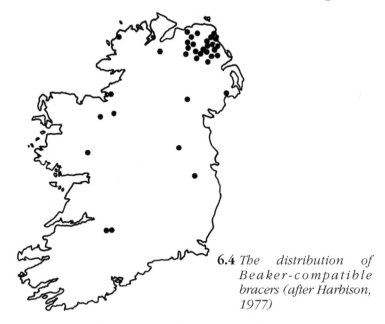

6.4 *The distribution of Beaker-compatible bracers (after Harbison, 1977)*

The combined evidence of the stream sediment analyses and the native copper and groups of metals exceedingly low in copper and arsenic, amounting to over 10 per cent of the analysed metal objects of the Irish Earlier Bronze Age, suggest that the absence (up to now) of Beaker material from the undeniably copper-rich south-west may not after all have presented such an obstacle to the Beaker People in introducing metallurgy to Ireland.

There are, however, other apparent difficulties in establishing the nature of the Beaker People's colonisation of Ireland, particularly if the assumption is made that the Beaker People in Ireland had simply moved across the Irish Sea from Britain. If this was so, how do we explain away so many of the features of Beaker society in Britain that simply do not appear to exist in Ireland? Where are the round barrows with crouched, unburnt burials? (It is worth recording here that in a cist in a slightly oval round cairn with food vessel at Cornaclery, County Derry, the flexed skeleton of a man 1.88 m [6 feet 2 inches] tall was found, who is described in the report as 'typifying the race of Beaker Folk.') Where are the relatively frequent associations of

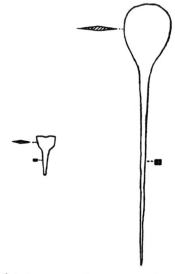

6.5 *Bronze fragment from Largantea, Co. Derry, and intact 'palmella' point (after Herring, 1938)*

beaker pottery with metal tools and weapons?

Perhaps the concept of colonisation directly, and solely, from Britain should be discarded, or at least modified—even though the distribution not only of Beaker pottery but of the rest of the Beaker-compatible equipment does seem so strongly to suggest it. For example, a fragment of a bronze blade (fig. 6.5) found with a beaker in the wedge tomb at Largantea, County Derry (in fact the first excavated site in Ireland to produce Beaker pottery), has been likened to the 'palmella' points of Iberia. Again, the relative scarcity of beakers, and of Beaker-compatible material of any kind, in the south-west would seem to be an obstacle to any argument in favour of colonisation directly from Iberia, or even from France, which has been suggested.

BEAKER POTTERY IN IRELAND

One of the most interesting features of certain types of beaker is their universality: a beaker from Poland, say, is unmistakably a beaker, showing its affinity with a beaker from Holland or from England (fig. 6.6). The beaker pottery that has been found in Ireland includes representatives of almost every type.

A fairly recent classification of Beaker pottery in Ireland and Britain, based on refined analyses of all relevant factors, 'stratigraphy, typology, material and ritual associations, statistical tests, distribution and absolute chronology' (mainly, it must be said, based on data from Britain), has distinguished seven intrusive beaker groups and, evolved from them, three groups of purely insular character that, while partly regional, were to enjoy lengthy popularity. Five of the intrusive groups appear in Ireland: the European bell beaker, the all-over cord beaker, the Northern British/ Middle Rhine, the Northern British/North Rhine, and the Wessex/Middle Rhine (fig. 6.7).

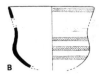

The European bell group is represented at such sites as the wedge tombs at Kilhoyle and Largantea, County Derry, at Moytirra, County Sligo (again, possibly, in connection with a wedge tomb), and from a settlement site at Gortcorbies, County Derry, and another on Dalkey Island, County Dublin, as well as on settlement sites in the Boyne Valley in the shadow of the great passage tombs of Newgrange and Knowth.

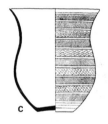

6.6 *Beakers from (A) La Halliade, Hautes-Pyrénées, France, (B) Emmerzand, Drenthe, Netherlands, and (C) Ledce, Moravia, Czech Republic (after Case, 1993)*

All-over cord beakers are represented again on settlement sites in the Boyne Valley and on Dalkey Island, as well as in settlements among the sand dunes at White Park Bay, County Antrim; they are also present among the assemblages at Lough Gur, County Limerick. The other three intrusive groups are represented at such sites as Gortcorbies and the wedge tomb at Kilhoyle, County Derry (Northern British/ Middle Rhine); the settlement site at Ballynagilly, County Tyrone (Northern British/North Rhine); and the settlement site (D) on Knockadoon, County Limerick (Wessex/ Middle Rhine).

Other varieties of beaker pottery are also represented. There is a so-called 'giant' beaker from Cluntyganny, County

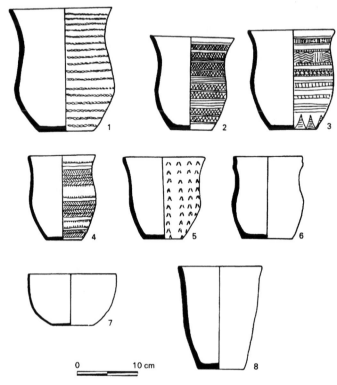

6.7 *British beaker types:* (1) *all-over cord;* (2) *European bell beaker;* (3) *Wessex or middle Rhine;* (4) *north British or middle Rhine;* (5) *rusticated beaker;* (6) *cordoned beaker;* (7) *undecorated bowl;* (8) *flat-based coarseware (after D. L. Clarke, 1970)*

Tyrone (fig 6.8), and there is 'rusticated' or beaker domestic ware from sites such as the enclosure at Monknewtown, County Meath.

BEAKER-COMPATIBLE MATERIAL
Flint arrow-heads
While there are many thousands of flint barbed-and-tanged arrow-heads in Irish museums, many of them are un-deniably of 'post-Beaker' form, of types that have been found on many occasions in association with later types of Earlier Bronze Age pottery. There is a form on which the tang projects little further than the barbs, which seems to

bear closest comparison to the forms found in association with beaker pottery not only in Britain but on the Continent as well. One was found—without beaker or any other pottery—in the wedge tomb at Boviel, County Derry (fig. 6.9); another was found in one of the settlement areas rich in beaker pottery (concentration C) at Knowth, County Meath. Flint barbed-and-tanged arrow-heads occur also at site C, with a small amount of beaker, at Knockadoon, County Limerick, as well as with formidable quantities of beaker at the settlement site at Ballynagilly, County Tyrone.

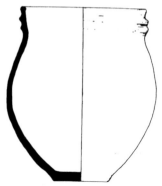

6.8 *Giant beaker from Cluntyganny, Co. Tyrone (after Brennan, 1978)*

6.9 *Barbed-and-tanged flint arrow-head from Boviel, Co. Derry (after Herring, 1940)*

Wristguards

Small rectangular slabs of stone, usually well polished and perforated at each end, are commonly found in association with beaker ware in burials in Britain and the Continent (fig. 6.10). Ethnographic parallels long ago suggested that these were worn on the left wrist to protect it from the backlash of the bow-string. They are surprisingly common in Ireland, though none has been found in direct association with a beaker here. Records do exist, however,

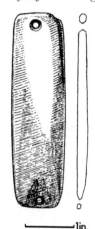

6.10 *Stone wristguard from Moss-Side, Co. Antrim (after Flanagan, 1970)*

that may suggest an association with burials, even possibly with Beaker burials.

The first is from Drumstaple, County Derry, where what appears to have been a bracer was found with an 'urn', bone, and ashes; unfortunately the 'urn' fell to pieces and the apparent bracer was lost. We do not know, therefore, what the 'urn' really was—it might even have been a 'giant' beaker, like the one from Cluntyganny; we do not really know whether the bone was cremated or not—though the fact that it was contained in the 'urn' makes it likely that it was. The second was from Forenaghts Great, County Kildare, where, in the Longstone Rath (where the 'rath' is likely to have been a henge of some sort, named after the standing stone at the base of which the find was made), a fragmentary bracer was found with sherds of coarse pottery, a small flint arrow-head of unspecified type, and cremated bone. Unfortunately the pottery has disappeared, so we cannot tell whether it too might have been a giant beaker or undecorated beaker rusticated ware. The third was from a 'burial', somewhere in County Antrim; there is no record of any other finds.

The only other recorded instance of bracers in Ireland in association with other objects is from Corran, County Armagh, where a pair of bracers were found in a bog (so it is unlikely to be from a burial), 'in a box bound with a gold band, together with some circular gold plates, and several jet beads of various shapes.' Again the ill-luck that seems to dog bracer associations in Ireland struck. The bracers are the only part of this discovery known to survive, though it has been suggested, fairly convincingly, that the gold discs were probably similar to those found in a Beaker burial at Mere, Wiltshire, and therefore that this pair of bracers are likely to be among the earliest bracers known from Ireland.

Gold ornaments

In addition to the postulated pair from Corran, County Armagh, there exist in Ireland seven other provenanced gold discs bearing 'wheel and cross' motifs, reminiscent of racquet-headed pins from eastern Europe (fig. 6.11) and of course of those found in Beaker contexts in Britain, such as the Beaker burial at Mere, Wiltshire. These—in contrast to

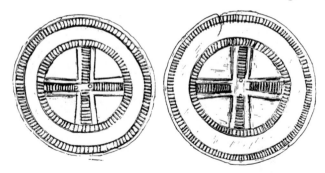

6.11 *Pair of gold discs of Beaker-compatible types from Ballina, Co. Mayo (after Armstrong, 1933)*

other beaker-compatible material—do at least enjoy a more general distribution throughout the country, though still without really penetrating the gold-rich areas of the south-west. There was a suggestion that these discs functioned as button-covers, but their flatness, and the presence of perforations round the edge as well as in the middle, presumably for sewing the disc in place, seem to suggest more or

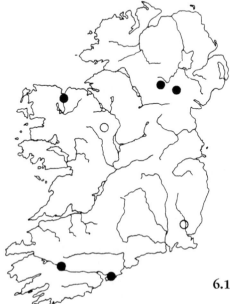

6.12 *The distribution of Beaker-compatible gold discs*

less permanent attachment to a garment of some kind, presumably to indicate status, if not actually rank.

Another gold ornament made from thin sheet gold, the disc from Deehommed, County Down, variously described as an ear-ring or a pin-head, is quite clearly an import: not only does it parallel very closely a pair of ear-rings from Ermegeira, Portugal, but the composition of the gold suggests that it comes from a non-Irish source.

The rivetless tanged copper dagger has already been mentioned as being Beaker-compatible, in that it has been found in association with Beaker pottery in other parts of Europe, though not, so far at least, in Ireland. It has been found in a couple of the small hoards of metal objects so typical of the Earlier Bronze Age in Ireland: those from Whitespots, County Down, and Knocknague, County Galway.

Unfortunately, in both of these associations the tanged daggers are accompanied by metal implements that would suggest a 'post-Beaker' date, that is, a date later than the initial phase of Beaker People's activity in Ireland: the dagger or halberd with a mid-rib from the Whitespots hoard and the axe with slight side-flanges from the Knocknague hoard. A tin-rich axe, of a type not normally to be expected in a Beaker context, was found at Newgrange, County Meath, in an area that apparently produced Beaker pottery.

Stone battle-axes and flint discoidal knives

In addition to the artefacts already described, two other types of object might be described as Beaker-compatible. One is the stone battle-axe—a rather boat-shaped piece of stone, about 150 mm long, with (usually) an 'hour-glass' perforation (a perforation drilled from both sides) about one-third of the distance from the 'stern' along the median line. The front is usually quite pointed, the rear end rounded, though occasionally nearly straight.

Nearly thirty such battle-axes have been found in Ireland; in Britain and on the Continent, but not so far in Ireland, they are sometimes found in association with Beaker pottery. About two-thirds of the provenanced Irish examples have been found in the northern part of the country, but, unusually for Beaker-compatible material, four have come from the south-west: two from County Clare, one from

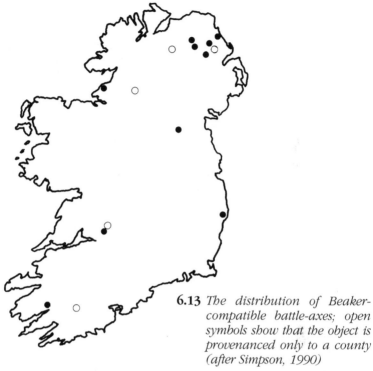

6.13 *The distribution of Beaker-compatible battle-axes; open symbols show that the object is provenanced only to a county (after Simpson, 1990)*

County Kerry, and a fourth from County Cork (fig 6.13). This last is recorded as having been 'found in the old working of a Copper mine.' Unfortunately the site of the mine has not survived in the records. Nonetheless, the existence of this specimen, particularly in the light of the Beaker pottery from Ross Island, does breathe life into the idea that the Beaker People may after all have been responsible for introducing metallurgy to Ireland.

The other type of object that may have a claim to Beaker-compatibility is the polished flint discoidal knife, usually roughly circular or D-shaped, about 100 mm across (fig. 6.14). This has occurred in Beaker contexts in Britain.

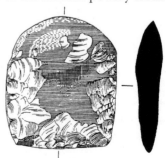

6.14 *Flint discoidal polished knife from Navan, Co. Armagh (after Flanagan, 1959)*

The surface of the flint has been roughly shaped by careful knapping, then virtually the entire surface has been carefully polished, presumably to make the knife more comfortable to hold in use. Unfortunately these objects have not been systematically studied, so no firm conclusions can be drawn about their distribution. There seem to have been no associated finds recorded in Ireland.

BEAKER SOURCES
Wedge tombs

Some four hundred wedge tombs are known in Ireland, their distribution showing a marked concentration in the west and south-west (fig. 6.15). Half the known tombs, indeed, are in Counties Clare, Cork, Kerry, Limerick, and Tipperary, while a quarter of the total are in County Clare, areas where other types of megalithic tomb are very rare.

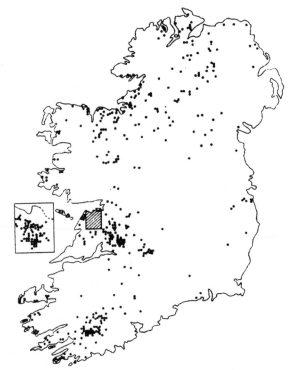

6.15 *The distribution of wedge tombs (after Ó Nualláin, 1989)*

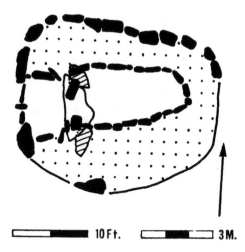

6.16 *Plan of the wedge tomb at Loughash, Co. Tyrone (after Davies and Mullin, 1940)*

Unfortunately, only a small proportion have been excavated—some twenty of the total, or approximately 5 per cent. In the past these tombs were known as 'wedge-shaped gallery graves', because the gallery, or sometimes simply chamber, was both higher and wider at the front; there was also generally a portico (fig. 6.16). The gallery was built of orthostatic stones, and the roof-slabs were set directly on these. Usually the gallery was set in a D-shaped cairn, and the orientation of the tombs was to the south-west, exactly the opposite of that of court tombs.

There are a number of difficulties connected with these tombs. In the first place, no convincing parallels can be found anywhere else. It has been suggested that the *allées couvertes* of Brittany, some of which have produced Beaker pottery and barbed-and-tanged arrow-heads, might be ancestral to the Irish tombs. Probably more authorities disagree with this derivation than agree with it. We are left with at least a suspicion that the wedge tombs are an indigenous invention.

But that is not the end of our difficulties. Once upon a time, wedge tombs were divided into two classes: northern wedges and southern wedges. Since, however, some of the most southerly wedges, such as Labbacallee and Island, both in County Cork, were quite acceptably 'northern' in

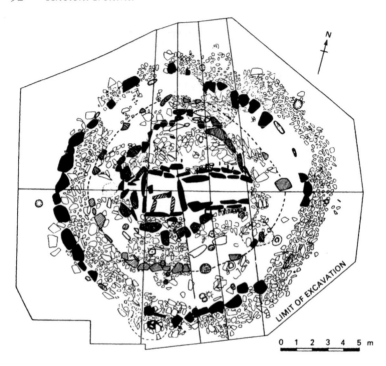

6.17 *Plan of the wedge tomb at Baurnadomeeny, Co. Tipperary (after O'Kelly, 1960)*

type, this classification had to be abandoned, or rather the terminology revised. The main difference between the two classes is that the former 'southern' tombs have a portico cut off from the rest of the tomb by a high septal slab, so that it may not be possible to pass from the portico into the main chamber, as is possible in the other tombs, and, in addition, they are contained in round or oval cairns, as at Baurnadomeeny, County Tipperary (fig. 6.17).

Of the excavated tombs, four, all in County Kerry, produced no finds, except for a cremated burial in one of them. Eight others contained no pottery as primary deposits; the remaining eight did produce Beaker pottery. One recently excavated example at Toormore, County Cork, is reported as having a decorated copper axe and two pieces of copper at its entrance. Of these, all except the megalith at Lough Gur and the Toormore tomb are in the northern

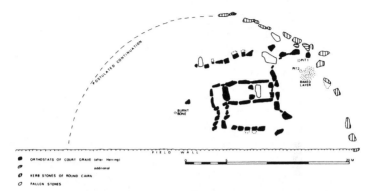

6.18 *Plan of the court tomb at Knockoneill, Co. Derry, showing 'wedge' modifications and superimposed Bronze Age round cairn (after Flanagan, 1980)*

part of the country. Moreover, a perfectly normal court tomb at Knockoneill, County Derry (fig. 6.18), seems to have been superficially converted into a 'wedge tomb' by the doubling of the entrance jambs to create a small porch or portico— not a standard feature of court tombs. This interpretation was reinforced by the discovery, in the re-excavation of the site, of sherds of perfectly acceptable unornamented bell beaker by the kerb of the court tomb, on the south side, notwithstanding the fact that the court tomb enjoyed the normal easterly orientation. The fact that the nearby court tomb at Tamnyrankin has an unusually high septal slab separating the chambers may suggest that in this area of Ulster, where court tombs and wedge tombs are both common, a fusion may have taken place; the addition of a subsidiary two-chambered gallery at the rear of this tomb, with a portico-like feature at the entrance, may also add weight to this argument.

If this 'conversion' of a court tomb to an admittedly two-chambered wedge tomb is accepted, an explanation of the origins of wedge tombs is suggested. It is generally agreed that portal tombs are derived from subsidiary chambers, or indeed galleries, inserted into court tombs. While substantive portal tombs generally show an orientation towards the east, the same clearly cannot be said of subsidiaries in court tombs, which, if the main gallery has an eastern orientation, must face in almost any direction except east.

The distribution of portal tombs, while densest in the north, alongside the parental court tombs, does, however, extend a little further south, particularly significantly into County Clare (fig. 4.8).

The chambers of portal tombs often narrow towards the rear; often, too, a slab closes, or partly closes, the entrance, which is not commonly a feature of court tombs, though it is a feature of wedge tombs, particularly of those that represent the remnant of the 'southern' wedges. The megalith at Lough Gur, as well as producing Beaker pottery, produced Western Neolithic pottery and the rather coarse, flat-bottomed ware described as class II ware. There would seem, therefore, to be a cultural continuity between portal tombs and wedge tombs.

Wedge tombs, incidentally, exhibit a longevity that may well be shared, in certain parts of the country, by Beaker pottery itself. The tomb at Loughash, County Tyrone, as well

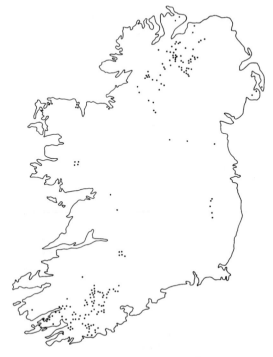

6.19 *The distribution of stone circles (after Ó Nualláin, 1995)*

as producing beaker ware also produced an encrusted urn and part of a stone mould for flanged axes; at Moylisha, County Wicklow, a wedge tomb had two valves of a sandstone mould for lozenge-bladed socket-looped spear-heads outside its kerb.

Stone circles

Stone circles, of which a considerable number exist in Ireland, are another great source of Beaker pottery. There are two main concentrations, one in mid-Ulster, the other in south Munster (fig. 6.19). In general, they seem, from the evidence of excavated examples, to be a phenomenon of the Late Neolithic Period and the Earlier Bronze Age—perhaps, indeed, a type of existing monument that attracted the later groups for some reason.

Those in the Lough Gur complex are conspicuous for their continuity or overlap. Of these the most impressive is the great stone circle at Grange: it is 45.7 m in diameter and is surrounded by a ring of 113 orthostats, placed contiguously, with a bank of earth nine metres wide built up against them on the outside, making the monument almost a hybrid of a stone circle and henge. Some of the stones are very large: one must weigh nearly fifty tonnes (fig. 6.20).

The circle is entered by a narrow passage, lined on both sides with contiguously placed standing slabs at the northeast. In the area excavated in the interior two hearths were found, with associated pottery. Throughout the excavated area some thousands of sherds were found—a mixture of Western Neolithic and class II ware (coarse flat-bottomed pots), but beaker and bowl food vessels as well. The flints recovered included barbed-and-tanged arrow-heads, as well as hollow-based forms, scrapers, and knives; there was also a bronze awl. While there was some human as well as animal bone, none represented a formal burial. The animals included cattle, pig, sheep or goat, horse, dog, and hare. The excavator considered this site to be solely ritualistic, in view of the absence of houses and burials.

There are other circles at Lough Gur. Circle J, which contained an unenclosed Late Neolithic habitation followed by a domestic site enclosed by a curved double wall, produced only a tiny proportion of Beaker ware in comparison with

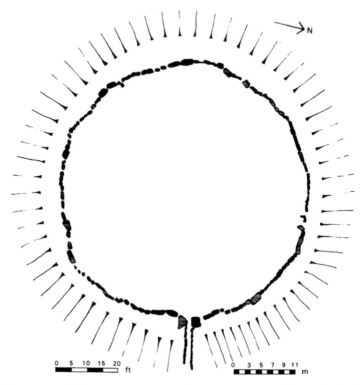

6.20 *Plan of the great stone circle at Grange, Co. Limerick (after Ó Ríordáin, 1951)*

the amounts of Western Neolithic and coarse flat-bottomed pottery typical of the Neolithic Period in the area. Circle K, as well as a number of burials, almost exclusively of children and young people (one of which, interestingly, was a crouched burial, suggestive of Beaker practice, of a woman with foetal bones in the pelvis), none of which were significantly associated with grave-goods, also contained two houses, one square, one rectangular. Between them these two houses produced not merely Beaker ware but also Beaker domestic wares, as well as two barbed-and-tanged flint arrow-heads. Interestingly, the first house, with a quantity of Western Neolithic and coarse flat-bottomed ware, produced a lozenge-shaped stone bead remarkably like one from the court tomb at Bavan, County Donegal, and the one from the portal tomb at Ballyrenan, County Tyrone.

Henges or henge-like monuments

There are quite a number of henges or henge-like earthen enclosures in Ireland (fig. 6.21), with a marked concentration in the Boyne Valley, in the area of the great passage tombs. While the classic definition of a henge requires that

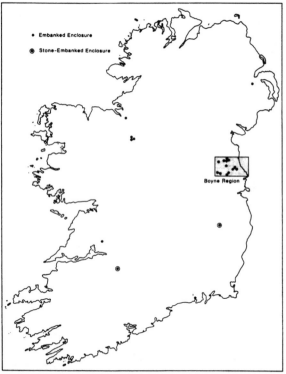

6.21 *The distribution of henges and henge-like earthworks (after Stout, 1991)*

it consist of a bank and a ditch, which is usually internal, enclosing a roughly circular area, few of the Irish enclosures conform to these requirements.

Only one of the Boyne examples has been excavated, that at Monknewtown, County Meath. This was originally a roughly circular banked enclosure, the interior about eighty-five metres in diameter, with no inside ditch; only about a quarter of the bank had survived. In the northern area, adjacent to the surviving portion of bank, eleven pits were discovered, three of which contained burials—two of them containing cremated bone but no grave-goods. The third was an unlined pit and contained portions of a large, flat-rimmed, very coarse bucket-shaped pot containing a few pieces of cremated bone.

An unusual find from this part of the site, in a shallow depression or hollow rather than a pit, was a Carrowkeel bowl containing cremated bone, the remains of a child. Much of this northern area had been covered with a layer of reddish-brown clay, deposited after the construction of the bank and after the pits and covering the Carrowkeel burial. Six hearths were found, as well as sherds of both Neolithic and Beaker pottery.

In the south-western part of the site, close to the original line of the bank, a curious pit-like feature was found, about seven metres by five metres, scooped out of the underlying gravel, with a hearth more or less in the centre and a number of irregularly placed post-holes. From and around this feature more than four thousand sherds of pottery, Neolithic and Beaker (including rusticated Beaker domestic ware), were found. A few metres from this pit-like feature was a shallow ring-ditch, about 4.5 m in diameter, in the centre of which was a shallow pit containing some cremated bone and a few sherds of very coarse pottery similar to that found in one of the burials in the northern part of the site.

SETTLEMENT SITES

Interestingly, the greatest bulk of Beaker pottery recovered in Ireland since the nineteen-forties has been from settlement sites. At Gortcorbies, County Derry, a small part of a settlement site was excavated, producing European bell beakers; but more recently a more extensive area of settlement was found at Ballynagilly, County Tyrone—oddly enough at a site known as 'the Corbie'. Here there were three distinct foci in an area covering about six hundred square metres. While no houses were identified, there were pits and hearths, around which occupation debris was thickly scattered. There was also a large pit containing blackened and heat-fractured stones and ash, suggesting that it might have been a large cooking-pit.

The pottery discovered included fine Beaker ware with comb or incised decoration and with motifs, as at Gortcorbies, suggestive of affinities with the Northern British/Middle Rhine group. There were also coarser wares. Included among the finds were scrapers and barbed-and-tanged arrow-heads. (Beaker ware on some settlement sites at Lough Gur has been discussed under 'Stone circles' above, since settlement was inside these features.) Two of the settlement sites on Dalkey Island, County Dublin, produced Beaker ware in quantity.

Newgrange
In some ways the Beaker settlement sites in the shadow of the great passage tombs of the Boyne Valley have constituted the most important discoveries. At Newgrange, after the successive collapses of the great cairn, on the stone and layers of turf that had spilled out from it there was intensive Late Neolithic or Beaker domestic activity. Over 3,600 sherds were recovered, representing at least two hundred individual pots, consisting of Late Neolithic wares, classical beakers (including bell beakers and all-over cord ornamented beakers), rusticated beakers, and other coarse wares—all of local manufacture. Among the flints were three barbed-and-tanged arrow-heads, as well as scrapers and knives.

Beaker Period farming at Newgrange
Perhaps even more important than the ceramic and lithic artefacts recovered was the wealth of information gleaned about farming practices, for as well as the implements there were considerable amounts of animal bone. The very first impression was that for food production, cattle and pigs were most important, but no evidence was found to suggest that the secondary products (manure, traction, milk, wool, hide, or even blood) were of any great importance in the economy. We are particularly fortunate that the evidence presented by this spectacular collection of animal bone was meticulously examined.

Knowth

At neighbouring Knowth too there was evidence of intensive Beaker settlement. Here there were four concentrations of Beaker activity, each in a different quadrant of the area round the great tomb, two on the eastern side, two on the western. In that in the north-eastern quadrant, concentration A, two hearths and some thirty-seven pits, of varying sizes and shapes, were found, but no definite evidence of structures. The pottery, consisting of some four hundred sherds, representing over thirty vessels, included a small group of Western Neolithic, another small group of fine beaker pottery, mostly of typical bell beaker form and decoration; the bulk of the pottery, however, derived from coarse, flat-bottomed vessels—at least seventeen, ten of them decorated.

Indications of the flint industry included a fine hollow-based arrow-head and a number of scrapers. The presence of many small fragments suggests that flintworking was carried out on the site. Concentration B was on the western edge of the great tomb; apart from a shallow depression it contained no structural features or hearths but about three hundred sherds, representing about thirty vessels, mainly bell beakers. The associated flint industry consisted mainly of flakes, blades, and scrapers.

Also on the western side but in the south-western quadrant was concentration C. While this area produced no evidence of structures, there were features such as rough cobbling, an oval pit, two oval holes, and an area reddened by burning. No finds were associated with these features, and it could not be shown that they were the result of Beaker activity. Over a thousand sherds of pottery were discovered in this area, representing something like eighty individual vessels. Surprisingly, only one coarse-ware pot was present, the rest being fine bell beaker vessels, about one-third of which bear decoration, mostly incised or made by impressed comb and cord. Accompanying the pottery was an assemblage of flint and chert, which included a flint barbed-and-tanged arrow-head and a chert leaf-shaped one. Scrapers are the predominant form of finished artefact, while two-thirds of the material is waste.

The final centre, concentration D, was in the south-eastern quadrant outside the great tomb. Some of this concentration was over primary slip from the cairn. The most prominent feature was a rather irregular hearth in a shallow pit. Only two post-holes were identified. About two thousand sherds of pottery were found, too small to permit any reconstructions. The great majority of the sherds were of fine ware, some of it decorated, mainly with incised lines. There was no really coarse ware, probably no more than four vessels of coarsish ware. There were, however, five crude lumps of clay, suggesting that pottery was manufactured on the site. Most of the flintwork was waste; of the finished artefacts most were scrapers.

In addition to these four areas of Beaker domestic activity there were a number of stray finds of Beaker pottery and a burial; this was in the passage of one of the satellite tombs (15). It consisted of the cremated bones of an adult and a young child, placed in the corner of a segment of the passage, accompanied by an undecorated bell beaker.

Beaker Period farming at Knowth
In contrast to the fairly abundant presence of animal bone among the Beaker areas at Newgrange, those at Knowth were almost devoid of such material. There was, however, enough seed and pollen present to suggest that there had been little change in the vegetation of the area from Neolithic times. The woods that had formerly been extensive but now were virtually confined to the river valley consisted of oak and elm on the higher ground, with hazel and birch and, in the valley, alder. Seeds and pollen of cereals indicate that cereal-growing had been established in the area in Neolithic times and remained during the Beaker Period.

THE EARLIER BRONZE AGE
2000–1200 BC

Despite its great richness in pottery, metalwork (both copper or bronze and gold), and even burials, the Earlier Bronze Age is still most conveniently considered in its different aspects, with an attempt to join these component parts into as cohesive a whole as possible. That this makes us rely largely on the typology of these components is in some ways regrettable, albeit inevitable.

POTTERY
In recent years there has been considerable reclassification of Irish Earlier Bronze Age pottery. The time-honoured division into 'food vessels', of bowl and vase forms, and cinerary urns—encrusted, collared, and cordoned—has been shaken up very thoroughly and with successive attempts to impose meaning on the typological divisions. The food vessels, so called originally on the supposition that—unlike the generally thin-rimmed 'beakers', regarded as drinking-vessels for this very reason—they were intended as containers for food, have perhaps suffered more. The most recent and probably the most effective and sensible reclassification of food vessels divides them neatly into two traditions, bowls and vases. The very term 'food vessel' is now discarded.

The bowl tradition
Pottery vessels of the bowl tradition are assigned to one of several categories. The simple bowl is a small, well-made

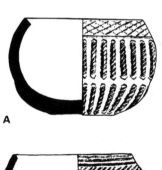

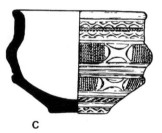

A   C

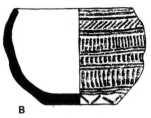

B

7.1 *Bowls:* (A) *simple bowl, Mount Stewart, Co. Down;* (B) *bipartite bowl, Slaghtneill, Co. Derry;* (C) *necked bipartite bowl, Rush, Co. Dublin (after Ó Riordáin and Waddell, 1993)*

bowl with a smooth, curving profile and a flat or slightly concave base. The decoration consists of two zones of matching ornament separated by one or two simple grooves or narrow bands of simple ornament. The ornament normally consists of a row of vertical lines, either incised or grooved or, more commonly, impressed—usually by a cord or whipped cord (fig. 7.1A).

Bipartite bowls are small vessels with a noticeable constriction at about the half-way mark; the decoration is similar to that on simple bowls (fig. 7.1B). A variant of the bipartite bowl, the necked bipartite bowl, has the addition of a nearly vertical or slightly out-curving neck; decoration is fairly similar to that on the first two classes but with the addition of comb-impressed decoration or false-relief chevrons (fig. 7.1C).

Tripartite bowls, as the name suggests, have a pair of horizontal ribs, sometimes dividing the vessel's profile into three broad zones, sometimes close enough to suggest a sort of shoulder groove, which may contain several lugs, with or without perforations. The decoration consists of parallel horizontal lines, false-relief chevrons, vertical lines, or oblique lines, which often form a chevron motif; it is most commonly by comb impressions or false relief, though incised and whipped-cord impression occur occasionally.

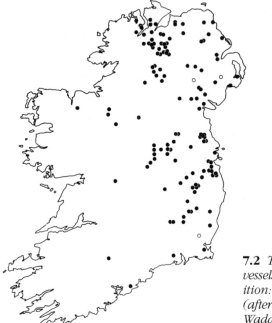

7.2 *The distribution of vessels of the bowl tradition: tripartite bowls (after Ó Ríordáin and Waddell, 1993)*

The final category is the ribbed bowl, which has three or more horizontal ribs on the exterior—most have three ribs, some four, and exceptionally five or six. The decoration consists of zones of horizontal lines or chevrons in false relief; parallel horizontal lines and vertical lines are slightly less common. Comb impressions and false relief are the commonest decorative techniques, though whipped cord does appear, and incised decoration more rarely.

Vessels in the bowl tradition occur over the whole country except the south-west (fig. 7.2). They are almost invariably from burials, either in cemeteries or from isolated graves; some, however, have been found inserted in existing Neolithic tombs, including the court tomb at Audleystown, County Down (a tripartite bowl), and in several instances in passage tombs, such as Carrowkeel, County Sligo (a tripartite bowl in tomb O and a ribbed bowl in tomb K). Examples have been found in wedge tombs at Loughash, County Tyrone (a bipartite bowl), and Kilhoyle, County Derry (a ribbed bowl).

Apart from these the great majority of finds were in cisted or uncisted graves (pit graves). The most interesting feature of these burials, however, is the remarkably high incidence of uncremated burials—over thirty examples—in both flat cemeteries and cemetery mounds, particularly at sites such as Keenoge, County Meath, where six graves contained bowls with uncremated skeletons, and Edmondstown, County Dublin, where two cists contained bowls with uncremated skeletons. It has been shown that the practice of burying uncremated skeletons with bowls was particularly widespread in the eastern midlands— Counties Kildare, Westmeath, Meath, and south Dublin.

The vase tradition
The vase tradition has been shown to be the principal ceramic, and therefore funerary, tradition of the Earlier Bronze Age. In addition to what used to be called 'vase food vessels' it includes vase urns and encrusted urns. The vases themselves divide into two classes, tripartite vases and bipartite vases. Tripartite vases have an angular profile with an everted (turned-outwards) vertical or near-vertical neck above a sloping shoulder. The distinct neck, shoulder and body produce a tripartite external profile. The decoration on the majority is incised, though impressed decoration, usually with whipped cord, appears as well. It is usually arranged in multiple horizontal zones. Oblique short lines forming a herringbone pattern, or filled triangles, are common (fig. 7.3).

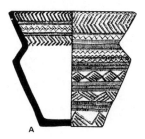 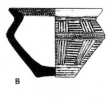

7.3 *Tripartite vases:* (A) *from Ballon Hill, Co. Carlow;* (B) *from Labbamolaga, Co. Cork (after Ó Ríordáin and Waddell, 1993)*

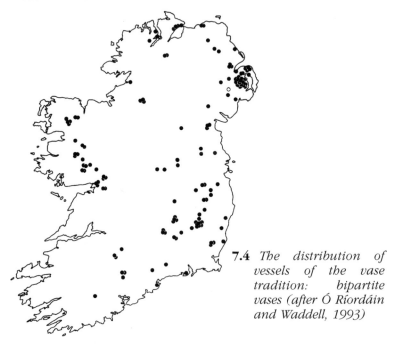

7.4 *The distribution of vessels of the vase tradition: bipartite vases (after Ó Ríordáin and Waddell, 1993)*

Tripartite vases enjoy a distribution that is densest in the north and the south-east; it does penetrate slightly into the south-west but has a curious void in the midlands. The burial rite, almost without exception, consists of cremation.

The majority of Irish vases belong to the second type—the bipartite vase. This class has a bipartite, biconical, often slightly curving profile and usually a slightly everted rim. The decoration is mainly incised, though twisted and whipped-cord impressions appear as well; it is usually placed in multiple horizontal zones, with short lines often used to produce a herringbone pattern. The distribution—while showing a clear northern, and particularly north-eastern, tendency—is more general than any of the other types of vase or bowl, filling in the west as well as the ribbed bowl, and penetrating the south-west better than any other form (fig. 7.4).

Very few of the burials containing bipartite vases have included uncremated skeletons, though one does occur at Glassamucky, County Dublin, and there is a small pocket in the west, in Counties Galway and Mayo. It would appear from the often inadequate records that rather more come from cisted graves than from simple pit burials. Seldom do vases occur in cemeteries containing bowls; two cemeteries, one at Cloghskelt, County Down, and another at Letterkeen, County Mayo, have produced a small proportion of bowls in otherwise vase-dominated assemblages.

The other components of the vase tradition, the vase urn (formerly known as the enlarged food vessel) (fig. 7.5) and the encrusted urn (fig. 7.6), also occur almost exclusively in burials. Some doubt has been expressed whether the occurrence of applied relief decoration on encrusted urns is a sufficiently diagnostic trait to merit their being regarded as a class by themselves, and so there has been a tendency to group these two types together. Their relationship to burials is very similar: vase urns, of which about eighty survive, usually occur either

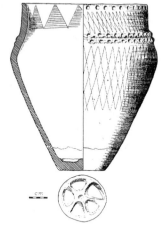

7.5 *Vase urn from Ballytresna, Co. Antrim (after Ap Simon, 1969)*

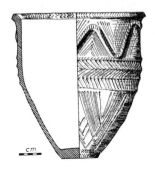

7.6 *Encrusted urn from Lyles Hill, Toberagnee, Co. Antrim (after Ap Simon, 1969)*

in pit (uncisted) graves or in cists, usually inverted over the cremated bone, though they are recorded from the court tomb at Clontygora, County Louth, and the wedge tombs at Kilhoyle and Largantea, County Derry, in all of which they were almost certainly secondary intrusions.

Apart from two possible, though unproven, examples, all are with cremations. Encrusted urns have a similar ritual history, normally inverted over cremated bone but on two occasions, at Edmondstown, County Dublin, and Brownstown, County Louth, mouth upwards, in either a pit or a cist. In general the distribution of encrusted urns, apart from a sizable area of dearth in the west and the north midlands, is fairly even over the country, with a tendency for sites producing more than one to be near the coast, particularly the east coast (fig. 7.7).

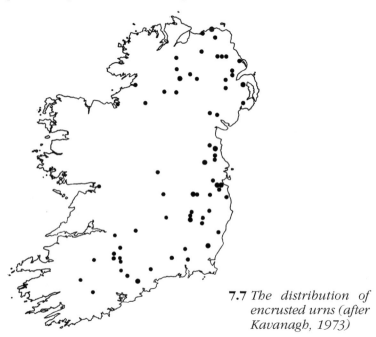

7.7 *The distribution of encrusted urns (after Kavanagh, 1973)*

Cordoned urns

Characteristic of this urn type is the presence of one or more external horizontal cordons encircling the vessel. Other decoration usually consists of either cord impression or incised decoration on the upper part of the body (fig. 7.8). While cremation was the rule, the preference is very much for simple pits, only five having been found in cists. Sometimes the mouth of the pit was covered with a slab of stone; in two instances the stone slab actually covered the mouth of the upright pot.

One burial site with a prodigious production claim, which, unfortunately, is impossible to corroborate, was

Killyneill, County Tyrone, where thirty urns were allegedly found, of which, sadly, only two remain. Unlike most of the funerary pottery so far discussed, cordoned urns have been recorded from domestic sites in several instances, most notably at Downpatrick, County Down, where the settlement included two round houses; lesser settlement sites include sandhills at White Park Bay, County

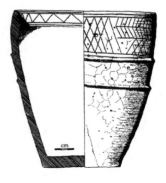

7.8 *Cordoned urn, Donaghmore, Co. Tyrone (after Ap Simon, 1969)*

Antrim, and Dundrum, County Down. The distribution is by no means even throughout the country: there is a distinct and distinctive northern and eastern focus, with a sort of trail across the midlands and a small cluster in Munster (fig. 7.9).

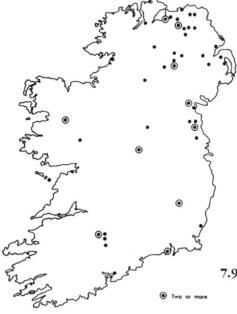

⊙ Two or more

7.9 *The distribution of cordoned urns (after Kavanagh, 1976)*

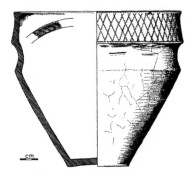

7.10 *Collared urn, Turnabarson, Co. Tyrone (after Ap Simon, 1969)*

Collared urns

These vessels—which at one time were known as 'over-hanging-rim urns'—are characterised by a sometimes fairly massive 'collar' or rim, often decorated with cord impression, plain, plaited, or whipped, or more rarely simple incised decoration (fig. 7.10). It is accepted as a certainty that they were introduced to Ireland, ultimately from what is now England but proximately from south-west Scotland. Again the burial rite appears to have been exclusively cremation. Most were inverted in pits, a few in cists. They show a marked preference for flat cemeteries; few have been found in mounds. The distribution of collared urns in Ireland is virtually confined to the east coast (fig. 7.11).

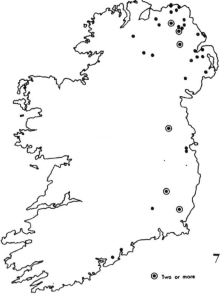

⊚ Two or more

7.11 *The distribution of collared urns (after Kavanagh, 1976)*

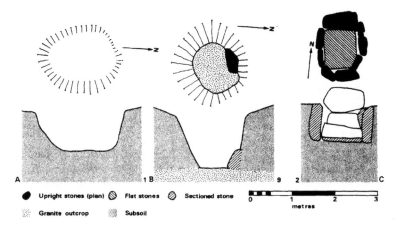

7.12 *Plans and sections of* (A) *an uncisted or pit grave,* (B) *a partially cisted grave and* (C) *a cisted grave at Cloghskelt, Co. Down (after Flanagan, 1978)*

GRAVES AND CEMETERIES

The individual graves in which the bodies of Earlier Bronze Age people were buried were usually of one of two kinds: a grave lined with slabs of stone to form a box or cist, or a simple hole in the ground, usually described as a pit or uncisted grave; sometimes a token stone or two was added (fig. 7.12). The cists were frequently covered with a slab, though simple pits sometimes received this treatment too. Pit or uncisted graves occur throughout the country but avoid the extreme south-west (fig. 7.13).

Most authorities would consider that the presence of two or more graves in fairly close contiguity constitutes a cemetery (though a very high proportion of Earlier Bronze Age graves has been found in apparent isolation—even when thorough searching has been made in the vicinity for other graves). The cemeteries are of two basic kinds. The first are those in which the graves (in this case usually cists) are incorporated in a custom-built mound or cairn of stone, often with a rather more imposing central cist, with the others grouped around it, like the famous cemetery mound at Mount Stewart, County Down, of which an early sketch-plan survives. The second category is known as a 'flat' cemetery, where no custom-built mound is used to contain

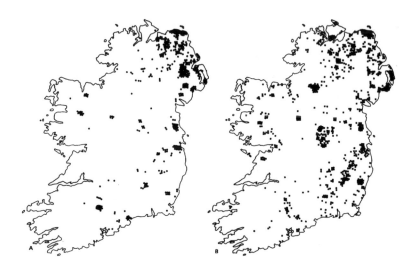

7.13 *The distribution of* (A) *simple pit or uncisted graves and* (B) *cisted graves (after Flanagan, 1978)*

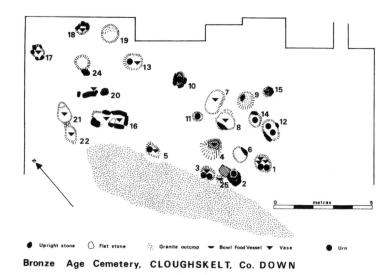

Bronze Age Cemetery, CLOUGHSKELT, Co. DOWN

7.14 *Plan of the flat cemetery at Cloghskelt, Co. Down (after Flanagan, 1978)*

the graves (though very often the 'flat' cemetery could be in a drumlin, creating a rather similar effect); an example of a flat cemetery on a drumlin is at Cloghskelt, County Down (fig. 7.14).

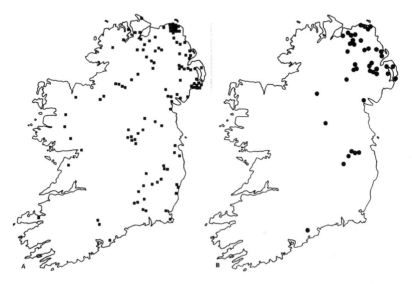

7.15 *The distribution of* (A) *cemeteries containing only cisted graves and* (B) *cemeteries containing only uncisted graves (after Flanagan, 1978)*

Normally, though not invariably, the burials were accompanied by pottery vessels in either the bowl or the vase tradition—though at Cloghskelt an otherwise exclusively vase cemetery did contain a single vessel of the bowl tradition. There is a tendency for cemeteries to be composed of either cists or pits (fig. 7.15), though 'mixed' cemeteries, containing both types of grave, do occur (fig. 7.16).

The human content

Information about the human remains found in graves and accompanied by pottery is neither copious nor consistent. However, in addition to the fact that over thirty of the burials in the bowl tradition were of uncremated skeletons, or parts of skeletons, some particulars of the occupant or occupants of the grave have survived. At Oldbridge, County Meath, one compartment of a double cist contained the

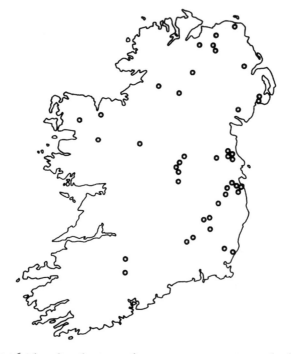

7.16 *The distribution of cemeteries containing both cisted and uncisted graves (after Flanagan, 1978)*

teeth of two men and a simple bowl, while the other contained the teeth of a woman. A cist at Dungate, County Tyrone, contained the disarticulated bones of a man, accompanied by a necked bipartite bowl and a few bones of a child, with part of a similar bowl. At Blackhill, County Kildare, a cist held the crouched skeleton of a child, with a necked bipartite bowl at its feet. At Woodend, County Tyrone, adult cremated bone was in a tripartite bowl. At Ballybrew, County Wicklow, a tripartite bowl accompanied the skeleton of a young man and some unburnt bones of a child. In a cist at Bolinready, County Wexford, a tripartite bowl accompanied a male skeleton and the fibula of a child. At Edmondstown, County Dublin, two cists each contained the crouched skeleton of a youth; and at Haylands, County Wicklow, was the crouched skeleton of a young adult with a ribbed bowl. At Fourknocks I, County Meath, a ribbed bowl accompanied the crouched skeleton of a child.

For the vase tradition, information seems even more unsatisfactory. However, at Cush, County Limerick, a young adult and a child were accompanied by a bipartite vase, while at Letterkeen, County Mayo, two adults and a child or adolescent were found in each of two graves, accompanied by bipartite vases. A cist at Cloghroak, County Galway, contained the unburnt bones of a young person and an infant, as well as the cremated bones of a man.

The position does not improve much regarding vase urns. At Ballinchalla, County Mayo, and Clonshannon, County Wicklow, the cremated remains were those of children, while at Caltragh, County Galway, and Cush, County Limerick, the bones of an adult with one or more children were accompanied by the urn. A cist at Knockroe, County Tyrone, contained a vase urn accompanying a man less than forty years old, an adolescent, probably female, of about sixteen, and three young children aged two, three, and four. Burials with encrusted urns are similarly rather scantily recorded, though several have been identified as adult males. At Crumlin, County Antrim, however, the cremated bone was that of a woman and a child, while there are several records of child cremations in Counties Limerick, Waterford, and Wicklow. At Moanmore, County Tipperary, two adults were together under an inverted urn, with a vase; while two adults and a child were with an urn and vase at Nevinstown, County Meath.

Bones of men have been identified at Urbalreagh, County Derry, and Harristown, County Waterford, with cordoned urn; women at Oatencake, County Cork, Gortfad, County Derry, and Aghascrebagh, County Tyrone. At Gortlush, County Donegal, a child, accompanied by one or two adults, was found; other children are recorded from several sites, including Fourknocks III, County Meath. At Kilcroagh, County Antrim, in a cordoned-urn cemetery, one burial contained the cremated bones of a man aged between twenty-five and thirty and a woman between twenty and twenty-five, tantalisingly suggestive of a husband and wife; while another grave contained a woman aged about thirty and an adolescent aged between fifteen and sixteen.

Collared urns have accompanied the cremated bones of men, women, and children, those of a man at Gortcorbies,

County Derry, and a woman at Ballymacaldrack, County Antrim. At Creggan, County Antrim, a collared urn accompanied the bones of a woman, a child, and an infant.

A recent detailed survey of Earlier Bronze Age cemeteries in the south-east has suggested that only a minority of children received formal burial and therefore that some form of social discrimination was practised. It further suggests that men were more likely to receive formal burial than women. Perhaps the recognition that an elderly male skeleton from a small cemetery containing both inhumations and cremations at Graney West, County Kildare, suffered from diffuse idiopathic skeletal hyperostosis—a condition of old age associated with obesity and suggestive of a sedentary life-style—reinforces these indications of social discrimination. In contrast to this fortunate individual, it should be noted that osteoarthritis is a fairly commonly encountered condition.

It has recently been calculated that the stature of the people in Earlier Bronze Age burials, from a study of the long bones that have survived, was, for males, between 157 cm (5 feet 2 inches) and 191 cm (6 feet 3 inches), with a mean at 173 cm (5 feet 8½ inches), and for females between 158 cm (5 feet 2 inches) and 174 cm (5 feet 8½ inches), with a mean at 165 cm (5 feet 5 inches). These statures are by no means impressive, though the female mean is in fact slightly higher than that of modern Irish women, at 164 cm (5 feet 4½ inches). An increase in the incidence of dental caries, in comparison with the Neolithic population, is thought to indicate a greater consumption of carbohydrates, possibly as a result of greater reliance on cereals.

The associations

By and large, the associations in graves of bowls are not numerous or very exciting for the most part. The only pottery type with which they are associated is other bowls, as at Letterbrick, County Donegal, Grange, County Roscommon, Rathbennett, County Westmeath, and Corrower, County Mayo. Flint objects have been found in several instances: a flint knife at Drudgeon, County Tyrone, and flint scrapers at Stranagalwilly, County Tyrone, Carrickbrack, County Donegal, and Ballybrew, County

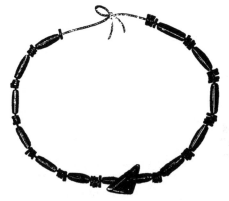

7.17 *Jet necklace from one compartment of a double cist at Oldbridge, Co. Meath (after Coffey, 1895)*

Wicklow. Beads of stone or jet have come from Oldbridge, County Meath—an ornate jet necklace from one compartment of a double cist, a simple bowl from the other (fig. 7.17). At Rathbennett, County Westmeath, a tripartite bowl was accompanied by two oval jet beads.

More helpful associations do, however, occur. At Keenoge, County Meath, a bipartite bowl was accompanied by a necked bipartite bowl, a (rather damaged) bronze knife, and flints; at Corkey, County Antrim, a tripartite bowl was found with a bronze triangular dagger; while at Carrickinab, County Down, a bronze dagger (badly corroded) and a rivet, as well as a copper or bronze awl, were found with a tripartite bowl. At Luggacurran, County Laois, a ribbed bowl was accompanied by two bronze bracelets and some beads.

For vases the picture becomes much more complex. They are found with vase urns, encrusted urns, collared urns, and cordoned urns. They are associated with various types of flintwork: knives at Curran and Magheraboy, County Antrim, Enniskillen, County Fermanagh, Moville, County Donegal, and Corrandrum, County Galway. They are found with beads of faience at Ballyduff, County Wexford. In several instances they have been found with bronze objects: a bronze dagger and awl at Annaghkeen, County Galway, a fine bronze dagger at Grange, County

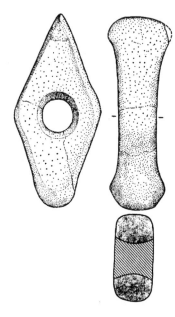

7.18 *Stone battle-axe found in a grave containing a cordoned urn at Ballintubbrid, Co. Wexford (after Kavanagh, 1976)*

Roscommon, and a bronze razor at Knockast, County Meath. Best of all, a tripartite vase was accompanied by a fine bronze dagger and a piece of ribbed gold, presumably part of its pommel-binding, at Topped Mountain, County Fermanagh.

Encrusted urns, apart from a bone pin at Coolnahane, County Cork, are accompanied usually by flint plano-convex (or 'slug') knives, on sites such as Killycarney, County Cavan, and Edmondstown, County Dublin. With cordoned urns, in addition to the repetitive presence of bronze razors at such sites as Pollacorragune, County Galway, Harristown, County Waterford, and Knockast, County Westmeath (in all about a dozen such associ-

ations are recorded), other novel items join the repertoire, such as stone battle-axes with shaft-holes from Ballintubbrid, County Wexford (fig. 7.18), and Laheen, County Donegal. Collared urns add their own contribution in addition to the types already listed, with barbed-and-tanged arrow-heads of flint from Creggan, County Antrim, as well as more battle-axes—from Tara, County Meath—and more daggers, also from Tara.

METALWORK
Bronze implement types

By far the most common metal implement of the Earlier Bronze Age was the bronze or copper axe. With regard to numbers recorded and preserved (by 1969), 1,886 examples, as well as 62 so-called 'ingots', are known. These are divided into four types. The first is the type known as

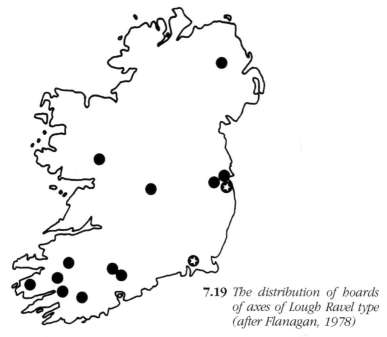

7.19 *The distribution of hoards of axes of Lough Ravel type (after Flanagan, 1978)*

'Lough Ravel', after a hoard found in County Antrim (although on other grounds it has been suggested that 'Cappeen type', after a hoard from Cappeen, County Cork, might have been a more felicitous name, since in County Kerry and neighbouring County Cork there is a cluster of hoards of this type of axe) (fig. 7.19). Of this type, with a thick butt and a rather torpedo-shaped long section, and its sub-type 'Ballybeg', 443 examples are known, representing a production of slightly more that 200 kg of metal over a then postulated period of 1,500 years. By the introduction of a principle applying the potential production of each conjectural mould, known as 'maximum postulable population', the theoretical production could be increased to rather more than two tonnes of metal over this period.

The next type, chronologically speaking, is the 'Killaha type', after a hoard found in County Kerry in which an example occurred: it could not have been more felicitously named, for, of the hoards of this type of axe, four are from County Kerry, with one from County Cork (fig. 7.20). It has a markedly splayed body and a rather thin long-section. The

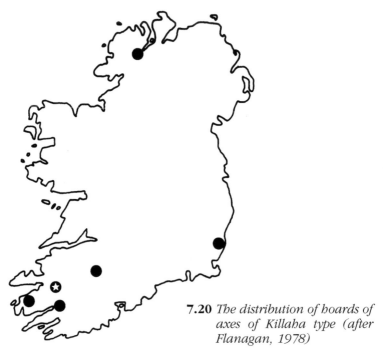

7.20 *The distribution of hoards of axes of Killaha type (after Flanagan, 1978)*

surviving population of this type, 303 examples, represents a production of some 160 kg of metal over slightly more than five hundred years; the application of the principle of maximum postulable population increases this to some 680 kg.

The next type of axe has been termed the 'Ballyvalley type', after a hoard from Ballyvalley, County Down; again, since there is a fairly marked north-eastern concentration of hoards of this type (fig. 7.21), the type name is very appropriate. These are much slimmer and less splayed than Killaha axes. A fairly massive total of 845 examples has survived, representing an actual production of nearly 300 kg, with a maximum postulable population suggesting a production of 1.3 tonnes over a period of slightly less than five hundred years. It is interesting to note that an axe of the Ballyvalley type from Culfeightrin, County Antrim, was recorded some forty years ago as having been cast in one of the matrices of an extant sandstone mould from Ballynahinch, County Down (plate 6).

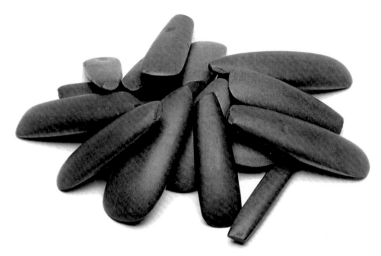

1. *The hoard of grand, large ground and polished porcellanite axes found at Malone, Belfast, Co. Antrim. (Reproduced by permission of the Trustees of the Ulster Museum, Belfast.)*

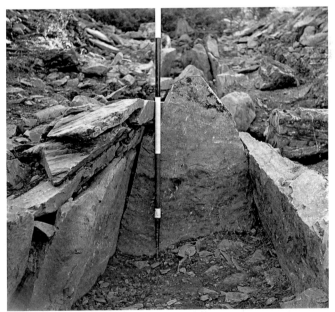

2. *Chamber 4 of the dual court tomb at Audleystown, Co. Down showing the gabled backstone with corbel slabs in position. (Crown copyright. Reproduced with the permission of the Controller of Her Britannic Majesty's Stationery Office.)*

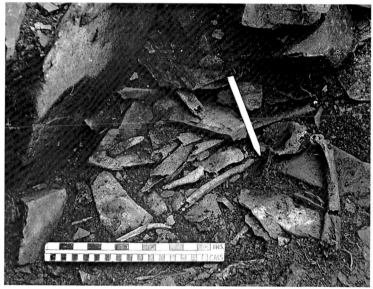

3. *Group of unburnt bones on top of the main burial deposit in one of the chambers of the dual court tomb at Audleystown, Co. Down. The white pointer indicates a sherd of Earlier Bronze Age pottery. (Crown copyright. Reproduced with the permission of the Controller of Her Britannic Majesty's Stationery Office.)*

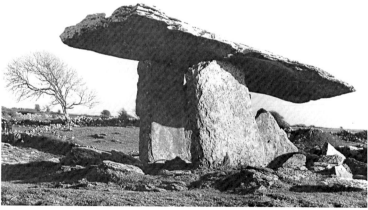

4. *Portal tomb known as Poulnabrone Dolmen, Co. Clare. Excavation showed that it contained the disarticulated unburnt remains of as many as thirty-three individuals. (Photograph: Dúchas, The Heritage Service.)*

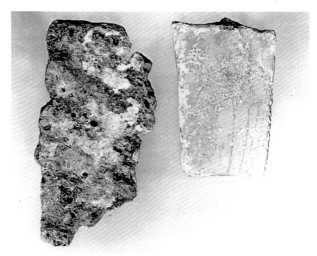

5. *Bronze hoard from Monastery, Co. Wicklow, containing a
    'copper cake' — more properly a copper ingot and an axe of
    Lough Ravel type. (Photograph: National Museum of
    Ireland, Dublin.)*

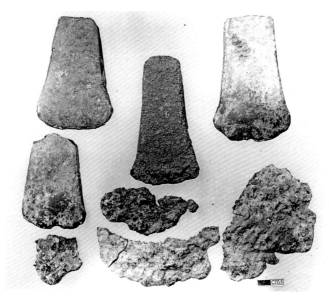

6. *Bronze hoard from Carrickshedoge, Co. Wicklow, containing
    a 'copper cake' — more properly a copper ingot and an axe
    of Lough Ravel type. (Photograph: National Museum of
    Ireland, Dublin.)*

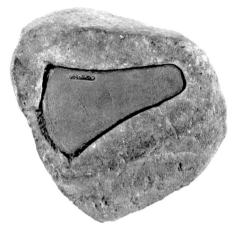

7. *Stone mould from Ballynahinch, Co. Down, with an axe from Culfeightrin, Co. Antrim, placed in the matrix in which it had manifestly been cast. (Reproduced by permission of the Trustees of the Ulster Museum, Belfast.)*

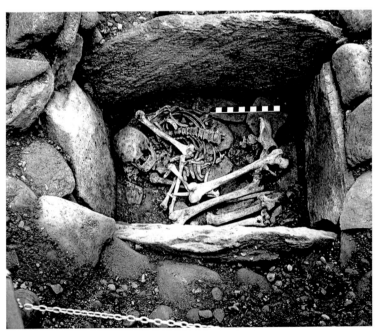

8. *The skeleton of a sixty-year-old man who had suffered from severe osteoarthritis, found in a cist at Stranagalwilly, Co. Tyrone. (Crown copyright. Reproduced with the permission of the Controller of Her Britannic Majesty's Stationery Office.)*

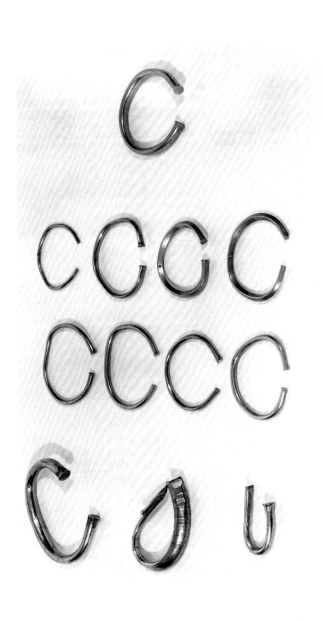

UM ▮▯▮▯▮ 10cm

9. *The first gold board found, in a pit, covered with a stone, on Cathedral Hill, Downpatrick, Co. Down. (Reproduced by permission of the Trustees of the Ulster Museum, Belfast.)*

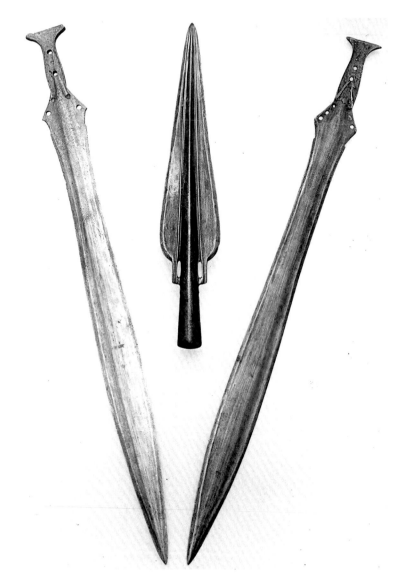

10. *Bronze hoard from Tempo, Co. Fermanagh, consisting of two particularly splendid swords and a spearhead. (Photograph: National Museum of Ireland, Dublin.)*

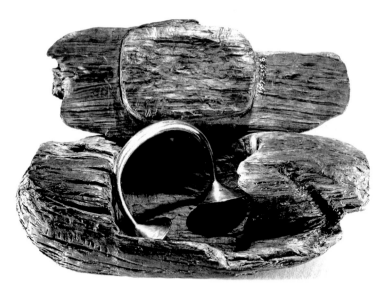

11. *Gold dress-fastener found in Killymoon Demesne, Co. Tyrone, and the wooden box in which it was found; probably due to shrinkage of the wood it is no longer possible to fit on the lid when the dress-fastener is in the box. (National Museum of Ireland.)*

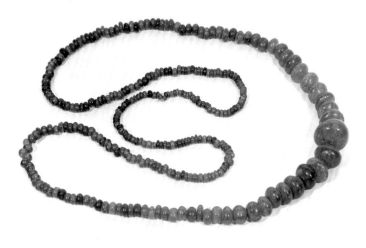

12. *Necklace consisting of over 300 beads of amber found in Kurin Moss, Co. Derry. (Reproduced by permission of the Trustees of the Ulster Museum, Belfast.)*

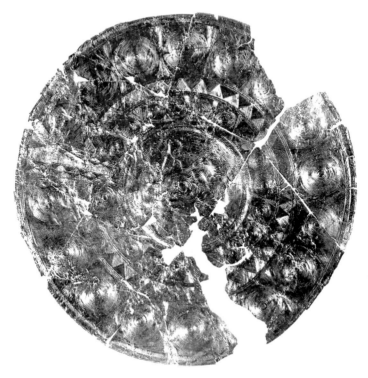

13. *Gold, elaborately decorated disc from Lattoon, Co. Cavan, found in a bog with two gold bracelets and two gold dress-fasteners. (Photograph: National Museum of Ireland, Dublin.)*

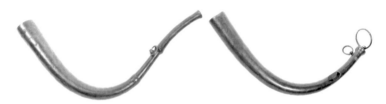

14. *Two of the four bronze horns found together at Drumbest, Co. Antrim. That on the left is blown through the end, that on the right through an opening on the side. (Reproduced by permission of the Trustees of the Ulster Museum, Belfast.)*

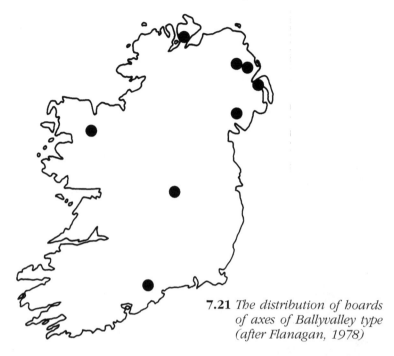

7.21 *The distribution of hoards of axes of Ballyvalley type (after Flanagan, 1978)*

The final type is named after a hoard from Derryniggin, County Leitrim (fig. 7.22). These tend to have at least embryonic flanges along their sides (which would have the effect of strengthening them) and are notably slimmer, and

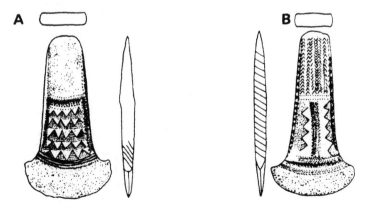

7.22 *Decorated axes of Derryniggin type* (A) *from Co. Limerick, and* (B) *from Scrabo, Co. Down (after Harbison, 1969)*

also lighter—on average half the weight of axes of Lough
Ravel type or Killaha type. They are also scarcer, with only
297 examples surviving, representing an actual production
of only 73 kg; even the application of the principle of
maximum postulable population brings this up to only
slightly more than 364 kg.

The fact that such a high proportion of Earlier Bronze
Age bronze production was concentrated on the manufacture of essentially useful and non-offensive tools casts
some light on what must have been an essentially peaceful
and non-aggressive populace. Weapons—or what may have
been used as weapons—were certainly manufactured, but
not in anything like the same quantities.

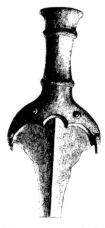

Daggers, of which some 174 survive,
have been divided into several classes,
of which the earliest, the 'Knocknague
type', the rivetless tanged dagger, has
previously been noted as a Beaker-
compatible type. Of this type, with a
similar one called 'Listack type', which
bore one or more rivets on their tangs,
only twelve are known.

Of the simple triangular form of the
next chronological type, Corkey, only
twenty-eight examples are known; of
the daggers of the type named after
the example from Topped Mountain,
County Fermanagh, a mere six
examples are known; while of the
bronze-hilted specimens (fig. 7.23) a
mere three examples are known.

7.23 *Bronze-hilted
dagger   from
Limerick (after
Evans, 1881)*

As the Earlier Bronze Age pro-
gressed, and so the skill of its metalworkers, there was a
move to lengthen the daggers into dirks or rapiers. Two
other types of weapon derive from daggers. Mounted on a
shaft, with the blade in line with the shaft, a spear-head is
produced. Only one example of the earliest form of tanged
spear-head is known from Ireland, allegedly from County
Westmeath; but a stone mould from County Tyrone does
indicate the casting of a ferrule to strengthen the hafting of
a form transitional between it and the ultimate socketed

spear-head (fig. 7.24), of which many examples are known, developing quite spectacularly (fig. 7.25).

If the dagger blade is mounted at right angles on a shaft, another type of weapon, the halberd, is produced. In their various types, some 174 examples of halberds are known from Ireland, ranging in type from the three-riveted representatives of 'Carn type' through the more plentiful 'Cotton type' to the more copiously riveted 'Breaghwy type'.

While the numbers of weapons in the form of halberds and, more spectacularly, spear-heads do slightly redress the balance between tools (in the form of axes) and weapons, there are a few other examples of tools. There are small copper or bronze awls, such as occur in the hoard from Knocknague, and of course there are

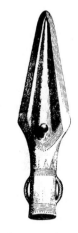

7.24 *A decorated form of early socketed spear-head with loops to secure the spear-head to the shaft (after Coffey, 1913)*

razors, which frequently occur with cordoned urns, which slightly tempt one to think that the men buried with cordoned urns may have been the first clean-shaven men in Ireland.

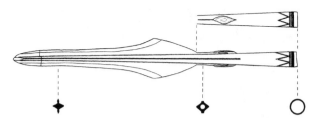

7.25 *A more developed form of socketed spear-head from Co. Cork (after Flanagan, 1961)*

Hoards

Some forty hoards of Earlier Bronze Age bronze tools and weapons are known. Unfortunately, nearly half of these contain implements of only one type; of the others, several show very useful and informative combinations. The hoard from Knocknague, County Galway, contains three axes of Lough Ravel or Ballybeg type (one of which, however, exhibits incipient side flanges), a rivetless tanged dagger, and three awls. That from Frankford contains three axes of Lough Ravel or Ballybeg type, a dagger of Corkey type, and a halberd of Cotton type. That from Killaha East, County Mayo, contains axes of Killaha type, a halberd of Breaghwy type, and a miscellaneous dagger.

Gold

While other forms of gold ornament do appear, there can be little doubt that the dominant form of gold ornament in the Earlier Bronze Age was the gold lunula ('little moon'), so called because of its crescent shape (fig. 7.26). Over eighty examples have been found in Ireland, a few outside it.

Some authorities have argued a Beaker context for lunulae, on the grounds that the decoration they bear, either incised or fully engraved, has more in common with Beaker motifs than with any other artistic repertoire; others

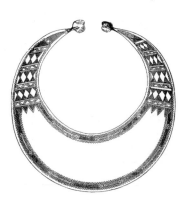

prefer to regard them as belonging to the full Earlier Bronze Age. The unfortunate feature of this argument is that lunulae are simply not represented in associated finds, apart from a flat bronze axe found with two at Harlyn Bay, Cornwall. They do not appear in graves.

Two types have been recognised among Irish lunulae. The ornament of the

7.26 *Elaborately decorated gold lunula from Killarney, Co. Kerry (after Coffey, 1913)*

classical type is precise and exhibits spectacular excellence of craftsmanship; while those examples that do not measure up to the high standards of the classical are relegated to an unaccomplished class. It is worth noting that the volume of gold used in Irish lunulae is greater than is to be seen anywhere else in Europe at the time. In barrows of the

Wessex culture in England, nineteen of which contain gold ornaments, the gold is so thinly beaten that in volume it is unlikely to exceed that of a mere two lunulae. Recent research has suggested that the gold they are made from may have been alluvially derived from a source in the Sperrin Mountains.

FLINTWORK

In addition to the finds of flint barbed-and-tanged arrow-heads mentioned above as associations of collared urns, many hundreds exist in museum collections, generally larger, coarser even, than their Beaker-compatible predecessors. A hoard of twenty-two examples was found some years ago at Ballyclare, County Antrim, ranging in length from 52 mm to 86 mm (fig. 7.27); with them were found seventeen 'blanks'—leaf-shaped pieces of worked

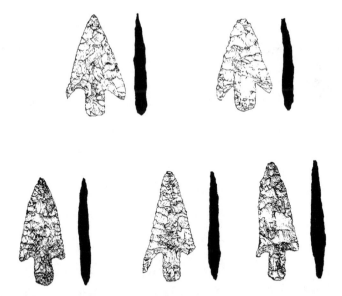

7.27 *Some of the twenty-two flint barbed-and-tanged arrow-heads found in a hoard at Ballyclare, Co. Antrim (after Flanagan, 1970)*

flint from which the arrow-heads were fabricated. A fragment of a bow found at Drumwhinny, County Fermanagh, showing that these barbed-and-tanged arrow-heads enjoyed a means of propulsion, has been confirmed as being of Earlier Bronze Age date by radiocarbon dating. Plano-convex flint knives, apart from their relationship with collared urns, also occur in great numbers in museum collections, as, of course, do flint scrapers.

STONEWORK

The kinds of perforated stone battle-axes found in association with cordoned urns are also well represented in museum collections. Many of the unassociated finds are in fact more handsome than the associated ones. Jet necklaces too are

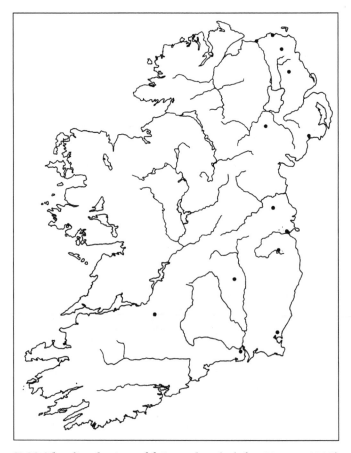

7.28 *The distribution of faience beads (after Magee, 1993)*

well represented—often, in fact, decorated in a fashion very reminiscent of that on gold lunulae but, with respect to the different material, usually executed in pointillé fashion, in which the lines are formed by distinct dots. The most striking feature of these necklaces is that the so-called 'spacer bead', actually a sort of trapezoidal plate, is perforated in a most complicated manner, to enable the lower elements in the necklace to hang properly.

OTHER ITEMS

Various kinds of beads and other objects that have been found in burials, accompanying the different forms of pottery, have been found in cists. At Kilcroagh, County Antrim, accompanying two cordoned urn burials, two handsome segmented beads of faience (earthenware with a glaze made from tin) were found.

It was once thought that faience found in Ireland had been imported from Egypt; now it is believed that it was produced locally. A recent re-evaluation of the finds of faience has shown it to be reasonably widespread (fig. 7.28). At Kinkit, County Tyrone, in a segmented cist that contained the cremated bone of two young adults, assured of a place in the Earlier Bronze Age by radiocarbon dating, were found a bone needle and a V-perforated button of bone. It is unlikely, however, that the bone needle could have served to sew the button onto anything, because of its girth (fig. 7.29).

DECORATION

While decoration on the various kinds of Earlier Bronze Age pottery and on such specifically decorative objects as jet necklaces and gold lunulae has already been referred to, it is worth drawing attention to decoration occurring on otherwise utilitarian objects, such as axes, daggers, and spear-heads. Many of the more developed forms of axe bear decoration. While sometimes this is simple, almost careless, consisting of either simple grooves cast in the surface of the bronze or simple overall coverage of dashes, more developed forms also occur, usually consisting of chevrons, triangles, and lozenges. These motifs occur also on daggers and rapiers (fig. 7.30) and on the razors found with

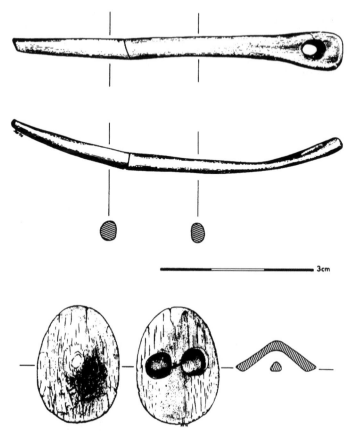

7.29 *Bone needle and bone V-perforated button found in the segmented cist grave at Kinkit, Co. Tyrone (after Glover, 1975)*

cordoned urns. They do also occur on spear-heads, but spear-heads share a form of decorative motif with jet necklaces: pointillé decoration. This form of decoration also occurs on one or two stones, such as that from Lyles Hill, County Antrim, where it was a component of a cemetery under a round cairn (fig. 7.31).

STONE MOULDS
Stone moulds were not merely a vehicle for the production of metal implements, like the mould from Ballynahinch, County Down (plate 7), but also serve in themselves as a

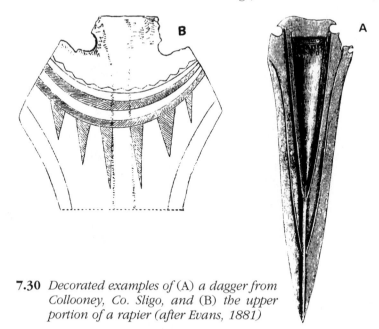

7.30 *Decorated examples of* (A) *a dagger from Collooney, Co. Sligo, and* (B) *the upper portion of a rapier (after Evans, 1881)*

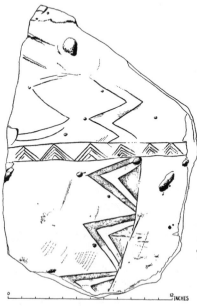

7.31 Decorated stone from the round cairn on Lyles Hill, Toberagnee, Co. Antrim *(after Evans, 1953)*

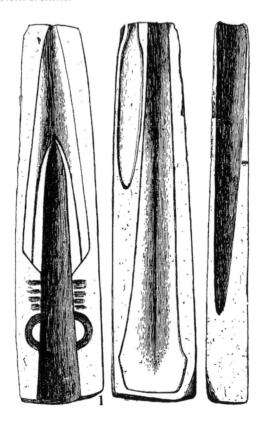

7.32 *Stone mould from Killymeddy, Co. Antrim, showing matrices for casting both looped spear-heads and daggers (after Coffey, 1913)*

sort of hoard. A stone mould—actually one valve of a two-piece mould—from Killymeddy, County Antrim (fig. 7.32), shows that it was capable of producing a fairly advanced form of spear-head and a reasonably advanced form of dirk. Moulds also have an important role to play in helping us to understand the distribution processes that were involved.

An investigation of the identifiable products of individual matrices of moulds shows that, somewhat surprisingly, the products of the mould in question were not clustered tightly around it but tended to be well dispersed (fig. 7.33). This suggests that the moulds (for axes at least, since these are the only implements so far to have been studied in this

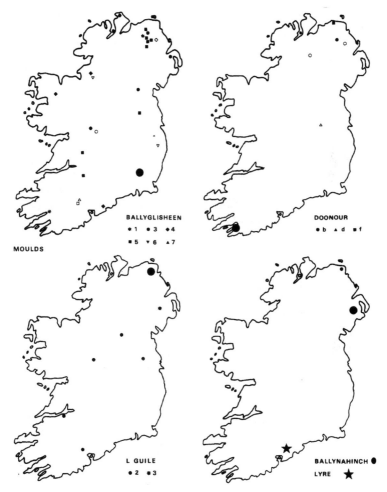

7.33 *The distribution of axes identified as having been cast in a particular matrix of a mould in relation to the find-spot of the actual mould (after Flanagan, 1978)*

fashion) were the equipment of an itinerant craftsman or group of craftsmen who carried around the country not only the mould but a supply of copper or bronze as well as the other tools required for finishing and decorating the implements produced by that mould. The existence of the smelting site at Ross Island in no way contradicts this hypothesis.

DWELLING-SITES

There are numerous sites where people of the Earlier Bronze Age have left evidence of settlement. Sandhill sites, at places like Dundrum, County Down, contain hearths and quantities of pottery. The complex of sites at Knockadoon, Lough Gur, County Limerick, showed signs of settlement; here there was also evidence of static early metalworking, in the form of crucibles and fragments of moulds for looped spear-heads, associated with fragments of pottery. At Downpatrick, County Down, two round houses, one about seven metres in diameter, the other about four metres, both with central hearths, were discovered; these belonged to people using cordoned urns and show that this form of pottery was not exclusively funerary.

An oval house at Carrigillihy, County Cork, built of stone with a thatched roof supported on posts, measured some 10 m by 6.7 m. Another oval house was at Cullyhanna, County Armagh, 6.5 m by 5.3 m. It was surrounded by a sort of stockade of posts enclosing an area nearly seventeen metres in diameter. On Coney Island, Lough Neagh, an Earlier Bronze Age level revealed two rectangular structures, with a series of pits and hollows associated with bowls; here also there was a cordoned urn, but in a later deposit.

8

THE LATER BRONZE AGE
1200–700 BC

Rather quaintly, the Later Bronze Age begins with a range of tools and weapons that really constitute a sort of residue from what used to be described as the Middle Bronze Age. These include tools such as palstaves, really a more developed form of flanged axe, which survived as well; palstaves were frequently fitted with side-loops as a further means of securing them to their haft. Elongated daggers, known as rapiers, also survived.

The true Later Bronze Age saw the introduction of a huge range of new and sophisticated tools and weapons. It is considered that these changes in technology and its products were a result of changes in the east, which caused repercussions that spread like ripples across the Continent, ultimately reaching Ireland.

The entire Irish metal repertoire has been examined and sorted, and three industrial phases have been identified, mainly on the basis of an analysis of the contents of hoards, and it is from key hoards in each of the three phases that the phases have got their names. The first of the three phases is known as the 'Bishopsland phase', after a large and important hoard found at Bishopsland, County Kildare. This consisted mainly of bronze tools: a looped palstave and a socketed axe, a series of socketed hammers (fig. 11.8), a couple of chisels, a double-edged saw, a non-socketed sickle, and various other items. Most of the other hoards of this phase contain only gold objects, such as that from

Derryvoy, County Cavan, consisting of fragments of ribbon torcs, or the two hoards of gold penannular bracelets from Downpatrick, County Down. The second or 'Roscommon' phase is named after a hoard found in County Roscommon. A more representative range of bronze objects appears. The Roscommon hoard itself contains two complete socketed axe-heads and portions of three others, a fragment of a sword blade, and three chapes (metal scabbard mountings) for swords. Interestingly, it also contains three pouring-gates for moulds, as well as a quantity of waste bronze. Almost inevitably, it is best described as a founder's hoard, the fragments and the waste obviously being intended for recycling. Another hoard of this phase, from Youghal, County Cork, contains two bronze swords and two plain leaf-shaped spear-heads—all of them damaged, so it too may well have been a founder's hoard.

It is with the third or 'Dowris' phase that hoards become both more common and more interesting. The hoard from Dowris, County Offaly, contained originally an estimated 218 objects, not all of which have survived. Of those that have survived there are 5 bronze swords, 36 bronze spear-heads, 35 socketed axes, 26 bronze horns or trumpets, and a staggering 40 of the rather enigmatic objects known as crotals, which appear to have been a kind of rattle (fig. 15.3). It also contained a number of tools (hammers, knives, and gouges) as well as several sheet-bronze buckets (fig. 8.1) and cauldrons—all in all, a vast array, which suggests that, since it was found in a place likely to have been under water when the hoard was deposited (not necessarily all at the one time), it had been a sort of votive offering.

Many of the other hoards of this phase contain formidable arrays of weapons. The hoard from Knockadoo, County Roscommon, consists of two swords and two spear-heads; one from Cullen, County Tipperary, is credited with originally containing some two hundred swords, of which only four survive, an unknown number of spear-heads, of which none apparently survive, and a few miscellaneous items, including a socketed gouge. The hoard from Relagh, County Tyrone (fig. 11.6), consisted of four slightly different swords.

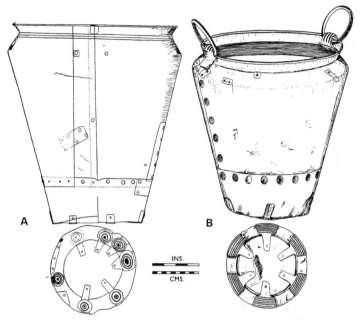

8.1 *Later Bronze Age buckets: (A) of Kurd type from Dowris,*
Co. Offaly; (B) a native copy with no recorded provenance
(after Eogan, 1964)

As if to compensate for the militaristic nature of these
hoards, a number exist that contain useful kits of tools. One
from Knockmaon, County Waterford, contains two looped
socketed axe-heads, two tanged chisels, a socketed gouge,
and two socketed knives, one of them with a curved blade,
which many think should be associated with leather-
working. It also contained a sword and spear-head, so that
the craftsman could at least defend himself. The hoard from
Glastry, County Down, is a neat little tool-kit: two socketed
gouges and a tanged chisel.

Many of the hoards, of course, consist mainly if not
entirely of ornamental objects, not always necessarily of
gold. The celebrated hoard of gold objects from Mooghaun
North, County Clare, is declared to be the largest associated
find of gold objects in Ireland and even in Bronze Age
Europe outside the Aegean. Part of the hoard, exhibited in
1854, contained 146 pieces; today only 29 objects can be
identified: one neck ring, six collars, and a whole collection

of penannular bracelets. The hoard from Derryhale, County Armagh, contained a fascinating selection of bronze sunflower pins and some cup-headed ones as well as series of solid bronze rings and some beads.

A surprising number of hoards consist of bronze horns or trumpets. One from Corracanvy, County Cavan, contained three, one only fragmentary; of the two intact ones, one was a side-blow, the other an end-blow. Another hoard, from Drumbest, County Antrim, consisted of four horns: two side-blow and two end-blow (fig. 15.2).

By no means all of the surviving Later Bronze Age arte-facts were found in hoards. Scattered all over the country are hundreds of objects such as swords, spear-heads, and axes. On the dwelling-site at Ballinderry, County Offaly, for instance, were found a sunflower pin and a socketed bronze knife, while among the Later Bronze Age material from Navan Fort, County Armagh, was a tiny socketed bronze axe and a socketed sickle. A very handsome amber necklace came from Kurin Moss, County Derry. There is also a series of bronze shields (fig. 8.2), mainly, it seems, from the Shannon area. All are circular, with raised concentric rings and central bosses. Examples in leather also occur, from Clonbrin, County Longford, while a wooden one was found at Cloonlara, County Mayo.

The pottery of the Later Bronze Age was coarse and unattractive, whatever type of site it was found at, both the

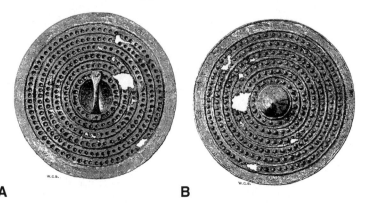

A   **B**

8.2 *Sheet-bronze shield from Co. Limerick:* (A) *back;* (B) *front (after Coffey, 1913)*

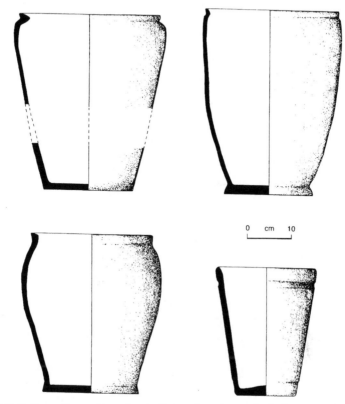

0   cm   10

8.3 *Pottery from Haughey's Fort, Co. Armagh (after Boreland, 1993)*

hilltop ones that seem to be such a feature of the period, at Haughey's Fort and Navan Fort, County Armagh, and Rathgall, County Wicklow, and lakeshore sites such as Lough Eskragh, County Tyrone, and Ballinderry, County Offaly. This type of pottery is bucket-shaped and devoid of decoration (fig. 8.3).

Evidence for Later Bronze Age metalworking has come both from hilltop sites, such as Rathgall, where it appears to have been extensive, and from the lakeside site of Lough Eskragh, where several log-boats were found (fig. 8.4). Evidence of other Later Bronze Age crafts includes the wooden shield-former, on which leather shields were formed, found at Kilmahamogue, County Antrim. Later Bronze Age burials, however, are a rarity, apart from

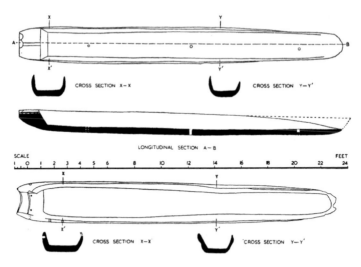

8.4 *Log-boats from Lough Eskragh, Co. Tyrone (after Collins and Seaby, 1960)*

Rathgall, where, in an area surrounded by a ditch, there were pits containing cremation burials, one of an adult, one of a child, and one of an adult with a child.

Evidence of Later Bronze Age farming comes not only from sites such as Haughey's Fort, County Armagh, where there was evidence not only of stock-rearing but also of the extensive collection of barley, possibly for redispersal, and Dún Aonghasa on the Aran Islands, where there was surprising evidence of sheep-rearing, but also in the form of the tanged-and-socketed sickles that appear in some hoards, like the tanged sickle in the hoard from Bishopsland, County Kildare, as well as individual finds (fig. 12.2). Surprisingly, the first appearance of saddle-querns for grinding cereals is in the Later Bronze Age, at sites such as Lough Eskragh, County Tyrone, and Ballinderry, County Offaly.

A rather bizarre feature introduced in the Later Bronze Age was the cooking-place or cooking-pit. (There is a tendency to describe this type of cooking-place as a *fulacht fia* or *fulacht fiann*. This should be avoided, because of the cultural impropriety of imposing on a patently Later Bronze Age structure an obviously later and inappropriate term.) These were first recognised at Ballyvourney, County Cork (fig. 8.5). Here and in neighbouring Killeen were found several examples. Typical was a trough measuring 1.8 m by 1 m, slightly wedge-shaped, lined with wood packed with clay. At the south-west end was a hearth, defined by erect slabs of stone; at the other end was a secondary hearth. To the north-east was a stone-lined pit 2 m in length and tapering in width from 1.8 m to 0.8 m; this was identified as an oven or roasting-pit. An irregular hut contained traces

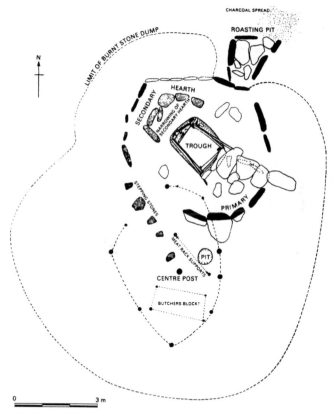

8.5 *Cooking-place at Ballyvourney, Co. Cork (after O'Kelly, 1954)*

that were identified as possible 'butcher's blocks' and 'meat-racks'. The principle suggested—and experimentally tested by the excavator, apparently with satisfactory results—was that heaps of stone were heated on the hearths and, when red-hot, cast into the water-filled pit to cause the water to boil. Cuts of meat (the excavator used a leg of lamb) were dropped into the boiling water, which was reheated when necessary by the addition of further pieces of red-hot stone.

Associated often with such cooking-places are heaps of burnt stone, used obviously as the heating element of the water. Such heaps, or 'burnt mounds', as they are called, are frequently suggested as having denoted the presence of a cooking-place. It is interesting that log-boats were sometimes used as part of the lining of such cooking-places, as at Teeronea, County Clare, and possibly Derrybrusk, County Fermanagh. Cooking-places of this nature are quite common, including such sites as Ballycroghan, County Down.

PART 2

THE SOCIAL PREHISTORY

INTRODUCTION

In 1903, P. W. Joyce remarked in his *Social History of Ancient Ireland*:

> Hitherto we have treated of the evidence afforded by written Literature. Material Remains constitute the other main source of information. They consist of antiquarian objects of various kinds, found underground from time to time, and now preserved in museums; and of numerous monuments and ruins of buildings scattered over the face of the country. These, so far as they go, and so far as we are able to ascertain their uses, give us perhaps the most certain and satisfactory evidence of all. Besides affording, of themselves, independent testimony, they serve to confirm, and in many cases to correct and tone down the written accounts. But in some cases we are unable to connect the remains with the literature; in other words, some articles are mentioned and named in the ancient writings which we cannot identify with any existing objects: and on the other hand we have several antique articles in the museums whose names and uses are unknown, and which we are unable to identify with any of those occurring in the records. These remarks apply to the ancient buildings and structures of various kinds scattered over the country: while a large proportion are identified and their uses known, numerous others are still a puzzle to antiquarians.

The great difference between us and Joyce is that in the background there existed for him a great body of written information with which he could attempt to reconcile such archaeological evidence as was available to him. For pre-history we have no such contemporaneous guidelines: we start off with an increasing volume of archaeological evidence, which we must assess in an attempt to extract from it as much information as possible.

Some of the information available to us is reasonably straightforward, in that we can arrange it archaeologically and draw conclusions directly from it. Much of the information about social prehistory, however, does not lend itself so conveniently to interpretation: it is either so scanty that it is not amenable to meaningful statistical analysis or, in many cases, so scanty that it constitutes more or less anecdotal evidence. The most useful manner in which to arrange such information as can be gleaned seems to be to consider all aspects of human social life as if there exist, and have always existed, government departments whose special responsibility is, and has been, that aspect of society.

9

SOCIETY

POPULATION

In many ways the assessment of the size of an ancient population is the most crucial—and the most difficult—problem to be encountered. The Scylla and Charybdis of population sizes are that on the one hand the population must be small enough for the natural resources at hand to be adequate to sustain it, while on the other hand it must be large enough to be genetically self-supporting. It is interesting to note that the legendary first occupation of Ireland, recorded in many of the early pseudo-historical accounts, was by Parthalón with a thousand companions, men and women. (This figure, of course, is not to be regarded as in any way normative.)

The Mesolithic Period

There seems to exist in the minds of many archaeologists a romantic notion that the first arrival of men and women in Ireland, in the Early Mesolithic Period, consisted of the landing, somewhere in the vicinity of Mount Sandel, County Derry (since it is the earliest dated site), of a small skin-covered boat containing a nuclear family, which was fruitful and multiplied and occupied the proximate areas of the earth. This notion is reinforced by the estimate that the site at Mount Sandel, occupying some seven hundred square metres, would have accommodated a family group of no more than fifteen people. Numbers of settlers of this order seem genetically unlikely to succeed—although it is extremely difficult to obtain any estimate of the genetically required minimum population. (These days even the legendarily lonesome Yeti of the Himalayas is denied its genetic solitude and allocated to a breeding pool at least one hundred in number.)

It would seem reasonable, therefore, to assume a minimum population, or genetic pool, in the immediate vicinity of Mount Sandel of something in the region of a hundred people. This would immediately convert the original landing to a more deliberate colonisation, implying the arrival in Ireland of considerably more than the contents of a single skin-covered boat.

Speculation about why such a colonisation took place at all must remain just that—speculation. Since the source of the colonists is most likely to have been Scotland (where, unfortunately, no sites culturally similar to that at Mount Sandel have been discovered, an absence that has been ascribed to inundation as a result of rising sea levels), it is unlikely that Mount Sandel—not visible from Scotland—was the primary target. An initial landing-place somewhere on the east coast of County Antrim, with a horizon profile visible across the narrow intervening strip of sea, would be much more likely.

The existence of an occupation site culturally closely comparable to that at Mount Sandel and chronologically more or less contemporary at Lough Boora, County Offaly, on the one hand complicates our problem about estimating the size of the population during the Earlier Mesolithic Period and on the other hand suggests that for the two sites so closely to share time and culture there must have been quite definite cultural and genetic links between them. Indeed it is virtually impossible to envisage their existing completely independently. Despite the present lack of an intervening series of sites providing such links, it is necessary to introduce the probability of a series of genetic 'puddles' covering the nearly 300 km (240 km as the crow flies) between them. If we assume only that the genetic puddles are placed at approximately 15 km centres, this would mean that the (so far as is known) scarcely existent sites would have been some twenty in number, suggesting a minimal developed population of over two thousand— only twice that of Parthalón's legendary colonising contingent. It has been suggested, however, that a population in the region of eight thousand may have been achieved during the Mesolithic Period. Not a single discovered and attested Mesolithic burial exists, so there is no direct, skeletal evidence of a single member of this population.

The Neolithic Period

The lack of burial sites and even of palpable skeletal remains for the Mesolithic Period fortunately does not apply as far as the Neolithic Period is concerned. There exist some

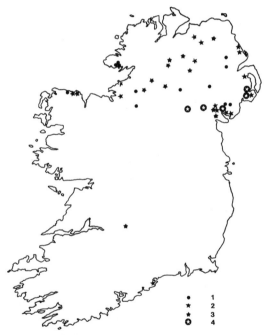

9.1 *Excavated and 'investigated' court tombs: the distribution of human evidence: (1) no bone; (2) bone unidentified; (3) bone partly identified; (4) unburnt bone*

300 examples of court tombs (fig. 4.1); of these, however, only some 36 have been excavated or 'investigated' (fig. 9.1). Of these, 13 produced no bone, burnt or unburnt, while of the bone yielded by a further 16 no information about the people it represents has been forthcoming.

The fact that no bone was discovered in so many sites is almost certainly due to the fact that the local soil was so acid as to prevent its preservation even had it been cremated. The dearth of information from such a number of sites that did produce bone may be due to a number of reasons: it could be that the bone was present in such small quantity that it could not be meaningfully identified, or that it was so decayed that the result was the same, or even that no expert was conveniently available to undertake the examination. On some of the sites where there is information about the remains it is scanty enough: at Clontygora Large, County Armagh, for example, the cremated bone was of one adult, while at Carrick East, County Derry, the one chip of cremated bone found was identified as simply being from one adult. In some cases the identifications have been fairly informative—always, it must be remembered, minimal, depending very strongly on the preservation of particularly diagnostic pieces of bone. At Ballyreagh, County Fermanagh, a woman aged between twenty-five and thirty-five was identified, while at Aghnaskeagh, County Louth, a woman and a girl were identified from the cremated bone.

On some sites where there was unburnt bone, much more information was recovered. At Audleystown, County Down, some 33 people were represented, including the unburnt remains of 4 women, 6 men, 4 adults whose sex was not determined, and 5 children—in addition to the cremated remains of 11 other people.

The total number of bodies so far identified from excavated and 'investigated' court tombs amounts to some 44 or 45 unburnt and some 52 cremated. This total of less than a hundred cannot possibly constitute more than a gentle indication that there were people living and dying in the period of the court tombs who, for some reason, were accorded burial according to one rite or the other in the court tombs that have so far been excavated or 'investigated'. The advantage—so far unexploited—of the presence of a reasonable proportion of unburnt skeletal material is that it represents a potential source of DNA, so that from the twenty-one or twenty-two individuals at Audleystown it could presumably be established whether any of the five children were related to the adult men or women also present.

There is, however, a rather devious method of calculating what might be described as a 'maximum postulable population'. Audleystown is the most productive excavated site with some bodies represented. The two burial galleries were each divided into four chambers, but the burials were not evenly divided between the chambers. One of the chambers—number 2 in the western gallery—does, however, contain the greatest number of occupants per chamber of any excavated or 'investigated' court tomb, with a total of thirteen or upwards; this chamber is followed by chamber 1 in the eastern gallery at Audleystown, with a total of eight, and then by chamber 1 at Ballyalton, County Down, with a total of seven or more. Since we are seeking a 'maximum postulable population', we shall use thirteen as the maximum observed number of occupants per chamber. About 330 court tombs are known to survive. While the majority have galleries divided into two chambers, many exist that have a gallery divided into three or even four; an appreciable number have two galleries, and many have additional subsidiary chambers. We shall therefore assume three chambers as a mean: this gives 990 as the number of chambers, and with an assumed thirteen bodies per chamber this suggests a 'maximum postulable population' of some 12,870.

In addition to the court tombs there are, of course, the portal tombs, of which over 160 have so far been listed. The number of these that possess two chambers is not excessive, so we shall accept 160 as the working total. Of those examples that have been excavated, some, such as Ballykeel, County Armagh, produced no bone whatsoever; a recently excavated example at Poulnabrone, County Clare, produced in contrast the amazing total of some 33 bodies. We thus arrive at a population, for those eligible for burial in court tombs or portal tombs, in the region of almost 13,500. This, of course, does not imply a 'census return' of that order for any given year: in fact this total has to be spread over the period when the use of such tombs was in vogue. There emerges a feeling that not every member of society was entitled to burial in a court tomb or a portal tomb, even in what has long been considered an extremely egalitarian Neolithic society.

The passage tombs

The sheer size and mass of the three hundred or so passage tombs of Ireland (most notably the mound of the great tomb at Newgrange) would suggest much higher numbers of burials. The irony is that while the construction of this one mound would have occupied an estimated work force of some four hundred people over a period of at least sixteen years, the actual burials found—admittedly the remnant of an originally larger total—amounted to a mere four or five. It is really only at Tara, in the Mound of the Hostages, that the number of burials—over a hundred—even begins to show a sensible relationship between the effort of building the tomb and the ultimate beneficiaries of the effort.

Burials in passage tombs, which were prone to disturbance partly because of their sheer monumentality and partly because of their accessibility, are therefore even less consistent than burials in court tombs and unlikely to be of much assistance in our efforts to estimate a minimum population. In any event, the size of a population relating solely to those worthy of or entitled to burial in passage tombs is genetically less critical (except perhaps in the eyes of those who granted the 'worthiness' or 'entitlement'), in view of the population size already postulated. The feeling, however, that not all members of society were entitled to burial in elaborate tombs seems to be considerably enhanced with regard to passage tombs.

The Later Bronze Age

It is perhaps tempting to view several aspects of the Later Bronze Age as evidence of increased pressure on resources, brought about by an expansion of population. The move to apparently more defensible settlement sites on hilltops, sometimes described as hill-forts, implies the existence, or at least the perception, of offence. The increased types, and numbers, of weapons would suggest a similar interpretation.

THE FAMILY

Whether the concept of 'family' was appreciated or observed among the prehistoric peoples whose social behaviour we are examining is perhaps questionable—or at best not proved. On balance, however, it seems likely to have constituted one of the building-blocks of society.

The Mesolithic Period

Despite the fact that even skeletal remains of our first social group in the Mesolithic Period do not exist—or have not so far been identified—which creates a sort of social, or at least sentimental, barrier between us and them, the size of the settlement at Mount Sandel, estimated by the excavator at 'fewer than fifteen', would seem to suggest a family unit, not particularly extended. We have no evidence whatsoever to suggest that the unit could have included grandfathers or grandmothers in addition to postulated parents and children: whether a primary family unit is likely to have consisted simply of a father, mother and twelve or thirteen children can be neither proved nor disproved. Modern examples of family units of this size are by no means uncommon.

The Neolithic Period

The almost dramatic increase in the availability of human remains from the Neolithic Period does make our task if not easier at least temptingly more approachable, especially when some of the burials consist of unburnt bones. Unfortunately the practice of collective burial, where a single chamber of a court tomb, such as chamber 2 in the west gallery at Audleystown, County Down, can contain the remains of thirteen individuals, twelve of whom had not been cremated (despite the fact that the unburnt bone tended to be placed in small groups and heaps), makes it difficult—although tempting—to allocate the remains of three children, three women and four men to family groups. It is circumstances like this that make the absence of DNA testing even more regrettable. Even in chamber 2 at Annaghmare, County Armagh, the presence of only (it would appear) the uncremated bone of a child and a woman does not inevitably imply a mother and child. The remains of those buried in passage tombs again could be either burnt or unburnt, and again buried collectively; it is even more difficult to detect potential family parties.

The evidence from the extensive field systems dubbed the Céide Fields at Behy and Glenulra, County Mayo, has been interpreted as inferring a large complex of family farms, forming a community that depended consistently, from the initial layout of the field system to the annual slaughter of beasts and the agreed staggering of such slaughter to ensure continuous production, on the active co-operation of the constituent families.

The Earlier Bronze Age

It is really only in the Earlier Bronze Age, with the appearance of the practice of burial in single graves, that the assumption of family groups becomes so tempting as to be irresistible, even where the bone has been cremated. The inferences that may be drawn from the evidence offered by even cremated bone make it even more regrettable that the surviving bone in nearly 250 of the recorded single graves has not undergone expert examination (fig. 9.2). (Perhaps the most surprising feature of this map is that it shows that many of the unexamined and unidentified remains were

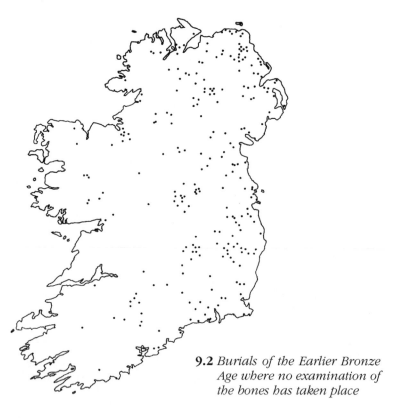

9.2 *Burials of the Earlier Bronze Age where no examination of the bones has taken place*

relatively close to centres where expertise should have been readily available—Dublin and Belfast in particular.) Thus at Creggan, County Antrim, the appearance of the cremated bones of three—a woman, a child, and an infant, accompanied by a collared urn, in a pit—is difficult to construe as anything other than a mother and her two children. The same could be said of the burial at Crumlin, County Antrim, of the cremated bone of a young woman and child accompanied by an encrusted urn.

The burial at Rossnaree, County Meath, of the crouched skeleton of a woman and foetus is very poignant; presumably the unfortunate woman died in childbirth. These examples do tend to suggest that the biological link between mothers and their children was recognised and appreciated— even that the concept of bereavement was known. At Labbamolaga, County Cork, the collocation of cremated bone of a man, a woman and a child aged between four and six in a cist makes it very tempting to view this as a family (though we may well speculate on what catastrophe caused their simultaneous deaths). Even at Drung, County Donegal, where three cists formed a small flat cemetery, one containing the crouched skeleton of a man, another the crouched skeleton of a woman, and the third fragments of the skeleton of a foetus or new-born child, it is again a strong temptation to view this as a family burial. The same could also be said of a single cist containing bones of a man, a woman and a child at Lodge, County Galway.

These are by no means the only examples of women having been buried with children, or even of putative family groups. They all illustrate an appreciation of the blood relationship on the part of Earlier Bronze Age society; and if one yields to temptation and interprets the groups as family groups, a suggestion even emerges that life-long bonding was in vogue—it is not, after all, unknown in other parts of the animal world. In human society, however, there could well be social ramifications and constraints arising from such institutions: 'adultery', rape, and the like.

The Later Bronze Age

In the Later Bronze Age the definition of 'family groups' becomes more difficult. The relative infrequency of Later

Bronze Age burials deprives us of one important field of investigation; by and large the family unit seems not to emerge at present as a distinct feature of Later Bronze Age society.

THE ORGANISATION OF SOCIETY

We have arrived at the conclusion that the family unit was, inevitably, one of the essential building-blocks of society and that genetic relationships—as of parents and children— were given due respect. We can try to establish how these features and others show us how society was organised.

The Mesolithic Period

The site at Mount Sandel, estimated by the excavator to have supported no more than fifteen people—a scarcely extended family—gives us our only available building-block for Mesolithic society. We have already suggested that the local breeding community, for simple genetic reasons, must have been at least a hundred in number, requiring at least a further six families of the same size in the immediate area. While each family group may have been responsible for their own needs—house-building, fishing, hunting, and collecting the fruits of the forest—we can at least construct a community consisting of several families and a labour force sufficient to undertake the exploitation of larger food sources: the deer whose hides are suggested as a possible covering for the frames of the huts, or the seals that could have been hunted or simply collected.

For the Early Mesolithic Period at least there seem few indications of specialised trades: it gives in general an image of a society in which 'DIY' was the rule. While co-operation between families may have been practised, for example in the building of huts, it is quite possible that for most of the time each family was an independent economic unit, responsible for its own food-gathering. In the Late Mesolithic Period, on the other hand, the existence of hoards of finished and unfinished flint tools could be construed as the emergence of specialist craftsmen, trading in flint and probably responsible for its spread into non-flint-producing areas—which is virtually everywhere in Ireland except flint-rich County Antrim.

The Neolithic Period

We are fortunate that for the Neolithic Period much more evidence is available. We know that Neolithic houses, particularly rectangular houses, were often considerably bigger than the 30 square metres represented by the round huts at Mount Sandel. The house at Ballyglass, County Mayo, was a comfortable 55.5 square metres in area, while that at Knowth was nearly 97 square metres. This increase in house size need not be interpreted simply as an increase in family size: it is more likely to be a result of the greater potential of rectangular houses, made possible by changes in the method of construction. Circular or oval houses did continue to be built, particularly at Lough Gur, County Limerick, where numbers of them existed—three of them at site C, ranging from 19.6 to 28.3 square metres.

The unfortunate fact is that, except at Lough Gur, Neolithic houses so far discovered have been found more or less in isolation. No convincing example of a Neolithic 'village' has so far been discovered. Yet there exists ample evidence that society did not consist solely of independent family units but that larger co-operatives were required for some aspects of communal life.

While a two-chambered court tomb, such as that at Shalwy, County Donegal, could well have been erected by a team of twenty to thirty able-bodied men (more than would appear to be available in a single not very extended family) over a period of two to three months, we have already seen that the construction of the great tomb at Newgrange would have required some four hundred. Spread over a period of at least sixteen years, that is a programme that requires considerable organisation, of consummate competence. Similarly, the construction of the walls for the field system of the Céide Fields, County Mayo, called for a highly organised and competently managed work force. There is therefore substantial evidence for the existence in the Neolithic Period of considerably sized social units. Whether this implies the concept of kingship in some form or other or merely the existence of individuals blessed with skill and strong 'officer' qualities is a matter that clearly depends on other information.

The organisation of a work force of some twenty to forty for the construction of court tombs (though larger teams would clearly have been required for the construction of larger examples, such as—keeping to the south-west Donegal group—Farranmacbride, which originally must have been one of the most splendid court tombs built) would not have been a feat in any way comparable to that of organising the construction of the tomb at Newgrange, either in number of workers or in the extended time involved. It is, moreover, difficult in the court tomb context to point at any object or objects that scream out 'kingship' or even exalted status for any individuals.

In the passage tomb context, however, there does exist an article difficult to interpret in any other way. This is the spectacular flint mace-head from Knowth, with its superbly conceived and superbly executed decoration. We must ignore the regal undertones suggested by its being described as a 'mace-head'; it does, however, in its own right and essence suggest even more than simply 'exalted status': even its excavator modestly (for the object) describes it as 'perhaps belonging to the most important person in the community—a political or religious leader—and therefore being the common possession of the community as a whole.' It is tempting to suggest a combination of the two functions: that the political and religious leader was in fact both—a sort of priest-king.

The time-scale involved in the grand plan raises another issue. An individual directing and overseeing a project lasting some sixteen years is not guaranteed the ability to remain alive for the duration of the project. This raises the problem of how the overseer was replaced if he did die. Was the office of priest-king a hereditary one? Did the inclusion in the mound of the 'mace', which could be interpreted as his symbol of power, imply not merely the death of a priest-king but the end of a dynasty?

While the construction of court tombs has been dismissed as a possible indicator of such exalted status on the part of its director, in comparison with the status of the person in charge of the construction of Newgrange and the other more grandiose passage tombs—especially in view of the lack, so far, of any court tomb equivalent of the flint mace-head—we must remember that the designer and director of the layout of the Céide Fields must have enjoyed a status not much lower. The Céide Fields are situated in what is, after all, a tract of countryside overwhelmingly dominated by court tombs. We appear to end up with a situation, therefore, where the societies that constituted the background to both court tombs and passage tombs were large and complex enough to merit leaders of considerable status, whether priest-kings or not, wielding some kind of power over quite considerable numbers of people.

The Earlier Bronze Age

While the relatively simple single burials have proved quite advantageous in other contexts, it may well be that their contribution to our knowledge of the organisation of society may be less secure. One or two examples do, however, leap out as suggesting high status for certain individuals. The first of these, patently, is at Topped Mountain, County Fermanagh, where in a round cairn that literally does 'top' the mountain there were three burials, one consisting of the crouched skeleton of a man, accompanied by a vase and a handsome bronze dagger with part of its gold pommel-binding. This clearly, because of the siting of the burial and the implications of the dagger (burials with daggers are not common in Ireland, burials with gold even less so), must have been a person of considerable importance.

By the same token, a rather extraordinary burial in a tumulus at Croghan Erin, Kiltale, County Meath, where a dagger accompanied what is described in the accounts as a perpendicular skeleton—as if the unfortunate deceased had been buried standing up—must have been that of someone of importance. Even the inclusion of part of a flat triangular dagger with a vase urn and cremated bone at Oldtown, County Dublin, must indicate some degree of status. Again, the skeleton of the man buried in a pit at Ballyenahan, County Cork, with a bronze dagger must be the remains of a person of some status. At Annaghkeen, County Galway, the same applies to the cremated bones in a cist under a round cairn with a vase and, in addition, a bronze dagger and a bronze awl; though in other contexts it might be assumed that the awl indicated that the person buried had been something like a leatherworker—hardly suggestive of great status.

The same apparently contradictory signals appear in a cist at Carrickinab, County Down, where the cremated bones of one man are again accompanied by a bronze dagger and a bronze awl, with a bowl and two flint thumb scrapers, which could reinforce the 'tradesman' image. (Of course there is a distinct possibility that we could be making a gross social error in assuming that in the industrial revolution of the Earlier Bronze Age a 'tradesman' would have been regarded as *déclassé*, when all around him other tradesmen were pumping away at their bellows or filling up their crucibles or heaving around heaps of copper ore.)

The existence of these and other burials accompanied by daggers does suggest a 'warrior caste', whether that implies inherited nobility or not. A couple of other burials are curious but make it difficult to exclude the possibility of high status or nobility. At Castlemartyr, County Cork, a skeleton was found in a cave, accompanied by gold plates and amber beads. In view of the relative absence of gold objects in Irish Earlier Bronze Age burials, this must confer on the deceased some claim to quality or nobility. Another burial, at Farta, County Galway, is surely the most extraordinary of all. In a tumulus was the extended skeleton of a woman accompanied by the remains of a red deer and a small seven-year-old stallion. (There was another burial in the tumulus, consisting of a cordoned urn and cremated bone.) It is difficult, indeed, to expel the notion of a huntress Diana from the mind, but inevitably this must be the burial of a woman of some importance—a truly exceptional woman.

Viewing the other Earlier Bronze Age burials, containing no such obvious indicators of apparent social status as daggers or gold, there is a feeling of slight helplessness. How, for example, in the status stakes should we rate burials with razors, as at Cush, County Limerick, accompanying cremated bone and a cordoned urn, or at Carrowbeg North, County Galway, where the cremated bones of what was considered to be probably a male adult, in a pit, were accompanied only by a razor; or at Carrowjames, County Mayo, where a central oval pit under a tumulus was occupied by a cordoned urn with the cremated remains of an adult and a razor?

Again with regard to status, how does a flint plano-convex knife compare with a bronze object? Examples are quite numerous: at Brownstown, County Kildare, such a knife was found in a pit with an encrusted urn and cremated bone. To make the equation even more difficult, at Glarryford, County Antrim, a collared urn burial with cremated bone was accompanied by two flint plano-convex knives, while in a cist at Coolmore, County Kilkenny, were the cremated remains of four people accompanied by one plano-convex flint knife. How do we evaluate these different kinds of grave-goods? Are they, after all, the 'actual commerciable products of society'? Do their differing values indicate their owners' rungs on the social ladder? Do we picture a finely stratified society, with nuances of caste defined by different types of artefact, of values whose difference we cannot appreciate?

Again, is there a well-defined difference of status between a person buried with only one vessel, as at Ballinvalley, County Meath, where an adult was cremated and buried in a cist with a single vase, and a person buried with several, as at Enniskillen, where the cremated bone buried in a sand-pit was accompanied by a vase and a vase urn? Finally, did those buried with no trappings at all occupy the lowest stratum of society, like the two people at Cuillare, County Mayo, where a cist contained nothing but the cremated bones of an adult and beside them the disarticulated bones of a man, or the man buried, crouched, in a cist at Park, County Galway, or the adolescent cremated and buried in a pit at Urbalreagh, County Antrim? Was there even a diminution in status between burial in a cist and burial in a mere pit?

Other evidence for an important 'ruling class' is difficult to unearth in the Earlier Bronze Age; but the fact that the Céide Fields apparently continued an active life into the Earlier Bronze Age—but in an area surprisingly deficient of Earlier Bronze Age burials—raises the question whether they were 'under new management' or whether the original owners continued to enjoy their pastoral life.

The Later Bronze Age
In the Later Bronze Age the move to potentially fortifiable hilltop sites (even if there is not always evidence of actual

fortifications having been erected) suggests the emergence of a new structure being imposed on society. There is an impression of a more 'clan'-type structure, with each clan vying with its neighbours for possession of or access to the means of livelihood or riches. This is strengthened by the enormous range of weapons available—some even described as 'ceremonial', suggestive of the existence of a sort of palace guard. A hint of this reorganisation may be discerned in the deliberate secretion of the first gold hoard discovered on Cathedral Hill, Downptrick, County Down, in a hole covered with stones, as if there was the threat of unrest, or even of warfare. Unfortunately, the goldsmith who had secreted the hoard was obviously prevented from recovering it.

VIOLENCE AND WARFARE

There has always been crime; sometimes and in some contexts it is described as sin. Unfortunately the only crimes that tend to leave evidence after three thousand years are those involving violence. Even in societies where no artefacts occur that could unequivocally be described as weapons there exist multitudes of objects that could be so used: lumps of wood, heavy stones—almost anything could be used to hurt, damage or even kill another person. Even if the violence is not restricted to one person using such simple, casual 'blunt instruments', it is still open to groups to use them against other groups, without any suggestion to archaeologists many thousands of years later that this was so. It is even more difficult to unscramble the reactions that were shown in the society in question, to know whether sanctions were employed against the offenders.

The Mesolithic Period

In the Mesolithic Period, while no specifically man-killing weapons have been identified, there do exist artefacts benignly and perhaps naïvely interpreted as tools to assist in hunting and fishing—items such as arrow-heads, fishing-spears, and harpoons. But of course any of these could equally be used for injuring or even killing people: the use today of such innocent pieces of equipment as spanners, hammers, even baseball bats and the like as weapons for the inflicting of injury on other parties is not unknown. Unfortunately, however, the lack of identified and attested Mesolithic burials again prevents any possibility of scientific or pathological examination to confirm or deny the existence of Mesolithic murder, manslaughter, or execution. Yet a casual glance at human behaviour throughout the millennia suggests that where two or three are gathered together, there exists a potential for acts of violence.

The Neolithic Period
The arrival in Ireland of Neolithic technology saw a great increase in the number of potentially offensive weapons, not merely a whole range of forms of arrow and javelin-heads (somehow javelin-heads convey the impression of weapons rather than tools) but also good, heavy stone axes, even mace-heads, which could very conveniently be turned to mayhem. The survival of so many burials—in court tombs, portal tombs, and passage tombs, both burnt and unburnt—provides a collection of material suitable for scientific examination. Unfortunately for us in our quest for evidence, fortunately for our Neolithic predecessors, little of this material has produced evidence of misbehaviour—except in the portal tomb at Poulnabrone, County Clare, where the tip of an arrow-head was found embedded in the ilium (hip-bone) of what was probably a male. This, though it must have been painful, is unlikely to have been life-threatening.

The Earlier Bronze Age
The Earlier Bronze Age brought with it a great range of new implement types, many of them, of course, manufactured from the wonderful new material, bronze. While by far the greatest weight of production was dedicated to the manufacture of useful tools, particularly axes, there was a fairly high level of production of daggers, of several types, which were manifestly offensive (and defensive) weapons. The role of these was so positive that on a number of occasions they were placed in graves, patently as an indication of the warrior status of the man whose grave they shared—almost in the same way as mediaeval coffin lids for men were embellished with a sword.

One of the most splendid examples was the one we have already seen at Topped Mountain, County Fermanagh, where the crouched skeleton of a man in a cist under a round cairn on the hill-top was accompanied by a handsome dagger together with part of its gold pommel-binding. Another example, though the dagger was not quite as splendid and had no gold pommel-binding, was at Ballyenahan, County Cork, where a skeletal man was accompanied by a dagger in a pit.

Another explicit weapon in use during the Earlier Bronze Age was the halberd—a dagger-like blade attached at right angles to its haft. One of these was found in a cist at Moylough, County Sligo, accompanying cremated bone that, although not identified, can hardly have been other than that of a man. Another type of weapon that developed rather late in the Earlier Bronze Age was the bronze spearhead, again, like the halberd, a development from the dagger but affixed in line with its shaft. One of these was found in a cist at Ballysadare, County Sligo, accompanying 'partly charred' bone—presumably of a man, though the remains were not identified.

Two other types of weapon also appear in Earlier Bronze Age burials. These are barbed-and-tanged flint arrow-heads and stone battle-axes. A stone battle-axe, for example, was found in a pit with a cordoned urn and cremated bone—again, although unidentified, presumably of a man—at Laheen, County Donegal; another was found with the cremated bone of an adult, again unidentified but presumably a man, with a cordoned urn at Ballintubbrid, County Wexford. Others apparently were found in a small cemetery at Ballynahatty, County Down, along with several urns and bones, as well as stone arrow-heads. Interestingly, at Stillorgan, County Dublin, one cist contained the skeleton of a woman whose death was due to a blow on the skull. It would be tempting—but without skilled scientific or medical examination totally unwarranted!—to suggest that this could have been inflicted with a battle-axe.

One Earlier Bronze Age burial of special interest, because a flint barbed-and-tanged arrow-head was present, was one of the five pit burials at Ballymacaldrack, County

Antrim, where the cremated remains of a young woman were found. The excavator suggested that the arrowhead may have been the cause of her death rather than a funerary offering. The temptation to speculate on a possible inquest verdict (if Earlier Bronze Age society had indulged in such institutions) is overwhelming. Was it accidental death? Was the unfortunate woman put to death—perhaps as a woman 'taken in adultery'? Sadly, we'll never know.

Three other burials raise similar questions. Two were at Sonnagh Demesne, County Westmeath, in pits, the other at Lehinch, County Offaly, also in a pit. What makes these three burials interesting is that of the two at Sonnagh Demesne, one was a headless extended burial, the other a crouched headless skeleton (a third burial, in a cist, was the cremated burial of a child), while that at Lehinch was an unburnt extended burial in a pit, also headless. In the same small cemetery there were five other extended unburnt burials in pits, an unburnt burial, and a cremation in a pit. What on earth was going on? we are forced to ask ourselves. One possible interpretation of the Sonnagh Demesne event is that the two headless people had been put to death as pederasts, the child—of whatever sex—their victim. Unfortunately the sex of none of the headless skeletons had been determined. The Lehinch situation offers no such glib interpretation.

The Later Bronze Age

The Later Bronze Age saw the introduction and manufacture of a much larger range of explicit weapons, not only new types of swords and spear-heads but also the continued production of types of weapon developed late in the Earlier Bronze Age: the enlarged daggers known as rapiers and the looped types of socketed bronze spear-heads, all in all constituting a formidable arsenal of weapons. The fact that, in addition to offensive weapons, shields of both leather and bronze were in production suggests a much more formally militaristic attitude and even makes it likely that in addition to random acts of violence actual warfare was possible. Unfortunately Later Bronze Age burials are rare enough to deprive us of any pathological evidence of the inimical use of these weapons.

WEALTH

The accumulation of wealth seems to have long been a human desire and practice. Obviously the nature of wealth varies from time to time and from culture to culture. For traditional pirates, for example, pieces of eight were a desirable commodity, while for Winnie the Pooh honey would have been much more to his taste. In any event, the accumulation of wealth, by its nature, may well have contributed to some of the violence, or even warfare, discussed above.

The Mesolithic Period

Even in the Mesolithic Period it is easy enough to envisage the short-term accumulation of wealth: he who was lucky enough to land a stranded seal, or to corner more food than was necessary for himself and his immediate family, could then share or trade with others in his immediate community and could be said to have accumulated 'wealth' in the short term. The accumulation of wealth in the long term, however, seems a concept difficult to apply to members of Mesolithic society, the normal desiderata of which—essentially food of some sort or other—were distinctly perishable.

The Neolithic Period

In the Neolithic Period the scope for accumulating wealth was, superficially at least, greater. The numerous hoards of flint implements, like that from Glenhead, County Antrim, consisting of 138 scrapers, while it could be construed as the stock of a flint-smith is nonetheless accumulated wealth. The same could be said of the famous Malone hoard of ground and polished large axes of Tievebulliagh porcellanite.

The difficulty comes when we start to consider the various aspects of agriculture and stock-rearing. Was the clearing of land for the planting of crops and the rearing of livestock carried out by communities at large for the benefit of the community, or was it carried out by individuals, and their immediate families, for the benefit of those individuals and their immediate families? Did the land so cleared belong to the community at large, or did it belong to an individual and his immediate family? The interpretation of the evidence from the Céide Fields put forward by the excavator seems rather to combine the answers to this question. It is suggested that the extensive field system formed by the building of long stone walls running up and down the hillside, about 150 m apart, was sub-divided by cross-walls; it is further suggested that family farms, each of about twenty-five to thirty hectares, would have constituted the components of the system. It has been postulated that the full known system would have supported as many as 200 or 250 families. The fact that the fields were clearly planned and constructed as a single entity implies that the planning and construction involved a consortium of families—possibly with a single leader who was able to inspire and direct them.

If, then, the fields belonged to the families by whom they were occupied, presumably the fifty head of cattle suggested by the excavator as a reasonable burden for the land area also belonged to the family. It should be stressed, however, that continual co-operation between groups of families would be necessary to ensure the rational staggering of slaughter times to ensure a continuous supply, and to participate in the consumption of each animal slaughtered, since each slaughtered beast would yield in the region of 300 kg of beef—too much, without some system of preserving, for a single family to consume. The land, at least, could thus be construed as accumulated wealth, even though the produce of the land could not be accumulated.

Of course the 'ostentatious consumption' involved in the construction of the larger passage tombs is a blatant example of wealth in the community, though this particular indication may be viewed not so much as the accumulation of material objects with enormous resale value but rather as the skilful husbanding of one particular resource—human labour—to achieve the desired result. Presumably also the skilful direction involved the active, willing, even enthusiastic co-operation of the work force.

The Earlier Bronze Age
The accumulation of wealth in the Earlier Bronze Age was greatly facilitated by the introduction of metal. Hoards of flint implements, such as that from Ballyclare, County Antrim, existed. It consisted of twenty-two large finished barbed-and-tanged arrow-heads as well as seventeen

'blanks'—leaf-shaped pieces of flint whose production was a preliminary stage in the manufacture of the arrow-heads. Their presence in the hoard was a sure indicator that it had belonged to a craftsman specialising in the production of such pieces. While the hoard hardly represented the craftsman's life savings, it did represent his trading stock, or part of it. Such barbed-and-tanged arrow-heads were considered sufficiently worthy to be included in burials as grave-goods.

Far more indicative of the accumulation of wealth are the bronze hoards from the period. Not only were they valuable in themselves at the time of assembly but they would retain (presumably decreased) value even if the artefact types represented in the hoard became outdated, as scrap with a potential for recycling. Examples of such hoards are quite common, such as the one from Whitespots, County Down, consisting of a beaker-compatible triangular copper dagger, whose hilt, unfortunately, has not survived, together with a rather later riveted bronze dagger with a slight mid-rib and a square-butted flat axe. (This hoard markedly conforms to the 'continued-value principle' suggested above.)

The Later Bronze Age

With the Later Bronze Age the evidence for accumulated wealth becomes even more conspicuous. Hoards became much more plentiful (over 160 are known), and bigger—though some probably do not represent the accumulated wealth of individuals. The famous hoard from Dowris, County Offaly, containing originally, it is estimated, over two hundred items, including swords, spear-heads, socketed axes, horns, cauldrons, and buckets, gives every impression of constituting a votive deposit—though it is still, undoubtedly, a staggering accumulation of wealth. Some hoards, such as that from Ballycroghan, County Down, consisting of three leaf-shaped swords at different stages in the manufacturing process, or that from Dreenan, County Fermanagh, consisting of a single sword, five spear-heads, an axe-head, a hammer, a knife, and a lump of bronze, were probably the stock of metalworkers. Other hoards, such as that from Athenry, County Galway, consisting of a spear-head and a shield, or that from Tempo, County Fermanagh, consisting of two swords and a spear-head, give the impression that they were the arms of warriors; while the small hoard from Glastry, County Down, consisting of a tanged chisel and two socketed gouges looks remarkably like the tool-kit of a craftsman.

In addition to hoards of bronze objects, however, there were also hoards of gold ornaments, some, like that from Newtown Forbes, County Longford, consisting merely of two similar gold bracelets, or that from Tara, County Meath, consisting of two dissimilar gold ear-rings, possibly the possessions of one person, while others, such as one of the hoards from Cathedral Hill, Downpatrick, County Down, consisting as it does of ten complete gold penannular bracelets, half of another, and half of a solid gold neck-ring, cut by a chisel before breaking and hammered and bent back, suggests that it was most probably the stock of a metal-worker and was probably destined for melting down, or recycling. It had been concealed in a hole dug into the otherwise undisturbed boulder-clay and covered with stones.

10

INDUSTRY

HOUSING

The 'private market', or the provision of homes for families or small groups of people, is the most immediate expression of the building techniques of our prehistoric predecessors. In a climate like that of Ireland, even with the fluctuations recorded, shelter from rain and cold was clearly a necessity from the first arrival of human colonists.

The Mesolithic Period

We have seen (p. 21) that the houses or huts built by the Neolithic settlers at Mount Sandel were round, varying in diameter from a mere three metres to about six metres. The method of construction—which lends itself particularly to circular buildings, as later on did corbelling—was interesting. A series of saplings were placed in holes and bent over, with each sapling meeting a corresponding sapling on the other side; to this it was secured. Eventually a hemispherical skeleton was created; branches were then woven through this framework. To help keep the interior watertight it is suggested that a covering of deer-hides may have been applied. The larger huts had an internal hearth, the smaller an external hearth.

The Neolithic Period

It is perhaps not entirely surprising that Neolithic houses show a much greater variety, not only in shape and size but in methods of construction. Round, D-shaped and rectangular house plans are found, even on the same site or set of sites, as at Lough Gur, County Limerick. Here there were rectangular as well as D-shaped, circular or oval houses, with sizes ranging from 14 to 48 square metres. At site A, a rectangular house 10 metres long by 5.5 metres wide was discovered. It had a wall-footing of stone, set between pairs of posts; it is suggested that the opposed posts would have been braced together with cross-ties and that the woven wall-facings applied to each row of posts would have held a filling of organic material, with the stone wall-footing serving as a kind of damp-proof course.

A circular house at site C and others in the complex appear to have been similarly constructed; the consistent presence of these features has been described as showing them to be 'characteristic of domestic architecture at Lough Gur.' The circular house had a central post to support the roof, while the rectangular house had a row of posts set inside the long walls, suggesting the possible use of purlins (horizontal beams supporting rafters). It is suggested that the rafters may have projected externally over the walls, helping to combat the internal weight of the roof. Thatching is considered to have been the most likely roof material.

Other circular houses have been found at Slieve Breagh, County Meath, where one with a diameter of six metres had two concentric lines of posts, suggesting a mode of construction similar to that of the Lough Gur examples. A smaller example on this site was represented by a single circle of posts. Outside the passage tomb at Newgrange, County Meath, what appears to have been a circular structure some fifteen metres in diameter may have been a Neolithic house, built from an outside circle of stake-holes with a circle of holes for stouter posts inside.

Rectangular houses have been found on other sites. At Ballynagilly, County Tyrone, a house was identified on a very early Neolithic site. It measured 6 m by 6.5 m; a series of stout wooden posts set along the middle of the house supported the inner ends of the rafters, while the long walls were composed of radially split oak planks set in trenches packed with stones, which would also have supported the outer ends of the rafters. The roof here was presumably of thatch too. Another house, at Tankardstown, County Limerick, appears also to have used oak planking set in trenches.

Under the west end of a court tomb at Ballyglass, County Mayo, were found indications of a rectangular house, thirteen metres long and six metres wide. The indications consisted of foundation trenches, 250 to 500 mm wide and some 200 mm deep; no trench appeared at the west end of the house, suggesting that it was possibly open at that end. There were, however, two transverse lines of posts and a transverse wall-slot dividing the house. At each corner of the house there had been a post.

At the passage tomb of Knowth, County Meath, a house plan 10.7 m by 9.1 m was again indicated by trenches along all sides. Only on the western side were there indications of posts, eleven in number. There was no indication of posts in the centre, though it has been suggested that prop-posts, merely resting on the floor, might have been adequate to support a roof.

The Earlier Bronze Age

Domestic structures of either Beaker or Earlier Bronze Age affiliations are by no means common in Ireland. No Beaker Period houses were discovered even at Ballynagilly, County Tyrone, despite the abundance of beaker pottery. Possibly the site at Ross Island, County Kerry, will provide some information about Beaker Period house construction.

Two rectangular structures with hearths are reported from Coney Island, County Armagh (fig. 10.1), associated with bowls, while at Downpatrick, County Down, two round houses, one about seven metres in diameter, the other about four metres, both with central hearths, were discovered on a site occupied by people using cordoned urns, apparently as domestic pottery, showing that this pottery was not exclusively funerary. An oval house at Carrigillihy, County Cork, measuring some 10 m by 6.7 m, was built of stone, with a thatched roof supported on posts. Another oval house, slightly smaller, at Cullyhanna, County Armagh, was surrounded by a stockade of posts, enclosing an area nearly seventeen metres in diameter.

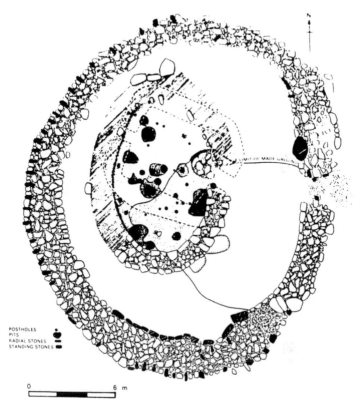

10.1 *Plans of Earlier Bronze Age houses at Carrigillihy, Co. Cork, where the original oval house enclosed inside a stone wall had been superseded by a square one (after O'Kelly, 1951)*

The Later Bronze Age

In the Later Bronze Age, in addition to the hilltop sites there were also lakeside ones. At Ballinderry, County Offaly, a fairly extensive occupation had not only nine wicker huts, of diameters ranging from 1 to 2.17 m—which could not have accommodated many residents and may have been for storage—but also a large timber structure, approximately 11.5 m square, built on a platform of broad oak planks fitted with holes holding vertical wooden posts, through which, presumably, pliable saplings were interwoven (fig. 10.2). At Lough Eskragh, County Tyrone, while no houses were recognised, a complex of three timber structures was established on the lakeshore, defined by piling.

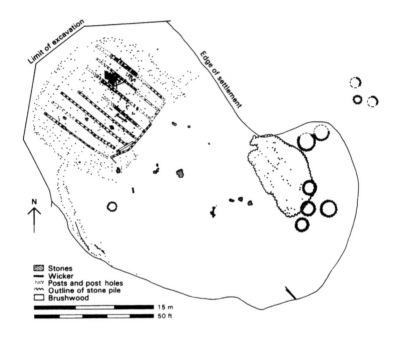

10.2 *The Later Bronze Age house-platform at Ballinderry, Co. Offaly (after Hencken, 1941/42)*

On the hilltop sites, on the contrary, circular houses seemed more in vogue. At Rathgall, County Wicklow, a circular area enclosed by a bank and external ditch contained a circular wooden house, some fifteen metres in diameter. At Navan Fort, County Armagh, a large timber structure, nearly forty metres in diameter, surrounded by a ditch, was found. Whether this constituted a large communal house or a ritual structure of some sort is not completely agreed. Structures at nearby Haughey's Fort have not been sufficiently excavated to reveal their function.

CONSTRUCTION

There are no manifestations of a construction industry in the Mesolithic Period; no examples of 'public works' have been discovered that may be related to this period—no elaborate tombs, no temples, no extensive enclosures. It seems, as we have said earlier, to have been a period when 'DIY' was the

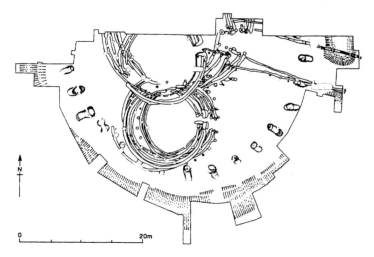

10.3 *Later Bronze Age structure at Navan Fort, Co. Armagh (after Lynn, 1986)*

normal procedure. It is only with the onset of the Neolithic Period, with the construction of elaborate tombs or temples and the creation of extensive enclosures such as the Céide Fields, County Mayo, that anything that could be described as a 'construction industry' is encountered.

Court tombs and portal tombs

Court tombs vary considerably in size and complexity, from basic two-chambered tombs like that at Bavan, County Donegal, to bigger and more complex examples such as at Creevykeel, County Sligo, itself basically also with a two-chambered gallery but with subsidiaries added to increase the accommodation, almost doubling the size of the original structure.

The erection of a two-chambered basic court tomb such as that at Bavan in a cairn some twenty metres long and with some twenty large stones to form the two chambers and the forecourt could probably have been carried out by some twenty to thirty able-bodied men over a period of two or three months. (This estimate is based on the time taken and the work force required to shift an equivalent amount of building material in the process of excavating a site of this size.) The stone used for the construction of court tombs and portal tombs was local and, in most cases, easily available. In south Donegal and south Derry, for example, at sites such as Bavan and Croaghbeg in County Donegal and Knockoneill and Tamnyrankin in County Derry, quartzite was available in quantity and in sizes of slab eminently suitable for the construction of such tombs. At Audleystown, County Down, on the other hand, shale was the stone used, because it was locally available—but not in the sizes in use in the quartzite areas, which is probably one cogent reason for the marked reduction in size of the constituent chambers.

It has been suggested elsewhere that the first part of the construction was to lay out the gallery and its two chambers, taking care to align the main gallery so that it faced towards the rising sun, or what we would describe as the east. (It would seem that often the presence of a hill to the east of the site caused the rising sun to be displaced, so that the orientation of the gallery is not true.) After the orthostats of the gallery had been set up, the roofing-stones could be set in position, either directly on the tops of the orthostats or on corbels placed on top of them, as at Shalwy and Croaghbeg, County Donegal. Sometimes, as at Audleystown, County Down, the roofing appears to have been simply of such corbelling.

It used to be commonly thought that the most sensible way of raising fairly heavy roof or cap-stones was by building a sloping ramp, up which the roofing-stones were moved on rollers until they were in position, when the ramp could be removed. Evidence from the court tomb at Shalwy suggests that the stones were more probably raised by a system of jacking, where one end of the stone to be raised was lifted by means of levers; when this end had been raised a certain amount, stones would be placed under it to hold it in position, then the other end would be similarly raised, and so on until the stone was at the right height to be shifted sideways into position. After this had been completed, the kerb of the cairn could be laid out and the cairn itself built. Now the tomb was ready to receive its occupants.

With portal tombs (which tend to be more impressively 'megalithic' than court tombs, with taller orthostats and more massive roof-stones) the main difficulty in construction would be the raising into position of the massive roof-stone. The roof-stone of a portal tomb at Brennanstown, County Dublin, has been estimated to weigh nearly a hundred tonnes. To raise such a stone into position would be a considerable feat, whichever method was used. Leverage and jacking, of course, would mean that only fifty tonnes would have to be raised at a time.

Passage tombs
It has been calculated that the great passage tomb of Newgrange, in its huge circular cairn, incorporates some 200,000 tonnes of stone—in addition to the 97 slabs forming the kerb (none weighing less than a tonne) and the 450 large structural stones used to form the passage, chamber, and roof. Fortunately, most of the rock of which the structural stones are composed is greywacke, available in the immediate vicinity of the site. We know it was not quarried specially for the monument, since the stones were already weathered at the time of the tomb's construction. The vast mass of cairn material too was available within a reasonable distance of the site, in the river terraces of the River Boyne.

While a court tomb, with its relatively simple orientation, could have been constructed under the supervision of a good jobbing builder, the construction of a tomb like Newgrange, with sophisticated details like the roof-box, through which the rays of the rising sun penetrate at the winter solstice, suggests that an architect, rather than a builder, was involved. It has been suggested that much of the building material was carried to the site in bags; how much more likely that a form of *travois*, a 'slipe' or slide-car, was used. Whether the slipes were drawn by human power or by oxen will remain a question for some time.

The Céide Fields
The layout and construction of the vast Neolithic farming landscape at Behy and Glenulra in County Mayo is another example of extensive and well-organised public works during the Neolithic Period. Here many kilometres of stone wall run up and down the mountainside, dividing it into long stripes, with occasional transverse walls to form indi-

vidual fields. It has been estimated that the field divisions absorbed some 250,000 tonnes of rock—rather more than what was required for the great cairn at Newgrange.

Despite the lack of sophistication involved in comparison with Newgrange, the planning and construction of this great field system must have required great skills of organisation and the exercise of a considerable amount of authority or persuasion. While nothing on the scale of the Céide Fields has been found elsewhere, and certainly not so deeply investigated, there are indications that the Céide Fields might not be unique. Just across Donegal Bay, at Malinmore, traces of stone walls under the bog have been observed, as they have been in other parts of the country.

TRANSPORT
Water transport
The fact that Ireland is an island, and had been before the first humans settled here, means that we can say without fear of contradiction that some form of water transport must have been available to them and to their successors.

No examples of possible sea-going craft have yet been discovered that could be related to any prehistoric context in Ireland. There are two potential choices for types of water transport. One is the log-boat or dug-out canoe; but log-boats are notoriously unsatisfactory as sea-going vessels, unless equipped with outriggers. Since there is no tradition of outriggers in western Europe, this possibility is virtually unanimously ruled out. The other possible choice is a skin-covered, wood-framed vessel rather like the curach, which was such a common feature of coastal life until fairly recently. It has even been suggested that for the transport of larger loads a version of the circumpolar *umiak* might have been used and even have proved capable of transporting cattle, in the prone position, to Ireland.

While log-boats have effectively been ruled out as sea-going vessels, it is quite likely that they were widely used on inland waters. A log-boat from Toome, County Antrim, at one time claimed to be of Mesolithic date, was not satisfactorily proved to be so. Log-boats were apparently connected to a Later Bronze Age complex in Lough Eskragh, County Tyrone, where the production of bronze swords was carried out. Unfortunately a recent survey, including radiocarbon dating, gives a very poor image of prehistoric log-boats. Of an estimated total of some 350 Irish examples, nearly 70 have been dated; the great majority of these are awarded dates well outside the prehistoric period.

While one small fragment of one of the boats found at Lough Eskragh appears a little too recent to co-date the Later Bronze Age material from the site, an example from Teeronea, County Clare, had apparently been reused as a trough for a typical Later Bronze cooking-pit, while two examples from Derrybrusk, County Fermanagh, are recorded as being found under a 'burnt mound', one on top of the other. A few do show respectably early dates, such as examples from Inch Abbey, County Down, Ballygowan, County Armagh, and, most respectably of all, an example from Carrigdirty, County Limerick, dated well into the Neolithic Period.

Land transport
While there is no direct archaeological evidence for their use, it seems highly likely that some sort of *travois* was in use during the Neolithic Period for the transport of the enormous quantities of building materials required, especially in the construction of the cairns of passage tombs. 'Slipes' or slide-cars were in common use in Ireland in the last century, particularly for 'off-road' purposes, and of course were employed in many other parts of the world. With the presence from the Neolithic Period onwards of cattle, it is quite possible that such cars were drawn by oxen as well as by humans. The introduction of the horse by the people who brought beakers with them made available another mode of land transport, probably implying a degree of status on the part of the rider.

Trackways
In the Later Bronze Age in particular there appear a number of timber-built trackways. One of these, at Annaghcorrib, County Galway, consisted of a sub-structure of logs, brushwood, and discarded planks, topped with two layers of oak planks, sometimes held in place by pegs inserted into mortice-holes. This track was followed for a distance of

some 1.5 km across Garryduff Bog, leading from dry land at the south end towards shallows on the River Suck, which might have been a ford. Another trackway is recorded from Littleton Bog, County Tipperary, and another from Corlea, County Longford. There is the possibility that these trackways were made to facilitate transport by horse-drawn wagons. Block wheels that might date from this period have been found at Doogarymore, County Roscommon, and Timahoe West, County Kildare. There is no evidence so far, however, for the form of the rest of the wagon.

The mere existence of these trackways shows a deliberation that is a new element in Irish prehistory. In some ways their construction might appear to be in stark contrast to the building of hill-forts, with the assumption of territoriality; we know so little about the 'territories' assumed to be under the control of the hill-forts. Are the trackways confined to single territories, or do they cross now-invisible boundaries? They do, however, show a purposiveness: a trackway was not built because someone said 'Let's have a trackway' but because it seemed a good idea to have a trackway joining two specific places.

QUARRYING AND MINING

To exploit the mineral resources of prehistoric Ireland it was necessary to extract the stone, or the ore, from the natural matrix in which it occurred. Apart from the fact that tools and implements of Mesolithic type are found on sites, for the Mesolithic Period there are no sites devoted to the extraction of even flint from the natural cretaceous limestone in which it occurred. In the Neolithic Period there are numerous examples of the procedures followed on an industrial scale.

Flint extraction: Ballygalley, County Antrim

On a promontory at Ballygalley Head, County Antrim, extensive traces of Neolithic settlement and industrial activity were discovered. In one area of the site evidence was revealed of open-cast flint-mining, or simply quarrying: the chalk had been quarried away to form a series of terraces corresponding to the bands in which the nodules of flint occurred. Basalt boulders lying in and on the boulder-clay had been used not only as seats and benches but as anvils as well.

The overwhelming majority of the finds from both the extraction site and the nearby occupation site were primary flakes and cores, with one, two or three platforms. 1,042 primary flakes came from the extraction site, 688 from the occupation site—adequate productivity to regard this as a truly industrial site. The cores totalled 208. Most of the flint appeared to have been produced by the stone hammer technique; yet only nine convincing hammer-stones were recovered.

Of the finished implements, mainly from the occupation site, the most frequent type found (as is usual on Neolithic sites) was the convex scraper. The second most frequent type was the leaf-shaped arrow-head. Strangely, no hollow scrapers—usually regarded as the characteristic implement of the Irish Neolithic Period—were found.

Flint substitutes
Flint is not evenly distributed throughout Ireland; instead it is virtually confined to a fairly thin outcrop of cretaceous chalk almost conforming to the boundary of modern County Antrim. There were two inevitable responses to this concentration of such a valuable natural resource in one limited area. One was the 'exporting' of flint from County Antrim to the other, less flint-rich areas. That this did happen is shown, quite transparently, by the presence of implements of flint on sites in other parts of the country. In the Neolithic Period this patently happened in the complex of sites in the neighbourhood of Lough Gur, County Limerick. The other response was the finding and exploitation of suitable (or sometimes not so suitable) substitutes for flint. This was the response indicated at the Mesolithic site at Lough Boora, County Offaly, where the local chert was used, with no indication of 'imported' flint.

Chert from the carboniferous limestone was the most widely used flint substitute—probably because it is the most widespread and most easily available. Interestingly, at Lough Gur locally derived chert appeared alongside the imported flint. The same mixture of local and imported raw material occurred at the court tomb at Ballyglass, County Mayo, and the court tomb at Creevykeel, County Sligo—though here the local material was felsite (a devitrified volcanic glass) as well as chert. In the Boyne Valley—including the spectacular passage tombs of Knowth and Newgrange—flint was quite common.

Sometimes fairly unsuitable substitutes for flint were used: arrow-heads and scrapers of rather coarse quartz have been reported. Presumably similar extraction processes were used for the exploitation of flint substitutes as were employed for flint itself, but possibly on a smaller scale.

Porcellanite and other axe materials

Although axes of flint were used by the earliest colonists in the Mesolithic Period, axes of rather unsuitable types of stone were used as well: mudstones and slates, neither of which was ideal for the purpose, the first being rather too soft, the other too liable to shatter in use. Again, in the Neolithic Period flint axes, some painstakingly polished, were in use. Possibly as a result of the need for fairly extensive forest clearance to provide open space for flocks and herds and for the cultivation of crops, a need for stronger and heavier axes was recognised. Sources of suitable stone were identified, and their exploitation was begun.

The best-known and most studied of these stones is porcellanite. This is a hard, fine-grained rock that, like flint, gives a conchoidal fracture, making it possible to readily shape it. The principal source of porcellanite had been known to collectors in the north for years—a fact that is almost as difficult to understand as the fact that Neolithic farmers could have found it in the first instance. This source is a mountain called Tievebulliagh in County Antrim, where there is a volcanic plug, the heat generated by which played an important role in the creation of the porcellanite.

The outcrops are now clearly visible on the surface (the stone is quite distinctive, blue-grey and speckled), and the scree on the side of the mountain contains abundant waste flakes. Although the site has been described as an 'axe factory', it could more properly be termed an axe quarry.

Another well-known source of porcellanite is Brockley, on Rathlin Island. There may be a third source near Limavady, County Derry. The rock was clearly quarried on the mountainside and fashioned into pieces of a suitable size for transporting to true 'factory sites'. Another well-known source of stone for axes is Feltrim Hill, County Dublin, while in County Limerick is to be found a group of axes of a distinctive straight-sided form, in a distinctive greenish rock, suggesting a local source and even a local style.

Copper

The distribution of copper in Ireland is nearly as unfair as the distribution of flint. It can be seen that the great concentrations of copper ores are virtually confined to the southern half of the country, particularly in Counties Cork and Kerry, Waterford, the Avoca area of County Wicklow, the Silvermines area of County Tipperary, and, to a lesser degree, County Galway. The midlands and the north are poorly supplied with known deposits of copper ores.

This distribution has caused great problems for archaeologists, because the most obvious choice for the introduction of metalworking is the people who did arrive here, complete with their distinctive style of pottery—the Beaker People. The core of the problem of attributing to them the introduction of metalworking has been that up till very recently the main distribution of Beaker pottery in Ireland has been in the north—in complete contrast to the principal sources of copper (fig. 10.4).

The sites of copper as ores, however, may be slightly misleading. In the late nineteen-sixties a survey of stream sediments in Northern Ireland (unfortunately restricted to the political entity) revealed many instances where copper was present in unexpected quantities—in some instances showing a presence of more than 150 parts per million, suggesting that these sediments were derived from fairly rich copper deposits further upstream. Unfortunately the sources of the copper in the stream sediments have not been found.

There are, in addition, records and actual specimens of 'native' copper (that is, copper occurring in its metallic form rather than incorporated in an ore) from several places throughout Ireland, with a particularly high incidence in County Antrim, at some seventeen localities. Among the specimens preserved is one from Woodburn, County Antrim, weighing 58.7 g, which, although small enough in relation

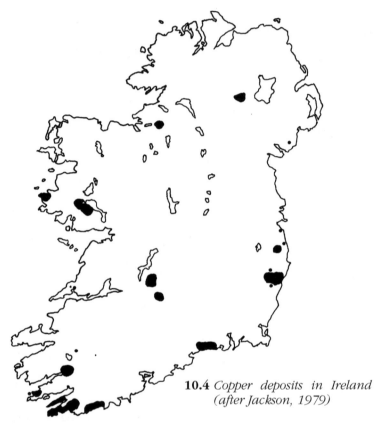

10.4 *Copper deposits in Ireland (after Jackson, 1979)*

to the weight of surviving metal tools (for the earliest axe types, average weights of 514 g and 373 g have been calculated), indicates the quantities of copper that may have been available to early metalworkers from this source.

Spread mainly along the south and south-west coast, as well as at Avoca, County Wicklow, and in County Tipperary, are the sites of mines, some of which are likely to have been exploited in the Earlier Bronze Age and some of which have been demonstrated to have been so exploited. Typically, the technique was to drive an adit or access tunnel into the mountainside, following the copper-bearing deposits. At Dane's Island, near Bunmahon, County Waterford, a cluster of a dozen such mines has been identified, one of which is typical.

At Mount Gabriel in County Cork an even more impressive assemblage has been discovered. On the eastern slopes of the hill, which is a mass of old red sandstone, at least three workings have been identified, often by the observation of large mounds of rock debris outside the mine openings. The excavation of one of the Mount Gabriel mines produced not merely a short-handled wooden shovel of alder but large quantities of roundwood of oak, ash, hazel, and willow, confirming that fire-setting was practised, whereby bonfires were set against the rock face, eventually causing it to shatter. The miners were then able to remove chunks of rock from the loosened structure of the mine face. Large quantities of resinous pine chips and brushwood were also found, suggesting that they had provided material for torches to provide the artificial light necessary. After the separation of the rock from the mine face, often by pounding with stone tools, it was taken out for crushing and sorting.

This type of mining would have required considerable quantities of fuel, as well as of human effort. Radiocarbon dating has confirmed that these mines were in use between 1700 and 1500 BC. It has been observed that 'the distribution of mine-workings on Mount Gabriel suggests a careful and systematic search for ore and shows that it had become possible to recognise the rock-formations which were most likely to contain copper.' The inevitable social conclusion to be drawn is that those involved in the mining industry must have been possessed of considerable specialist skills; mining as an industry would seem to have been an activity carried out by a work force with 'professional' supervision and management at least.

Tin

Many of the Irish copper ores included arsenic in varying proportions, from 1 per cent in one sample of tenorite from Ross Island, County Kerry, to a staggering 15 per cent upwards in a sample of tetrahedrite from an old mine dump at a site in the same area. In the earliest stages of the industry, therefore, it was unnecessary to consider the problems of tin supplies, the arsenic being a reasonably satisfactory alloying material.

When a preference for true tin-bronzes was established, however, a supply of tin was required. Not very long ago it was believed that any tin required by the bronze industry must have been imported, probably from Cornwall. It has been stated that 'the amount of tin used in Ireland must have been modest'—a statement borne out by calculations that the entire surviving total of axes produced by the Irish bronze industry in its first 250 years amounted to little over 6 kg.

Tin has, however, been recorded as being present in Ireland at seven authenticated sites. The most important of these is Gold Mines River in County Wicklow. For this site, records show that in 1795, 28 kg of tin was recovered in a mere six weeks. Since this amounts to over four times the quantity required for the production of the surviving axes manufactured in the first 250 years of bronzeworking, imports of additional tin would clearly not have been necessary; though in view of the other, less stable items imported in the Neolithic Period, such as cattle, importing tin from Cornwall would not have been a serious problem.

Gold

Gold is reasonably widespread as a natural resource in Ireland, occurring at some 130 recorded localities, scattered all over the country, from Counties Cork and Wexford in the south, Tipperary and Galway in the west and Dublin and Wicklow in the east to Donegal, Tyrone, Derry and Antrim in the north. County Wicklow has long enjoyed a perceived position as the main source, perhaps obscuring the importance of other localities.

The gold used in the Bronze Age was from placer deposits, in the form of nuggets and flakes in the sand and gravel of streams and rivers. The great advantages of this were that the gold required no mining and no smelting. Because of its relative softness and malleability it could be heated in a crucible until red-hot to facilitate the fusing together of the separate pieces or flakes, or the complete melting together of the pieces. The Earlier Bronze Age ornaments, being of flat or sheet gold, could be shaped simply by hammering or beating, processes termed 'cold working'. The Later Bronze Age ornaments would have required melting, to be cast in moulds. Recent research has shown, incidentally, that much of the Earlier Bronze Age gold is likely to be derived from a source, as yet unidentified, in the Sperrin Mountains in west Ulster.

11

MANUFACTURING

THE FABRICATION OF FLINT AND STONE IMPLEMENTS
Flint fabrication sites

At the Earlier Mesolithic site of Mount Sandel, County Derry, an area was designated an 'activity area'; this was the area in which the fabrication of tools and implements was carried out, evidenced by the profusion of waste material and cores. Without designated activity areas, flint fabrication was carried on at the type-site of the Later Mesolithic Period, Newferry, County Derry. Interestingly, at Glynn, County Antrim—a site that produced material including microliths typical of the Earlier Mesolithic as well as of the Later Mesolithic Period—both core and flake axes were found, as well as these microliths, and a series of flint cores, single-platformed, dual-platformed, and polyplatformed.

In the Neolithic Period, flint fabrication was carried on at most settlement sites. At site C at Knockadoon, County Limerick, part of the Lough Gur complex, flintworking was evidenced by a profusion of worked flakes and waste. Flint fabrication was clearly carried on also at Townley Hall, County Louth. Even at court tombs there is evidence of flint fabrication, usually most significantly in the form of the presence of flint cores, which occur, for example, at Audleystown, County Down, and away in the west at Bavan, County Donegal. In the passage tomb context there was a specifically designated 'flint-knapping area' among the features of the settlement at Knowth, County Meath.

The fabrication of flint artefacts on what might be regarded as an industrial scale occurred, as we have seen, at sites such as Ballygalley, County Antrim, where it was carried on as an adjunct to flint extraction, and at Madman's Window, County Antrim.

The flint mace from Knowth

Occupying a prominent niche in the history of flint artefacts, of course, is the flint mace from the passage tomb at Knowth, County Meath. It is, without doubt, the most splendid piece of flintworking in Ireland. Measuring only 79 mm long, it is elaborately decorated on all six surfaces. There is also a cylindrical perforation. It has been suggested that the main motif on one face represents a human face, with hair, beard, eyes, and mouth. To conceive of this design in flint, presumably executed by means of a sort of micro-pressure flaking followed by polishing, suggests an almost incredible standard of flintworking skill. Even the perforation is a masterpiece.

Stone axe manufacturing sites

For the fabrication of polished or ground stone axes, two things were ultimately necessary: abundant water and sharp sand. These are clearly not available on an exposed mountainside such as Tievebulliagh, County Antrim; so the raw material had to be transported to some site where they were freely available. At this stage two possibly conflicting factors had to be considered. A bare mountainside such as that of Tievebulliagh is not the most comfortable place to carry on prolonged axe fabrication; on the other hand, there is no point in carrying a greater weight than necessary down from the mountain. Therefore, as the debris that litters the scree on the mountainside suggests, the rock was reduced to usable pieces for the manufacture of axe-heads and then carried to the finishing sites.

Possibly the work on the mountainside was carried as far as the production of rough-outs, as the axes are called before the final polishing or grinding process. Since these had to be adjacent to large supplies of both sharp sand and water for the final grinding process, coastal sites on sandy beaches were clearly ideal. White Park Bay, County Antrim, was one such site; there, hundreds of axes, in varying stages of completion, have been found. The polishing or grinding was clearly an arduous and time-consuming process; nevertheless the finished products in many cases show that great pains were taken to ensure virtually perfect results. Some examples have survived complete with their original wooden hafts, like one preserved in a bog near Carrickfergus, County Antrim. Here the haft is nearly 300 mm long, widening from a mere 30 mm at the butt end to about 100 mm to permit the excavation of a hollow to receive the butt end of an axe some 180 mm long. Perhaps originally the axe-head was additionally secured by a leather thong lashed round it.

METALWORKING

While native copper enjoyed the enormous advantage of not requiring any pre-treatment (that is, smelting), since it was already metallic, it is unlikely that it existed in sufficient quantity to satisfy the needs of the industry or to constitute the main resource of an expanding metal industry for long. Metal implements of Earlier Bronze Age type do, however, exist, with metal compositions that suggest that they might have been made from native copper. An axe from Cloonmullin, County Roscommon, consisting of virtually pure copper with mere traces of antimony, silver, and bismuth, could fall into this category. Even the use of the oxide ores that occurred in the so-called 'zone of secondary enrichment', which were to be found at or close to the surface of the ground and which could be smelted directly and fairly easily, was not likely to satisfy the growing needs of the industry. Attention had to be directed, therefore, to the sulphide ores that were to form the main source of copper used by early Irish metalworkers.

Smelting

Normally at the mine-heads there was no indication that smelting took place in the immediate locality, which makes sound industrial sense, as does the evidence that the ore was well broken down and sorted before being transported to the smelting site. The reason for this is the sheer amount of fuel required: to smelt one tonne of ore would require an incredible 2,500 tonnes of fuel. Obviously transporting the single tonne of ore to the smelting site is 2,500 times less arduous than transporting the fuel to the mine-head.

The exception to this pattern is the fairly recently discovered site at Ross Island, County Kerry. It is not, like most mine-heads, on a mountainside, with suitable trees at a premium (the fuel required even for the fire-setting would have had to be transported to the mine-head); instead it is on a level escarpment, on the eastern shore of Lough Leane. Here, immediately next to a Bronze Age mining complex, was a site that produced spreads of crushed mineralised limestone, associated with stone hammers and anvil blocks. There were also pits connected with on-site metalworking activity.

Since the mined ores were mostly sulphide ores, they required roasting even before the true smelting process was begun. Assuming an average copper concentration of 2 per cent in typical Irish copper ores, if the desired amount of copper is 20 kg (as seems to have been the minimum annual requirement in the earlier stages of the metal industry, in the light of the surviving corpus of axes), one tonne of comminuted, sorted and roasted ore will be necessary for the production of this quantity of smelted metal. To smelt one tonne of ore, at the necessary heat of at least 1,200°C, requires 2,500 tonnes of wood—the equivalent of 100 mature forest oaks, felled, logged, and converted into charcoal. (The amount of fuel will remain *pro rata* for smaller quantities of ore: 2,500 times the amount of ore involved.)

Eventually, when the copper has been run from the waste, it is formed into ingots—the so-called 'copper-cakes' known from such hoards as those of Monastery, County Wicklow, and Carrickshedoge, County Wexford (plates 5 and 6).

Earlier Bronze Age casting
For the manufacture of the product, for example an axe-head, two other pieces of equipment are required: a crucible in which to melt the copper, and a mould in which to cast the object. No example of an Earlier Bronze Age crucible has survived, though it has been reckoned that since the weight of one of the surviving ingots, that from Knockasarnet, County Kerry, is just under 750 g, the normal crucible is likely to have been capable of holding this amount of copper.

For Earlier Bronze Age moulds, however, several examples have survived, made of stone, usually sandstone, and invariably of the type known as a 'single-valve' or 'open' mould. Essentially the mould consists of a block of stone, and the actual matrix a cavity whose shape is that of the object to be cast and whose depth is sufficient to accommodate the desired thickness of the axe. Although these moulds are described as 'open', in practice a simple lid or covering slab would have been used, leaving an opening at one end to serve as a 'gate' through which the molten metal could be poured from the crucible and a further opening at the other end to serve as a 'riser', to permit the escape of air and gas. The use of such a lid would also have prevented excessive oxidation. Further supplies of fuel would, of course, be required. To melt the 20 kg of copper derived from our original tonne, at a heat of slightly over 1,000°C, fifty tonnes of wood would be needed, the equivalent of a mere two forest oaks.

After casting, some finishing had to be performed. Unfortunately, metallographic examination of finished implements has not been carried out on a wide scale; we do know, however, that post-casting treatment included 'cold working', 'heating and cold hammering', and 'heat-treatment carried out as an annealing operation to facilitate forging.' Any decoration desired, as it fairly commonly was, could now be carried out as well.

The organisation of the Earlier Bronze Age industry

Products of moulds can be traced back to the parent mould, even if that mould no longer exists. This was first suggested by the chance discovery that an axe from Culfeightrin, County Antrim, fitted precisely into one of the matrices on a mould from Ballynahinch, County Down (plate 7). It is confirmed by the precise identity of outlines of other axes, as shown by a comparison of two axes, one from County Cork, one from Portrush, County Antrim (fig. 11.1). This discovery, followed by a survey comparing all known axes of the Earlier Bronze Age, made it possible to examine the dispersal of axes from a common parent mould. This formed the basis of a guide to the means by which such products could be distributed through the country. One

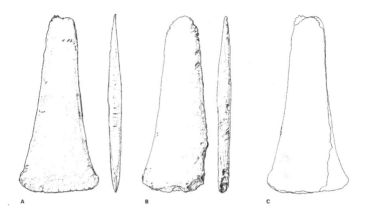

11.1 *Bronze co-matrical axes:* (A) *from Co. Cork;* (B) *from Portrush, Co. Antrim;* (C) *the two axes superimposed (after Flanagan, 1978)*

result that emerges quite clearly is that dispersal was fairly widespread (fig. 11.2).

An examination of the distribution of hoards of axes was made, with the notion that the presence in such hoards of an ingot or 'copper-cake' was a reasonable indication that that hoard was at a manufacturing site, even if no mould was present (fig. 11.3). An examination of matrical links between axes in hoards seemed to contradict that notion and, on the contrary, to suggest that concentrations of objects in hoards of axes with a parent mould in common were more indicative of the possible place of manufacture (fig. 11.4). Finally, an examination of the distribution of axes from an existing mould suggested that the one place where products of a parent mould are not to be found is the immediate proximity of the mould (fig. 11.5).

All in all, the evidence, confusing though it may appear, suggests that in the Earlier Bronze Age the manufacture and 'retailing' of axes was in the hands of itinerant bronzeworkers. Perhaps the discovery some day of an actual manufacturing site, fully equipped with ingots, moulds, crucibles, and unfinished axes, will either confirm or disprove this suggestion.

Later Bronze Age casting
During the transition from the Earlier Bronze Age to the Later Bronze Age—in what used to be described as the

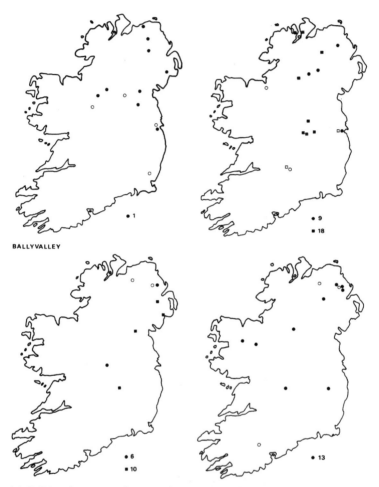

11.2 *Distribution of axes from several postulated moulds of Ballyvalley type axes. The open symbols indicate that the axe is provenanced only to the county in which it was found (after Flanagan, 1978)*

'Middle Bronze Age'—there developed a preference for, and therefore a need to introduce the means of manufacturing, bronze tools and weapons that were cast 'in the round'— objects such as flanged axes, palstaves, and socketed spear-heads. This necessitated moulds quite different from the 'open' mould in use in the Earlier Bronze Age. Two-valve moulds became necessary for the production of daggers,

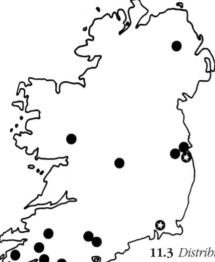

11.3 *Distribution of hoards containing axes of Earlier Bronze Age type. A symbol with a star indicates that the hoard contained an ingot (after Flanagan, 1978)*

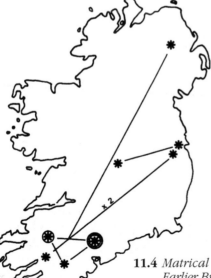

11.4 *Matrical links between hoards of Earlier Bronze Age axes. Surrounding circles indicate the presence in the hoard of one or more siblings (after Flanagan, 1978)*

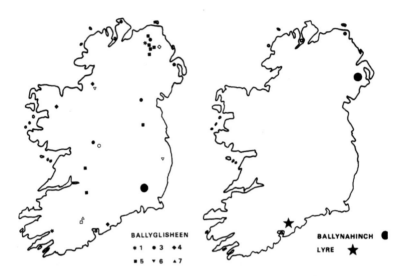

11.5 *Distribution of products of surviving moulds. The large symbol shows the site of the parent mould; the numbers and letters refer to the different matrices on the mould; open symbols indicate that the axe is provenanced only to the county in which it was found (after Flanagan, 1978)*

shaped on both faces; flanged axes or palstaves, shaped on both faces; and socketed spear-heads, where an additional development was necessary. This was the insertion of a core of clay, held in position by metal pins, for which location points were provided on the two halves of the stone mould, for the provision of the socket. The ingenious metalworkers rose to the solution of these problems, whether by native ingenuity or by help and advice from outside Ireland.

Two-valve moulds for these purposes have survived, at first of stone. Moulds of sandstone for flanged axes or palstaves have been found at Loughash, County Tyrone, in a wedge tomb, and for a palstave at site D, Knockadoon, County Limerick. Moulds, usually of steatite (sometimes known as 'soapstone', because of the comparative ease with which it could be carved) or talc-schist, for socketed spear-heads, which required the insertion of a clay core to form the hollow socket, have been found at places such as Killymaddy, County Antrim.

For the production of true Later Bronze Age weapons and tools, such as leaf-shaped swords and socketed spear-heads, another innovation appeared: the clay mould. This type of mould did not necessarily replace the stone mould but rather supplemented it where it seemed more suitable. For example, for a long object like a sword, the finding of easily carved pieces of stone suitable for the manufacture of moulds could have been difficult, and the ensuing mould heavy and cumbersome.

The clay mould had both advantages and disadvantages. The advantages were that an existing weapon or implement could be readily replicated by producing a mould from it by covering first one side, then the other, with a thin layer of finely levigated clay to give a close impression of the shape, then covering this with a layer of coarser clay, which might incorporate strengthening rods, particularly in the case of longer weapons, like swords and the larger spear-heads. If a suitable example of the item was not readily available the clay mould could be built up instead on a carefully made wooden model, examples of which have been recorded. The great disadvantage, on the other hand, was that almost invariably the mould had to be broken to remove the casting. These clay moulds incorporated in their design the 'gates' and 'risers' needed to admit the molten bronze and to let the surplus bronze, and the air and gas, escape.

Later Bronze Age moulds of this type have been found at a number of sites. At Lough Eskragh, County Tyrone, fragments of clay moulds for leaf-shaped swords, along with a pouring gate and fragments of crucibles, were found; on the hill-fort at Rathgall, County Wicklow, were found some four hundred fragments of clay moulds for leaf-shaped swords, spear-heads, and possibly socketed axes. The finding of fragile clay moulds, together with crucibles, on sites such as these suggests a significant change in the structure of the bronze industry between the Earlier and the Later Bronze Age. Unlike the situation in the Earlier Bronze Age, where the evidence seems to suggest itinerant metalworkers, manufacturing their pro-duce as they travelled the country, the evidence in the Later Bronze Age seems to favour the idea of fixed manufacturing sites.

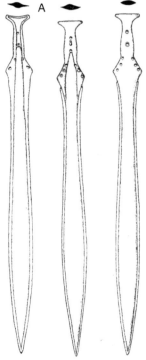

11.6 *Hoard containing three leaf-shaped bronze swords, of slightly different type, from Relagh, Co. Tyrone (after Eogan, 1983)*

It is possible, however, that some of the Later Bronze Age's numerous hoards may have been the stock in trade of peddlers, who hawked the produce of the 'factories' around the countryside. The hoards might have been actual merchandise or have constituted a sort of three-dimensional catalogue of items that could be ordered for later delivery. The hoard from Relagh, County Tyrone, consisting of three swords of the same type but slightly different styles, could fit either category (fig. 11.6). The hoard of fragments of gold ribbon torcs from Derryvony, County Cavan, could easily be interpreted as a three-dimensional catalogue, showing designs of torc and terminal, on the basis of which orders could be placed.

Later Bronze Age sheet-metalworking

While the working of sheet metal had clearly been practised in the Earlier Bronze Age—the lunulae, for example, were beaten in thin sheets from ingots of gold—it was in the Later Bronze Age that it reached its acme in the production of huge cauldrons and buckets. The cauldrons in particular were vastly desirable objects and regarded as precious heirlooms. One, originally thought to be from Portglenone, County Antrim, but now convincingly re-provenanced to Cape Castle, County Antrim, shows its desirability and heirloom status by having been repaired some thirteen times, with patches of sheet bronze riveted over damaged areas.

There are two basic types of sheet-bronze cauldron: those with necks and those without necks. The ones with necks (ascribed to class A), an example of which occurs in the famous hoard from Dowris, County Offaly, are invariably formed from three sheets of bronze, one circular to form the bottom, the other two rectangular to form the top. The neck itself is ribbed. The ones without necks are commonly made from a number of sheets of bronze riveted together. An example of this type is known from Castle Derg, County Tyrone. Both types are fitted with a pair of free-moving cast bronze ring-handles.

The almost equally impressive sheet-bronze buckets, based on a type found in a well-known hoard from Kurd in Hungary, were imported into Ireland during the Dowris phase of the Later Bronze Age; again one appears in the famous hoard from Dowris. Soon after the arrival of these imports, local sheet-metalworkers began to copy them.

Costs

In calculating the costs of production of an average implement (for our purposes a typical axe of Earlier Bronze Age type has been chosen), it is necessary to make one great assumption: that the copper (in whatever form), and later the tin (from whatever source), was not 'owned' by another party and was therefore available freely for the taking, that the same applied to the trees used to provide the enormous quantities of fuel involved, and that therefore the only true cost was the human labour involved.

Those who mined the ore, felled the trees, smelted the metal and made the tools and axes had to be sustained in full health and strength to enable them to carry out their labours and practise their skills. It is not possible to accurately calculate the amount of labour involved in the production of the axes for which the 20 kg of copper derived from the tonne of ore was required. We can, however, reasonably estimate that the production of that 20 kg absorbed some eight hundred work-days, including mining, smelting, tree-felling, and the production process, which means that the average axe, of some 500 g, has cost the equivalent of twenty days' labour—meaning that every person involved in the process had to be fed and housed for twenty days to compensate him or her for this expend-iture of energy in the production of each axe. This can then be translated into the cost, in any culture and any currency, of the average axe.

Without any proven evidence of the nature of Bronze Age trade, the simplest conclusion is that the communities to which those involved in this work belonged supported them, and that subsequently the products of the metal industry were traded for other goods or services. The same system would apply also to gold ornaments, with the rather strange proviso that the cost of producing a gold ornament is a small fraction of that involved in producing a bronze axe. The only factor that would have increased the value of a gold ornament, even in the Earlier Bronze Age, was the fact that gold was a much rarer metal, and objects made from it there-fore were not only attractive in themselves but, because of the rarity of the raw material, constituted 'status symbols'.

WOODWORKING AND CARPENTRY

While even in the remote Mesolithic Period woodworking was clearly practised, not only in the felling and trimming of saplings for the construction of huts but also in the prepa-ration of shafts for harpoons and arrows, the evidence for it is not always readily discovered, mainly because the wood itself has not survived.

In the Neolithic Period, woodworking skills were clearly demonstrated not only in the clearing of forest to provide open space for stock-rearing and agriculture but also in the construction of rather more commodious houses. Perhaps the most ambitious example of this skill was the creation of the cleft oak planks used for the houses at Ballynagilly and Tankardstown. The provision of shafts for arrow-heads and javelin-heads was also a notable need, as was the provision of hafts for axe-heads. It has been suggested that the flint hollow scraper, the tool unique to the Neolithic Period in Ireland, may have been used for the shaping and smooth-ing of arrow-shafts. Used examples frequently display lustre along the working or scraping edge, caused by organic silicates, which could have been occasioned by such use.

In the Earlier Bronze Age, needs and their fulfilment were similar, although the axe-heads were of bronze, as were the javelins or spears. The arrow-heads, on the other hand, continued to be of flint. The bronze axes and knives would have been the tools used for woodworking.

There were, however, some objects whose manufacture could be described as a *tour de force* on the part of Earlier Bronze Age woodworkers. These are the versions in wood of pottery polypod bowls, of which some six examples are recorded. One of these, from Tirkernaghan, County Tyrone, has been shown by radiocarbon dating to share a date with pottery counterparts and therefore to belong to the Earlier Bronze Age. The body was originally some 250 mm in diameter, standing on four legs, evenly spaced. It was carefully made and finely finished; no tool marks are visible. The bowl was probably polished, even—literally—sanded (fig. 11.7).

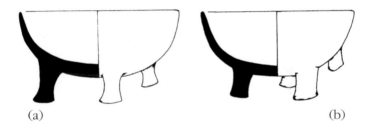

(a)   (b)

11.7 *Wooden polypod bowls:* (a) *from Tirkernaghan, Co. Tyrone;* (b) *from Lecklevera, Co. Monaghan (after Earwood, 1991/92)*

It is really in the Later Bronze Age, with its quite incredible array of newly introduced tools as well as weapons, that we see the apparatus available to woodworkers and carpenters in all its glory, as well as, occasionally, the results. The variety is almost endless. At Lough Eskragh, County Tyrone, fourteen of the stakes used to create the lakeside platforms showed recognisable marks of axes, and of these, four were demonstrably cut by the same axe. The production of the broad oak planks forming the foundation of the square Later Bronze Age structure at Ballinderry, County Offaly, shows one level of performance executed by Later Bronze Age craftsmen.

On a smaller scale, the production of wooden models for the creation of bronze-casting moulds showed a different level of skill, while the carving of the wooden former for a leather shield showed another. The production of wooden vessels, like those from Lough Eskragh, showed consummate skill, somewhat akin to that of making log-boats at the same site.

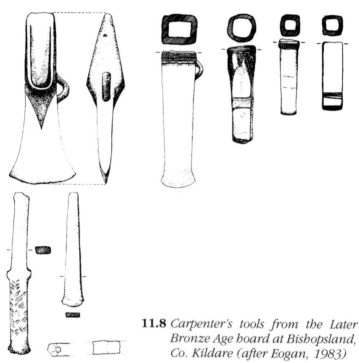

11.8 *Carpenter's tools from the Later Bronze Age hoard at Bishopsland, Co. Kildare (after Eogan, 1983)*

From the evidence of the surviving dated examples, log-boats seem to have been originally produced during the Neolithic Period. Most of the surviving examples, however, date from much more recent times. Some are found in association with Later Bronze Age cooking-places, where they were recycled to form part of the trough, as at Teeronea, County Clare. Unfortunately, the examples from Lough Eskragh seem chronologically incompatible with the Later Bronze Age material from the site.

The digging out of a log-boat was not merely highly skilled but quite a formidable job. From a tree trunk, say, ten metres long a large quantity of wood had to be removed, care being taken that there was sufficient thickness of wood left to keep the finished boat waterproof and intact. There is evidence that when the log-boat was nearing completion, holes were bored through it to serve as reasonably accurate gauges of the thickness of the remaining wood. These could then be closed with wooden plugs when the craft was completed. The types of wood used range from oak, in the sample from Ballygowan, County Armagh, to poplar, in the example from Carrigdirty, County Limerick. It is possible that the task of hollowing out the logs may have been facilitated by the careful use of fire.

In the earliest phase of the Later Bronze Age there appear in the Bishopsland hoard (fig. 11.8) several items unambiguously associated with carpentry: three socketed hammers, two chisels, and a portion of a double-edged saw. A small hoard from Glastry, County Down, clearly the kit of a craftsman, adds two socketed gouges to the workshop. The axes used by the stake-cutters at Lough Eskragh, for example, were of several different forms, though a particularly Irish type, usually described as 'bag-shaped', had developed (fig. 11.9).

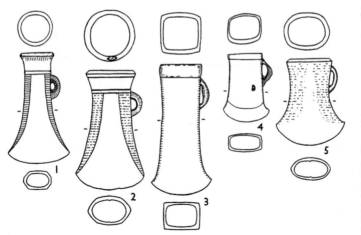

11.9 *Socketed bronze axes:* (1) *from Kish, Co. Wicklow;* (2) *from Mountrivers, Co. Cork;* (3) *from Rosconnor, Co. Down;* (4) *from Meeavally, Co. Donegal;* (5) *an Irish bag-shaped example from Glenstal, Co. Limerick (after Eogan, 1964)*

12

THE FOOD INDUSTRY

FISHING AND HUNTING

The mere fact of the introduction of agriculture and stock-raising does not mean that fishing and hunting died out at the onset of the Neolithic Period. Of the many varieties of river and sea fish exploited by Mesolithic colonists, however, only shellfish are recorded from later prehistoric sites—almost certainly because the shells are more likely to be preserved and identified.

The shell of a razor-clam was found (in fact under the back-stone) in the court tomb at Shalwy, County Donegal—in an area where such delicacies continue to be enjoyed; and in passage tomb contexts, scallop and oyster shells were found at Fourknocks, County Meath, and a pile of unidentified seashells under the mound at Knocklea, County Dublin. In Earlier Bronze Age contexts a mussel shell was found in a cist at Claretuam, County Galway, while others were found in a cist containing a crouched skeleton and a vase at Kinard, County Mayo.

While red deer was used to a very small extent at the Mesolithic site at Mount Sandel, County Derry, it was exploited to a markedly greater degree at Lough Boora, County Offaly. From the Neolithic Period, bones of red deer are reported from the site at Lyles Hill, County Antrim. There are also records from several court tombs: Aghanaglack, County Fermanagh, Legland, County Tyrone, and, appropriately enough, Deerpark, County Sligo. Red deer, usually in the form of antlers, is recorded from several passage tombs, notably a handsome antler pin from Fourknocks I, County Meath, and, of course, at Newgrange. During the Beaker occupation at Newgrange a total of nine individual antlers were represented; this may perhaps be explained as a result of the deliberate collection of cast antlers, carried out in April and May.

In the Earlier Bronze Age our attention returns to the woman buried under a tumulus at Farta, County Galway, not only with her seven-year-old stallion but with the remains of a red deer. The Earlier Bronze Age cemetery at Knockast, County Westmeath, in a round cairn containing some forty-four burials, produced both antler and bone; this is also one of the relatively few sites that have produced tusks of wild boar. In the Later Bronze Age levels at Ballinderry, County Offaly, red deer was present, although in fairly small quantities.

Despite the abundant assortment of game exploited by the residents of Mount Sandel during the Mesolithic Period—mallard, widgeon, teal or garganey, red grouse, capercaillie, snipe or woodcock, and wood-pigeon—there is little surviving evidence of its exploitation in later pre-historic times, apart from the appearance of bird bones of unspecified type in the Neolithic court tomb at Audleystown, County Down, and bones of wild duck in a Later Bronze Age context at Ballinderry, County Offaly.

STOCK-REARING

The presence of cattle, presumably imported in significant numbers from Britain, is attested by the discovery of cattle bones on Neolithic sites such as the court tombs at Annaghmare, County Armagh, Audleystown, County Down, and Ballyalton, County Down—all in primary deposits. Cattle bones were also found in other court tombs, such as Ballymarlagh, County Antrim, and Legland, County Tyrone, though on these sites not in demonstrably primary deposits. They are also associated with passage tombs at Knowth and at Fourknocks, County Meath. They occur in the tomb of Linkardstown type at Ashley Park, County Tipperary, as well as on settlement sites like those at Lough Gur, County Limerick. The great complex of the Céide Fields in County

Mayo has been interpreted as a well-designed and highly organised series of farmsteads, primarily for the rearing of cattle in considerable numbers, in herds of about fifty, each herd grazing on about thirty hectares.

In the Beaker or Earlier Bronze Age, cattle are attested on a reasonable number of sites, including several of the barrows at Carrowjames, County Mayo, and at the cairn of Knockast, County Westmeath. The most abundant material, however, and the best analysis, comes from the Beaker settlement at Newgrange. Here cattle were evidently the most important: a total of 7,067 cattle bones were recovered and examined, representing at least 106 to 114 individual animals.

While there was no direct evidence to suggest that castration was practised, the equal proportions of male and female suggest that it was. If the males were required only for breeding purposes, only one bull for every ten cows would have been required. This impression is strengthened by the advanced age at slaughter; since steers have a slower growth rate, they require a longer time to attain their optimal body weight, and at Newgrange most of the cattle seem to have been slaughtered at three to four years of age. The fact that only 10 per cent of the cattle survived beyond the age of four makes it unlikely that the use of steers as draught animals was extensive.

The absence too of really old animals suggests that cows were not kept specifically for milk production; and if heifers had their first calves in the spring of their third year, milk would not have been available all the year round. It seems, therefore, that dairy products did not play a great part in the diet of the inhabitants of Newgrange during the period of the occupation by Beaker people. The fact that 75 per cent of the cattle survived to their fourth year does suggest, however, that the procurement of adequate winter fodder presented no great problem. All in all, the impression is of a well-managed herd, with careful consideration given to its planned maintenance.

Curiously enough, pigs were the second most important animal in the stock list at Beaker Newgrange. A total of 4,208 pig bones were found, representing some 206 to 208 animals. They were large, long-legged, mobile animals, with males and females of a similar size and a live weight of 75–100 kg. It seems likely that both sexes were killed in equal numbers, probably before they reached the age of two-and-a-half. About 70 per cent of the slaughtering appears to have taken place between October and April. There is a strong indication of a specific breeding scheme aimed at meat production. The product of a pig is reckoned to be some 80 per cent of the live weight, and this is likely to have included between 40 and 50 per cent of fat—an important and calorie-rich item of diet.

Sheep and goats were poorly represented among the animal remains. This could partly be explained by the fact that rearing sheep for meat is considerably less profitable than rearing pigs for the same purpose. Pigs have a reproduction rate at least four times that of sheep: they also have a higher growth rate, as well as a higher proportion of usable meat. If sheep or goats were kept primarily for milk production, one or two would have been adequate for the needs of a single family, which may be another reason for their low representation. There is no archaeological evidence, either directly, through the presence of fragments of woollen fabric, or indirectly, through the presence of spindle-whorls, to suggest that such animals were kept primarily, or at all, for their wool.

In view of the scanty economic importance of sheep or goats among the Beaker stock-rearers at Newgrange, the presence of dog bones among the animal remains comes as something of a surprise, particularly since hunting seems to have formed an insignificant part of the economy. These dogs were medium-sized and may have been used as guard-dogs, or simply as pets. This second explanation would cast light on the fact that some survived to a fairly advanced age, seven or even older. Alternatively, of course, they could simply have been 'hangers-on', scrounging on the scraps to be obtained from the humans.

The presence of horse bones—about twelve individuals are represented—suggests that they were probably used as pack or riding animals. It is thought that there existed in southern Spain a local domestication centre for horses perhaps as early as the third millennium BC. (Wild horses did exist there in Mesolithic and Neolithic times.) It is thought too that horses, present occasionally in graves more or less from the time of their first domestication, may have been seen as a status symbol among the Beaker People, which would explain their rapid expansion in number. Again we are forced to remember the woman from Farta, County Galway, buried with her seven-year-old stallion.

The Later Bronze Age evidence seems to do little more than confirm that these stock-rearing habits continued. The site known as Haughey's Fort, on a low hill near Armagh and therefore in the Navan complex, has produced evidence of stock-rearing with a similar mix to that at Beaker Newgrange. Cattle constituted some 64 per cent of the domestic animal bones, with pig following at 30 per cent and sheep or goat tailing along at a mere $6\frac{1}{2}\%$. Only on one site, at Dún Aonghasa in the Aran Islands, has a Later Bronze Age occupation layer revealed a stock-rearing situation where sheep were the dominant species, constituting 52 per cent of the recovered bone, with cattle constituting 34 per cent and pigs 12 per cent. We must remember, of course, that certain landscapes are more suitable for sheep than for cattle, which have less ability to graze on mountainsides. The traditional picture of Later Bronze Age life, with great stews bubbling away in the sheet-bronze cauldrons typical of the period, capable of containing more than 150 litres of stew (fig. 12.1), seems set to persist.

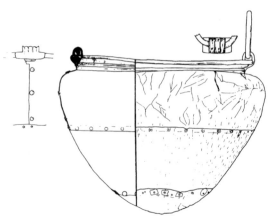

12.1 *Sheet-bronze cauldron from Portglenone, Co. Antrim (after Briggs, 1979)*

One factor we have to bear in mind is that these pre-historic stockmen had to serve as their own veterinary surgeons. Unfortunately, the examinations we possess of animal bones from prehistoric sites stop short of telling us whether animal diseases, such as foot and mouth disease, were present—though only those that left distinctive impressions on bone would now be discernible.

AGRICULTURE
The main cereals introduced to Ireland by Neolithic farming colonists were wheat and barley, each represented by two varieties: emmer (*Triticum dicoccum*), bread wheat (*Triticum aestivum*), barley (*Hordeum sativum*), and naked barley (*Hordeum polystichon*). Evidence of these cereals has been found in court tombs, passage tombs, and settlement sites. The Earlier Bronze Age saw the introduction of hulled barley (*Hordeum vulgare*) at Jamestown, County Dublin. These cereals have not been recorded in enormous quantities, and sometimes only in individual grains. There is no evidence of whole fields of cereal.

It is only in the Later Bronze Age that evidence of agriculture on a larger scale is forthcoming. At the important hill-fort known as Haughey's Fort, County Armagh, large quantities of barley were recovered from storage pits. Even more startling was the recovery from this site of an apple, perhaps indicative of Armagh's future role as an orchard county.

Inedible plants whose cultivation has been identified include flax (*Linum usitatissimum*) from a site possibly of Earlier Bronze Age date at Agfarrel, County Dublin, and at Carrowmore, County Sligo, in a passage tomb complex.

FOOD PREPARATION
Meat
The Beaker Period occupation at Newgrange, because of the thoroughness of the examination of the animal remains, gives us our best insight into the butchering techniques in use. Unfortunately the cattle bones were not well enough preserved to yield much information. The pig bones, however, yield evidence of slaughtering and butchery: the animals were slaughtered lying down and opened up from

the rear. The slaughtering of even a single pig is a highly organised process, inevitably with strict time limits. Killing, scalding (removing the bristle) and butchering require the services of two or three people, while the cleaning of the intestines and making of sausages entails the labour of two people for two days. If meat is to be smoked, the fire must be tended for three days. The whole slaughtering and butchering process for a single pig, therefore, takes between seven and twelve worker-days.

In the light of the present anxiety about hygiene in food preparation, it is perhaps worth considering how stringently hygiene was observed in prehistoric times. Possibly the answer is simply that natural immune systems compensated for any shortcomings.

Cereals

The evidence for cereal cultivation in the Neolithic Period is fairly sparse. The palaeobotanical evidence consists for the most part in the recognition of individual grains of cereal, scattered over the country, mainly in the north-east. The archaeological evidence is not much greater.

For the processing of cereals, two implements are essential: a sickle to cut the crop, and some kind of mill-stone to grind it. Only one flint sickle of a type frequently found in Neolithic contexts in England has been found in Ireland. It has been suggested, however, that sixteen flints from nine Neolithic sites, all court tombs, exist. Many of these are short rectangles of relatively thin section. Of these, two bear lustre—evidence of organic silica occasioned by their use with organics, possibly as a result of cutting cereals. (The same lustre occurs on the cutting or smoothing edges of flint hollow scrapers, which could have been used as sickles, but awkwardly.) These came from the court tombs at Ballybriest, County Derry, and Aghnaskeagh B, County Louth.

Unfortunately there are no finds of mill-stones until the Later Bronze Age, when they appear at such sites as Lough Eskragh, County Tyrone, and Ballinderry, County Offaly, and, happily, at the site known as Haughey's Fort, County Armagh, where large quantities of carbonised barley were also recovered. There is therefore no evidence for the processing of cereals until the Later Bronze Age, when not only the necessary saddle-querns (always regarded as the most primitive form of grain-rubber or mill-stone) appear but also bronze sickles in relative abundance, at first in a tanged form, then in a socketed form (fig. 12.2).

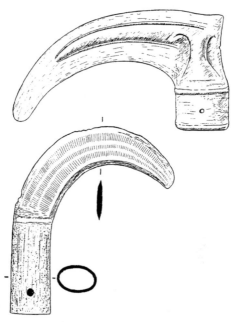

12.2 *Bronze-socketed sickles:* (a) *from Co. Westmeath;* (b) *from Athlone, Co. Westmeath (after Eogan, 1964)*

13

Nutrition and Health

Nutrition

It has been more or less customarily considered since the discovery of Mount Sandel—the type-site of the Earlier Mesolithic Period—that the residents there, despite a lack of carbohydrates, enjoyed a reasonably healthy diet. However, it has recently become evident that many people are allergic to fish, many others to nuts. Often they are the same people; so that living at Mount Sandel, such people would have had, literally, a thin time.

It has also been customarily considered that the introduction of cereals by Neolithic farmers would have meant a most useful and welcome supplement to their diet. Recent pathological examinations of skeletal material has more or less repudiated this customary belief and shown that in the Neolithic Period a diet low in carbohydrates resulted in a virtual absence of dental caries and that in general the population was a healthy one, attaining, for men, a mean height of 171 cm (5 feet 7 inches).

In the Bronze Age, while there was an increase in dental caries, suggesting a greater dependence on cereals and therefore a greater consumption of carbohydrates, the rate was still low, indicating that cereal cultivation was still not as important as animal husbandry. Statures similar to those in modern Ireland were attained, with a mean height for men of 173 cm (5 feet $8\frac{1}{2}$ inches) and for women of 165 cm (5 feet 5 inches). It is interesting in this context to recall that at

Lecarrow, County Roscommon, by a central stone in a stone circle the skeleton of a 'powerfully built young adult male' was recorded, while at Carnfeehy, County Westmeath, in a small flat cemetery of five cists, one cist was found to contain the bones of a person 'of a size greatly above the common proportion of men.' Possibly as a response to the need for ascorbic acid (vitamin C), in an oval cairn at Aghnaskeagh A, County Louth, under the floor slab of a cist containing cremated bone, was found a deposit of blackberries.

HEALTH

It would not be surprising that in prehistoric societies, which would generally be regarded as 'primitive', perinatal mortality would be common. While from Neolithic burials, both in court tombs and passage tombs, there is quite an incidence of child burials, it is only in Earlier Bronze Age burials that we really get a picture of how common it must have been. In a pit at Rossnaree, County Meath, was the crouched skeleton of a woman with a foetus; in a cist at Gortafludig, County Cork, was the cremated bone of an adult with an infant or newly born child; in a cist in a small flat cemetery at Drung, County Donegal, were the fragments of the skeleton of a foetus or new-born child (in the next cist was the crouched skeleton of a woman); in a cist with a vase urn at Ballinvoher, County Cork, were found the bones of a foetus, an infant, and an adult; while at Halverstown, County Kildare, in a cist were the cremated bones of a small adult and an unborn child.

For the mortality of children under ten, records from the Neolithic Period do exist. From court tombs come the cremated remains of seven children under the age of ten, at sites such as Annaghmare, County Armagh, Aghanaglack, County Fermanagh, and Tully, County Fermanagh, where there were three. A total of ten unburnt burials are recorded from court tombs, such as Annaghmare, County Armagh, and Audleystown, County Down, where there may have been as many as four. They occur also in passage tombs, most spectacularly at Fourknocks, where there were three cremated children and eighteen unburnt remains.

In Earlier Bronze Age graves there is impressive data. In a pit with a cordoned urn at Urbalreagh, County Antrim, was the cremated bone of a man and the cremated bone of a child; in a pit at Keenoge, County Meath, was the crouched skeleton of a child and in a cist in the same flat cemetery the crouched skeleton of another with a bowl.

Apart from accidental injury (such as that to the man who had broken his leg and some time later was buried in a cist at Ballybrew, County Wicklow, having died before his leg had healed) and inflicted injury (such as that to the woman whose skeleton was found in a cist at Stillorgan, County Dublin, and whose death had been caused by a blow on the skull), it is really only those ailments that show clearly on bone that are detected. This is why osteoarthritis—a progressive and irreversible disease in which the protective cartilage between the bones of a joint wears away—is one of the most commonly observed ailments. At Kilcroagh, County Antrim, a man over forty was buried, with a cordoned urn. He had suffered from osteoarthritis of the spine and the metatarsal (foot)—a little on the young side for a man. Again, at Stranagalwilly, County Tyrone, in a cist with a tripartite bowl was the crouched skeleton of a man approximately sixty years of age who had suffered from general osteoarthritic degeneration of the hip, knee, spine, and shoulder joints.

The worst recorded was a man of only thirty-five buried, without burning, with a vase urn at Straid, County Derry. He, poor thing, had suffered from diffuse degenerative arthritis, worst in the knee, shoulders, and spine. 'The destruction of the joint surface in the knee would give rise to much pain and he would probably have been unable to pursue any active occupation.'

14

Domestic and Personal Life

Domestic life

While presumably in Mesolithic society flint knife-like forms could be used for the preparation and consumption of food, few other pieces of equipment have survived that could be unequivocally described as 'domestic equipment'. There is of course a huge range of organic equipment that has not survived that might have been so used.

Looking back to the nearest contemporary substitute for life in Mesolithic times—for example camping as a boy scout—one remembers using pointed sticks for cooking, in the manner of toasting-forks, or making simple spits on which something could be roasted over the fire. Skin or wickerwork containers have not survived but would have been necessary for holding liquids and solids, respectively, for domestic use.

Even in the Neolithic Period the range of palpable domestic equipment is not extensive. Flint plano-convex knives again could be pictured in a completely domestic milieu. It is really only pottery that suggests itself, in bulk, as domestic equipment. The range of sizes of bowls, of Western Neolithic form, lends itself to the idea of some of the smaller ones having served for individual portions, while the larger ones played a communal role. One pottery spoon is recorded from a court tomb—these were much more common in English Neolithic contexts; it is possible, however, that other examples may exist but have not been recognised. It is quite feasible that horn or wooden spoons, which have not survived, could have been in use.

In the Earlier Bronze Age, including the Beaker Period, pottery vessels clearly could have fulfilled domestic roles, not only beakers but beaker coarseware and some of the pottery that showed itself as domestic as well as funerary— the cordoned urn from the dwelling-site at Downpatrick, County Down, for example. There were many items of bronze that could have served domestically, such as the tanged knives or daggers of the Beaker Period, as well as the knives or daggers of the true Earlier Bronze Age. Whether bronze awls could be classed as domestic rather than industrial equipment is arguable: the great majority found in burials are with men, which does suggest an industrial application. One, however, was buried with a woman at Fourknocks II, County Meath.

When we come to bronze 'razors' accompanying burial in the Earlier Bronze Age we come upon another problem (or two). Razors at some sites accompanied merely cremated bone: at Pollacorragune, County Galway, with a cordoned urn; at Ballinashurock, County Westmeath; at Cush, County Limerick; at Burren, County Mayo; and at Newcastle, County Wicklow. At only two sites has the sex of the buried people been identified: at Carrowbeg North, County Galway, it was an adult, 'probably male,' who accompanied the 'razor'; at Reardnogy, County Tipperary, on the other hand, it was an adult, 'probably female.' On the one hand it becomes a problem with which Joyce would have sympathised: are Earlier Bronze Age 'razors' really razors, presumably an almost totally male requirement? Was there an Earlier Bronze Age unisex chain of barber-shops; or were there exceedingly hirsute females?

In fact it is only in the Later Bronze Age that we come upon items, apart from pottery, that can unequivocally be identified as domestic. There is of course a continuing series of domestic pottery. There are also, however, surviving vessels of wood, like those from Lough Eskragh and Haughey's Fort (fig. 14.1). There are also a series of bronze implements that would suggest 'domestic' as their intended role. And there are knives, both tanged and socketed, like those from the famous Dowris Hoard, County Offaly.

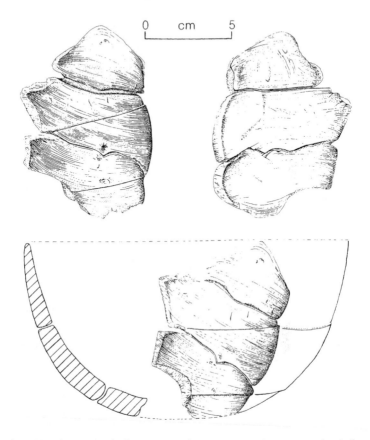

14.1 *Wooden vessel from Haughey's Fort, Co. Armagh (after Mallory, 1991)*

Whether the vast sheet-bronze cauldrons and buckets should be classified as domestic or communal is perhaps debatable. The same doubt must also hang over those strange objects, even more strangely described, the so-called 'flesh-hooks'—U-shaped objects with curved and pointed ends, one of which occurs in the hoard from Bishopsland, County Kildare.

PERSONAL DRESS AND ADORNMENT
For the Mesolithic population of Ireland, apart from assuming that they wore garments made of skin and fur, derived

from the animals that were present during the early post-glacial period, it must be said that we have no information whatsoever about either dress or personal adornment.

In the Neolithic Period, in court tomb contexts, the situation improves very little. We have no direct or indirect information about clothing and are forced to conclude that, with the addition of raw materials from domesticated animals, the clothing situation must have remained rather similar. For personal adornment, on the other hand, we have got some information. Beads, of various types of stone but also of bone, appear at a number of sites. At Ballymacaldrack, County Antrim, a disc-bead of bone and a bead of serpentine were recovered; at Ballymarlagh, County Antrim, a disc-bead of bone was found; at Bavan, County Donegal, two rather coarse spherical beads were found, as was a rather elegant lozenge-shaped bead of schist with a perforation drilled through its long axis, which showed signs of wear, presumably as a result of having been worn. At Tully, County Fermanagh, a bead, also of schist remarkably similar to the Bavan example though not with such a pronounced lozenge shape, was found; at Aghanaglack, County Fermanagh, a small disc-bead of serpentine was found; while at Creevykeel, County Sligo, was found a disc-bead of igneous rock.

The total number of finds is not impressive but does show that personal adornment was in vogue. We do not know, however, whether it was among men or women. Stressing the relationship between court tombs and portal tombs, beads virtually identical to those from Bavan were found in the portal tomb at Ballyrenan, County Tyrone. A bead similar to the Bavan lozenge-bead was found on a settlement site at Lough Gur, County Limerick.

Passage tombs
In the passage tomb context the range of items of personal adornment increases greatly, both in range and in quantity. Items showing a connection with dress styles also appear. The range of beads and pendants increases enormously, not just those of stone but also of bone and baked clay, as well as a range of different types of stone, including steatite, jasper, and serpentine. Many of them bear decoration.

For dress requirements a whole range of often highly decorated and decorative pins appear, usually made of bone or antler (fig. 14.2). It was usually assumed, with a degree of perception, that pins as cloak-fasteners served better with garments of woven material than with garments of skin, fur, or hide. If the passage tomb farmers at Newgrange, for example, had observed a similar pattern of stock-rearing to that employed by their Beaker successors, with a small incidence of sheep and no evidence, direct or indirect, for the use of their wool, there would seem to be a possible conflict. Of course, while pins might be

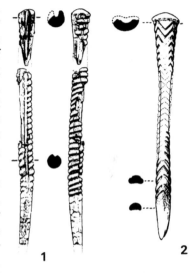

14.2 *Bone and antler pins from passage tombs:* (1) *from Knowth, Co. Meath;* (2) *from Fourknocks, Co. Meath (after Eogan, 1986)*

construed as handier with woven textiles, their use with garments of skin or hide cannot be ruled out: the provision of prepared holes in the skin garment would permit the continuous use of pins.

Earlier Bronze Age

In the Earlier Bronze Age, including the Beaker Period, the picture becomes a little more complex. Often associated with beakers in countries other than Ireland are V-perforated buttons; while none has been found in association with beakers in Ireland, a number do exist (fig. 14.3), made of materials as diverse as steatite, jet, jasper, shale, and bone. In addition during this period faience beads occur (fig. 14.4), often singly, even in graves, as at Knockboy, County Antrim, where a quoit-shaped bead was found with cremated bone and a large urn. At Tara, however, they formed part of a necklace. Jet beads have been found in several graves of this period, for example at Keenoge and at

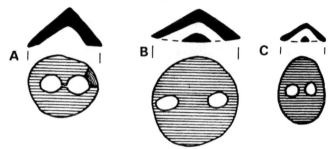

14.3 *V-perforated buttons: (A) of steatite, from Carrowmore, Co. Sligo; (B) of jet, from Lissan, Co. Tyrone; (C) of bone, from Kinkit, Co. Tyrone (after Harbison, 1976)*

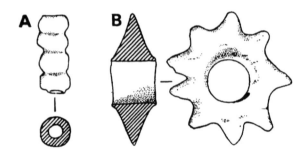

14.4 *Faience beads from Dundrum, Co. Down: (A) segmented; (B) star-shaped (after Jope, 1966)*

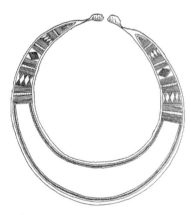

14.5 *Gold lunula (after Coffey, 1913)*

Oldbridge, County Meath, in both instances with a crouched skeleton in a pit.

This, however, was the period when gold ornaments started to appear as quite stunning items of personal adornment. The most spectacular are of course the gold lunulae (fig. 14.5), but there are also the even earlier circular gold discs, with Beaker affinities, which, because of the usual presence of small holes in the centre, are assumed to have been stitched to garments. There are also examples of even more exotic pieces of gold jewellery, such as the ear-ring or pin-head of Portuguese type from Deehommed, County Down.

Later Bronze Age
It was in the Later Bronze Age, with its impression of vastly conspicuous consumption, that both dress accoutrements and other aspects of personal adornment reached a quite devastating level. For dress accoutrements there was a whole range of pins. Sunflower pins, usually of bronze, with conical heads, usually bent over at right angles to the shank and frequently bearing elaborate ornament, and cup-headed pins, where the head is concave rather than conical, usually in bronze though occasionally in gold, were fairly obviously intended as garment-fasteners. So too were sleeve or cuff-fasteners, made of gold and functioning in a very similar fashion to modern cuff-links, being passed through two holes—palpable button-holes, with the decorated bow placed externally to show it off.

The range of ornaments, usually of gold, was quite extra-ordinary. There were gold torcs made of flat gold ribbons, either simple or with another element soldered on to create a triple-bladed ribbon. Strictly speaking, a torc has to be twisted; there is, however, a hoard from Coolmanagh Upper, County Carlow, composed of an untwisted triple-ribboned 'torc' and a twisted simple ribbon torc.

Later in this period cast-gold ornaments appear, such as the cast-gold armlets or bracelets, sometimes quite massive, often with expanded terminals and sometimes decorated, like those in the two hoards from Downpatrick, County Down. These are quite numerous and in fact are probably the most common form of Later Bronze Age ornament. There are, however, a number of rather rare and exotic forms of ornament, such as the broad ribbed bracelets that appear in the hoard from Derrinboy, County Offaly. The same hoard also contains a most intricate and skilfully made necklace, which consists of a cylindrical leather core, a thin leather strip folded over and sewn with gut with zigzag stitches. Over this a thin gold wire, of D-shaped cross-section, was closely wound. The two ends of the core were enclosed within a single cylindrical cap.

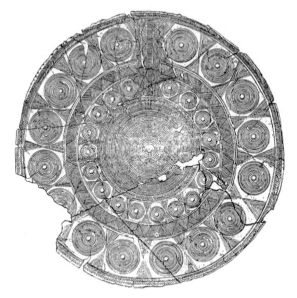

14.6 *The intricately decorated gold disc from Lattoon, Co. Cavan (after Armstrong, 1933)*

Perhaps the most 'artistic' of the Later Bronze Age goldwork, however, is the celebrated disc from Lattoon, County Cavan (fig. 14.6). It measures 121 mm in diameter, with a small central boss, around which are concentric circles, the outer two of which are filled with diagonal hatching. Outside this is a ring of small circles, eighteen in number, then two concentric circles infilled with herringbone, then a ring of larger circles, sixteen in number. The rim is decorated with herringbone. Breaking through the ring of circles is a tapering ornament that runs through from the rim to the outside of the cross-hatched circles. The disc is broken, with a small portion missing; all in all, however, it is a consummate achievement both of design and execution. It was found in a hoard containing two armlets with slightly expanded terminals and two with cup-shaped terminals.

Actual dress remnants
At last, in the Later Bronze Age, we catch a glimpse of actual items of dress. A hoard from Cromaghs, County Antrim, found in a bog in 1904 contained a socketed axe-

head, a socketed gouge, and a sunflower pin—all of which testified to the genuine Later Bronze Age date of the find— and some portions of Later Bronze Age dress. Also in the find, interestingly, was a razor with a leather case.

The textiles are two pieces of woollen cloth (fig. 14.7). Unfortunately some was destroyed at the time of finding and immediately afterwards when it lay on the surface of the bog. The two pieces that have survived are roughly 470 mm wide and 710 mm long. Technically there is no apparent difference between the two pieces of cloth, and it might have been assumed that they had been woven as one piece; there are, however, differences in the position of the selvedges, which make it more likely that they were woven separately. It is suggested that they could have been woven on a small braid loom, or on a special warping apparatus, or even by tablet weaving. Only a few stitches of the sewing by which they were joined have survived. It is interesting that despite the paucity of evidence for extensive sheep-rearing throughout prehistoric Ireland, both of these pieces are of wool.

With the textile fragments was found an extremely fine and delicately made ornament of black horsehair, which

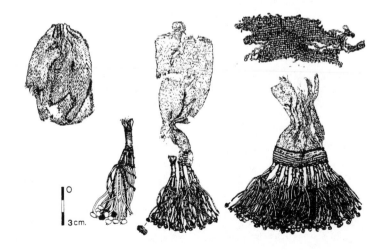

14.7 *Woollen textiles and horsehair fringe from Cromaghs, Co. Antrim (after Coffey, 1906)*

might have been part of a belt. It is made of unspun single hairs, which formed both the warp and the weft, done as a herringbone twill. To this woven fabric are attached tasselled fringes, also of horsehair; the preserved perfect tassel consists of bunches of horsehair bound round with more horsehair. Unfortunately there is not enough evidence to reconstruct the costume or even to state categorically that it was of a man or a woman, though the bronze items in the find would suggest that it was probably a man.

ENTERTAINMENT AND HOSPITALITY

It is of historical interest that beakers were so called by antiquarians because their usually thin lips suggested that they had been used specifically as drinking-cups, in contrast to the usually rather thick-rimmed 'food vessels'. Traces of a drink resembling mead have been identified in a Scottish example, and it may well be that Irish examples contained similar potions, introducing a note of conviviality to the otherwise rather sober chapters of Irish prehistory.

15

RELIGION AND THE ARTS

ART

If we include as 'art' the application of simple decorative
features (or sometimes complicated arrangements of simple
motifs) to objects such as pottery and metalwork, the history of art begins with the Neolithic settlers. For the Mesolithic
Period, as so often, we have no evidence whatsoever, for
the simple reason that nothing on which decoration might
have existed has survived. For all we know they may have
painted their bodies or their skin clothing or even the skin
coverings on their huts.

It is, therefore, to the Neolithic potters we have to look
for the first appearance in Ireland of decoration for its own
sake. Here we find very simple stroke decoration on 'plain'
Western Neolithic pots (fig. 3.4), developing into quite
complex arrangements on Ballyalton bowls, usually of
'imitation whipped cord', where a blunted piece of stick has
been pressed into the surface of the pot before it is fired,
creating a series of lines that do indeed resemble whipped
cord. Often the technique is used to create quite complex
patterns, with arc motifs as well as straight lines.

It is with the introduction of passage tombs, however,
that decorative art really emerges. Not only are many of the
stones of the tombs heavily decorated but the bone and
antler pins used to fasten clothes are too. A repertoire of
motifs (fig. 5.6) is used to decorate the structural stones in
passage tombs and so to create some of the undeniably

impressive masterpieces of passage tomb art to be found not merely at the best-known sites, such as Newgrange and Knowth, but at their far humbler relatives at places like Knockmany, County Tyrone. The great entrance-stone at Newgrange (fig. 5.5) is but one example of how awe-inspiring these pieces can be.

The fact that must be considered incomprehensible is how the people under whose aegis these fantastic tombs—in many ways adding 'art gallery' to the more commonplace terms like 'temple' or 'tomb' attributed to them—could produce some of the worst pottery ever seen, the so-called Carrowkeel ware (fig. 5.10). Not only is the fabric of the pots coarse and crude but so too is the decoration.

The Earlier Bronze Age

With the introduction of 'beakers', and their exemplary and meticulous decoration (on very finely made pots, it may be added), and the consequent practice of metalworking, the range of durable materials on which decoration might be practised enlarged considerably. Of this pottery it has been said 'the finest Beakers must have taken many hours to make and decorate, they were highly prized,' and 'it is generally thought that the wide distribution of this pottery type is due mainly to the fact that these pots were prestigious vessels (maybe even part of some cult), much sought after by certain elements of society.'

The habit of decoration spread to all sorts of metalwork: axes, daggers (fig. 7.30), spear-heads (fig. 7.24), and of course gold objects, such as the circular gold discs (fig. 6.11) and the lunulae, which were fashioned purely for decoration (though possibly also as virtual badges of rank or status). In the established Earlier Bronze Age, pottery of all types was heavily and richly ornamented—the bowls (fig. 7.1) and vases, even the cinerary urns (fig. 7.5, 7.6, 7.8, 7.10).

The Later Bronze Age

Curiously enough, in the Later Bronze Age decoration was virtually confined to decorative objects. It is true that some socketed axes, for example, have cast ribs, even cast cable motifs, round the socket; apart from that, however, it is to

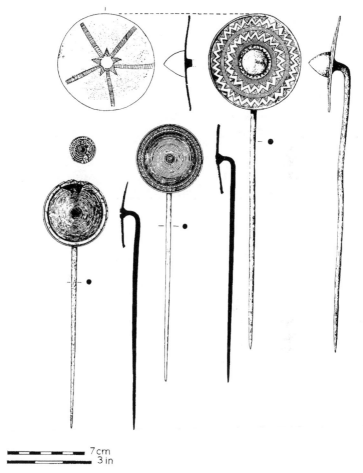

15.1 *Decorated heads of sunflower pins from Ballytegan, Co. Laois (after Eogan, 1983)*

specifically ornamental pieces, such as sunflower pins and the decorated terminals of gold bracelets or the gold ribbed bracelets, that we have to turn for usually fairly simple decoration, consisting for the most part of herringbone motifs, or triangles, or concentric circles. As we have already noted, possibly the most elaborate and satisfying item of Later Bronze Age art is the gold disc from Lattoon, County Cavan, with its well-laid-out design and its careful execution.

MUSIC

It is only in the Later Bronze Age that we get any evidence of music, in the form of the celebrated bronze horns or trumpets that have survived in quite surprising quantities. In the hoard from Dowris, County Offaly, for example, a total of twenty-six examples have survived. They are of two basic types: *end-blow*, shaped like cow-horns, where the air is applied through a fairly small aperture at the end of the horn, and *side-blow*, where the air is applied through a fairly large aperture on the side of the horn. It has been suggested in recent years that these horns functioned almost like Australian didgeridoos; but experiments in Belfast with two of the surviving examples from a hoard at Drumbest, County Antrim, one end-blow and one side-blow, possibly the only surviving pair of Later Bronze Age trumpets still in a playable condition, demonstrated that even without the use of modern mouth-pieces both horns could be played. Together they proved musically compatible and were quite capable of producing a recognisable simple tune (fig. 15.2).

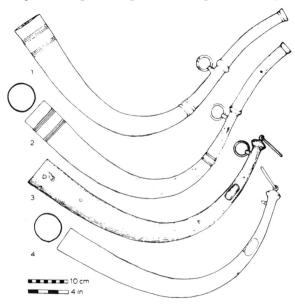

15.2 *The four bronze horns constituting the hoard from Drumbest, Co. Antrim; (3 and 4) the two side-blow horns (after Eogan, 1983)*

Whether the objects known as crotals—rather egg-shaped hollow objects of bronze, with a loose 'rattler' of bronze or stone inside—were intended as instruments to form a sort of rhythm section in a Later Bronze Age band is not, of course, known. There were, however, forty-eight of these objects in the hoard from Dowris (fig. 15.3).

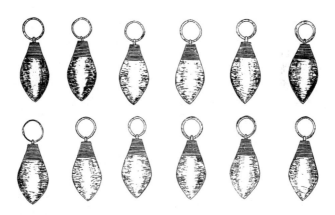

15.3 *Bronze crotals in the hoard from Dowris, Co. Offaly (after Eogan, 1983)*

RELIGION

While there is no surviving evidence of any religious belief on the part of the Mesolithic settlers, it is difficult to avoid the conclusion that the construction of court tombs, portal tombs, passage tombs and even wedge tombs is an expression of some sort of religious belief on the part of their builders. Obviously the first tenet of their religious beliefs that comes to mind is the ancestor element. These tombs presumably were built to contain the bones or ashes of the dead and, by their monumental nature, even to commemorate them.

It is difficult to separate their construction from some awareness of the influence of the sun in the people's lives. Court tombs show a strong tendency to be aligned so as to face the rising sun, as do portal tombs. Passage tombs are shown to share this feature and even to enhance it by the inclusion in their structure of 'sun-awareness devices', such as the roof-box at Newgrange, cleverly designed and built to permit the rays of the rising sun at the winter solstice to strike the very back-stone of the passage. This shows not only great skill but a keen interest in the sun and perhaps a devotion to it and its effect on humankind.

The fact that wedge tombs have an equal and opposite tendency to face west could be construed in several ways. It could (but not very seriously) be said that their builders had simply 'turned their back' on the sun; more seriously, it is not easy to understand why they preferred the setting sun to the rising sun. It does, however, still seem to indicate an awareness of its existence and position.

In the established Earlier Bronze Age there is scant evidence of any awareness of the sun or its position in relation to the graves. In the Later Bronze Age, because of the rarity of discovered graves, it is not possible to say even this with any degree of confidence.

The most puzzling thing about prehistoric religion is its 'ecumenism': the fact that what would to us appear to be completely conflicting rites are permitted in the same tomb. Cremations and inhumations were put to rest side by side. In court tombs, cremations seem to enjoy a preference, though this could, after all, be because cremated bone enjoys a slightly greater chance of survival in our rather acid soils. Of the human remains in court tombs, slightly more than 52 were cremated, while 44 or 45 were not, which is not really a great preponderance of cremations.

As far as passage tombs are concerned, it is less easy to find universal statistics, though it is confidently said that 'cremation is the predominant rite at all the Irish sites.' Taking individual sites, it is seen, for instance at Fourknocks I, that of the minimum of sixty-five individuals present, 40 per cent were cremated.

In the Earlier Bronze Age, while many cemeteries—such as those at Letterkeen, County Mayo, Knocknacart, County Derry, Scarawalsh, County Wexford, Drumnakilly, County Tyrone, Corrower, County Mayo, and Cloghskelt, County Down—are occupied exclusively by cremations, others—such as Oldtown and Ploopluck, County Kildare, and Carryglass, County Tyrone—are exclusively occupied by unburnt burials. Other cemeteries, however, do not exhibit this kind of exclusivity. At Carrownacaw, County Mayo, a small cemetery contained two skeletons and five cremations; at Poulawack, County Clare, there appear to have been sixteen uncremated burials and two cremated remains; while at Ballyenahan, County Cork, a small flat cemetery revealed five cremations and two uncremated burials.

Even the pottery 'affiliations' of the deceased show a similar degree of ecumenism. While the majority of crouched, unburnt skeletons are accompanied by bowls, as at Sliguff, County Carlow, where the crouched skeleton of a young man is accompanied in a cist by a bowl, at Knockiveagh, County Down, a bowl accompanied the cremated remains of an adult and a child. On the other hand, at Glassamucky, County Dublin, a vase accompanied a crouched skeleton in a cist, while at Ballyduff, County Wexford, the vase in a cist was accompanied by the cremated bone of two adults, possibly one male and one female.

It has been suggested that cremation was common in Ireland because of a stronger inclination towards pastoralism or stock-rearing, with its nomadic undertones, than towards agriculture in the fuller sense. While at the moment it seems that pastoralism held sway throughout the Neolithic Period and Earlier Bronze Age, it was certainly not nomadic, if we observe the evidence of the Céide Fields and the Beaker farming at Newgrange.

16

Technology and Science

Technology
There are many aspects of technology revealed in Irish pre-history—for example in the spheres of prospecting, metal extraction, surveying, and architecture—of which we can say little more than 'They did it.' The height of their achievements, however, can possibly be more deeply appreciated if a brief examination is made of the problems facing them.

Prospecting
While the finding of flint supplies by our prehistoric ancestors may have been easy, by recognising great outcrops of cretaceous limestone, with the knowledge that this mass of white rock was likely to contain flint, this would be so only if in their previous homeland cretaceous limestone with flint had been a common feature. If in fact they came to Ireland directly from Scotland, this would not have been so, because of the complete absence of extensive outcrops of cretaceous limestone with flint there. It therefore entailed a certain degree of cleverness to recognise that in this new land the great masses of white rock did in fact contain large nodules of flint, from which they could fashion their tools and implements.

The discovery of sources of suitable, even ideal, stone for the manufacture of axes could perhaps be ascribed to 'happy accident'. The discovery of suitable sources of copper as the necessary raw material for metalworking is not so easily written off. Native copper—golden and shiny—would have been relatively easily recognised and exploited by people with a knowledge of metalworking but unfortunately did not exist in sufficient quantity to satisfy the needs of the growing industry. It was therefore necessary to find sources of ores. In an area of some 84,000 square kilometres, this would have been no easy task, but they did it, presumably after months, even years, of combing the countryside, necessarily with a fair degree of knowledge of the tell-tale indications of what they were looking for.

Surveying

The laying out on the ground of the form of even a simple two-chambered court tomb to ensure that it would face the rising sun would entail a knowledge of basic surveying and, presumably, some method of recording. The laying out of the forms of stone circles would introduce the relatively simple procedure (to us) of using a taut string tied to a central peg.

But it is the massive problems of surveying involved in the construction of passage tombs on the scale of Newgrange and Knowth, observing the various astronomical requirements found to have been used, and over the length of time involved in their construction, that imply greater knowledge and skill and, even more necessarily, some means of recording the necessary information for the many years involved in their complete construction. The Céide Fields dramatically show prehistoric society's ability to survey, and create, straight walls over long distances.

Measurement

While it is not necessary to invoke the elusive 'megalithic yard', our prehistoric ancestors must have availed of some method of measurement, in the first instance in their surveying. There is no need to assume a universality in their basic units. Units of length with a completely local and transitory value would have been quite adequate: the height of one of the workers, or simply a piece of wood, could possibly have served as this basic unit.

As far as the metal industry is concerned, there must presumably have been some method of assessing weights and, on that basis, calculating, say, the amount of tin required to alloy satisfactorily a certain amount of copper.

ASTRONOMY

It has been known for a long time that court tombs show a strong tendency to face the rising sun; it has also been known for some years that the passage tomb at Newgrange is so aligned that on the morning of the winter solstice the rays of the rising sun pass right down the twenty-five metres of passage and illuminate the back-stone.

There have been several attempts to impose astronomical observations on megalithic structures. The complex of stone circles and alignments at Beaghmore, County Tyrone, were examined for evidence of astronomical significance. The conclusions were not by any means indicative of any convincing solar or lunar alignments. It was reported that 'the fairly short rows do not point to any obvious markers or foresights on the horizon and so it is not possible to give much weight to their use for accurately observing the moon at major standstill.' The question was even posed, 'Were the erectors beginners and learning about the moon's movements or were the rows put there for other purposes?'

A great deal of eloquent argument has been raised about the astronomical attributes of passage tombs. It would be nice to believe that at Lough Crew not only does cairn T indicate the spring and autumn equinox but that by using the two satellite cairns S and U the 'cross-quarter' days (dividing the year into quarters at intervals between the solstices and equinoxes) are indicated, so that 'together the two satellite mounds of cairn T serve to announce the four seasons of the year and in themselves form an agricultural and pastoral calendar.' However, it is easier to agree that 'as the number of sites surveyed increased so did the panoply of alternative orientations on celestial bodies in an effort to keep the original theories intact.'

A recent study of stone alignments and their astronomical significance in the south-west of Ireland has produced a number of alignments that do indicate significant astronomical orientation, mainly, as at Monavaddra and Cloonshear Beg, County Cork, and Dromteewakeen, County Kerry, of the summer solstice or, as at Cabragh, County

Cork, and Eightercua, County Kerry, of the winter solstice. At Newcastle, County Cork, both solstices were properly indicated. Exceptionally, at Gneeves, County Cork, the equinox is recorded, which, considering the amount of time and effort involved in counting the days between the solstices to deduce their mid-point, is quite impressive. It is interesting to note the incidence of western as well as eastern orientation.

EDUCATION

While it would be highly fanciful to picture rows of little pre-historic children sitting in front of a teacher, there remains the fact that information and skills had to be passed on from generation to generation. Even the Mesolithic hunters must have had a system whereby their children were taught how to hunt, and what to hunt. Neolithic farmers had to teach their children how to look after stock, how to keep the wolves away, and how to cure any of the more common diseases of cattle.

Even more, miners, smelters and other metalworkers had to inculcate in the next generation their knowledge and skills: how to identify a promising source of copper ore, how to construct safe adits, how much tin would be needed as an alloying material for a certain amount of copper. All the new generations of every period would need to be taught how to build huts and houses. Presumably, in fact, at adolescence the young would be incorporated in the work gangs, join in the hunt, help clear out the mines, and fetch smaller amounts of fuel, and thus, by a sort of generalised apprenticeship, learn the tricks of the various trades.

17

THE ENVIRONMENT

The environment encountered by Mesolithic people when they first arrived in Ireland was totally unspoilt. It was people who began spoiling it. The first fire lit by our Mesolithic ancestors saw the first emissions by human agency of carbon dioxide into the atmosphere; the first small clearings saw the beginning of the destruction of the natural means of combating these emissions. The vastly more extensive forest clearance engaged in by Neolithic farmers to provide space for their crops and herds helped to hasten the effects. To this, in the Earlier Bronze Age, was added the emission of arsenical vapours, and then, with the smelting of sulphide ores, sulphur dioxide. Acid rain had been invented.

Among the blessings enjoyed by Irish prehistoric people were supplies of flint and stone, as well as good soil for grazing and a fairly generous supply of natural foodstuffs, to which was added a generous provision of minerals for the metal industry.

One blessing they all shared was an abundant supply of clean, wholesome water. Sometimes it may have seemed that this was available in excessive quantities, as the inhabitants of the Later Mesolithic site at Newferry found to their cost when the River Bann periodically expanded and inundated their dwelling-sites.

CLIMATE
As the weather changes from day to day and from season to season, so too, over longer periods, does the climate. The

first great example of this climatic change occurred some time about 13,000 BC, when the temperature gradually started to rise and to melt the great ice-sheet that covered virtually the whole of Ireland. This process extended over about two thousand years and eventually prepared the country for the arrival of Mesolithic settlers in a land that was reasonably comfortable.

Most of the climatic changes are recorded in bogs and are discussed by palaeobotanists, ably assisted by palaeozoologists, studying the accompanying insect remains. In a period from about 11,000 to 8000 BC the pollen from a bog at Woodgrange, County Down, has shown a record of increasing temperatures, with a succession of plants that begins with grasses, sorrels, and a type of willow. This was adequate to support herds of reindeer.

This period was followed by a phase in which the climate became suitable for junipers and birches to spread through the country. The insects found relating to this phase suggest that the climate was at least as warm as, or at times warmer than, that of today. Towards the end of this phase, however, short periods of colder weather began to reassert themselves, breaking up the plant cover. These breaks of cold climate did not last long, however; and although the earlier high temperatures were not re-established, the grass cover was able to revive and lasted until nearly 8600 BC. It was during this period that the giant Irish deer made its brief appearance among the Irish fauna. Unfortunately this period of relative warmth was followed by a return of cold severe enough to see the return of ice to valleys such as that at Glenmalure, County Wicklow.

About 8000 BC, warmer conditions returned once again; deciduous forest established itself, and the scene was set for the arrival of the first humans. The temperature continued to rise, until somewhere about 5000 or 4000 BC average temperatures were higher than today's by about 1°C. From then on, apart from minor reductions in temperature, the greatest effects were periodic increases in rainfall, which encouraged the growth of peat towards the end of the Neolithic Period—helping to preserve for us Neolithic structures like the Céide Fields.

GLOSSARY

adits: access tunnels burrowed into an area deemed to be rich in ores, or indeed any material considered to be economically worth mining, providing an approach to the desired material and a means of extracting it. Abundant examples exist in Ireland, mainly in the south-west, at sites such as Mount Gabriel, County Cork, where indeed they have been shown to have been in use during the Earlier Bronze Age.

arsenic (symbol As): a metallic element frequently found in Irish copper ores, often in surprising quantities. Ores from Quin, County Clare, and Ross Island, County Kerry, have been shown to contain more than 15 per cent arsenic, while another from Faithlegg, County Waterford, was shown to contain more than 30 per cent. Many others from different areas contain more moderate quantities, between 1 and 5 per cent. This naturally occurring arsenic served to make, with the accompanying copper, a natural alloy, which could be described as an *arsenical bronze*, with much more hardness and strength than copper alone would have.

beakers: rather elegant and well-made pottery vessels, often, as so-called *bell-beakers*, with a characteristic S-shaped profile, found all over Europe with groups of similar material, including early bronze or copper implements, suggesting that it was the people who made these vessels who spread the knowledge of metal-working throughout the Continent, eventually bringing it to Ireland.

bowl: **(1)** the simple bowl-shaped round-based pottery of the first farmers in the Neolithic Period; **(2)** certain vessels of the Earlier Bronze Age that exhibit a basically curved profile, in contrast to the straight profile displayed by vessels of the *vase* tradition.

bronze: an alloy of copper, meaning that to improve the strength and hardness of the copper another metal has been added to it. The normal alloying metal is tin, but arsenic can successfully be used instead, though it produces a slightly less satisfactory alloy. In Ireland, since so many copper ores contain naturally a proportion of arsenic, bronzes of this composition were regularly used until supplies of tin were found and exploited.

bulbar surface: a term applied to the back of a flint flake. Flint gives what is known as a *conchoidal* fracture, so that when a flake is detached from the lump of flint—generally known as a *core*—the *face* (the outer side of the detached flake) often tends to be slightly hollow in section, while the back has at the bottom a slight rounded lump, known as the *bulb of percussion*. Because of the presence of this bulb, the back of the flake is known as the *bulbar surface.*

carboniferous period: a geological period that started some 345 million years ago, deriving its name from the fact that it was during this period that coal measures were formed. It is from limestones of this period that *chert*, used often by prehistoric peoples as a substitute for flint, is derived.

chalk: a white rock, also known as *limestone*, of the cretaceous period. It is from this cretaceous chalk, often displayed as cliffs in County Antrim, that flint, such a vital raw material for prehistoric peoples, is derived.

cists: usually smallish holes dug into the ground and lined with stone to receive burials of the Earlier Bronze Age. They can, however, be formed of stones erected on the surface, usually for incorporation in a mound or cairn.

copper (symbol Cu): a metallic element usually found, mixed with other elements, in ores of various characters; occasionally it is found naturally in its metallic state and is then known as *native copper*. It was the most important raw material for people of the Bronze Age and is fairly widely distributed through Ireland, but with a distinct sparsity in the north and a great abundance particularly in the south-west, where, indeed, evidence of its having been mined in the Earlier Bronze Age survives.

cortex: the skin, or bark, formed naturally in the parent chalk on nodules of flint. It was generally removed by its prehistoric users before fashioning implements by detaching what are termed *decortical flakes*.

court tombs: one type of tomb built by Neolithic people in Ireland and generally thought to be the first type. Essentially they consist of a burial gallery divided into chambers, two, three or four in number, interconnected and opening off a *court* or forecourt at the front, which usually faces in the direction of the rising sun. Sometimes two galleries are placed back to back, less often two galleries are placed side by side, and sometimes two galleries are placed front to front, each opening off a shared central court. Frequently subsidiary chambers are placed at the sides or ends of the long *cairn* of stone built over them.

cretaceous period: a geological period that began about 136 million years ago. It was in this period that chalk or cretaceous limestone was formed, containing the flint that was to be so important for prehistoric people as a necessary raw material for the manufacture of tools and implements.

dendrochronology: a technique of dating wooden objects by counting the growth-rings of trees, or of the wood derived from them, and making allowance for the different widths, which reflect the annual growing conditions, fitting the pattern formed into a master pattern.

faience: a sort of tin-glazed sub-glass originally developed in Egypt. Beads of this material, usually a greeny-blue in colour, of various forms—disc-shaped, star-shaped, and segmented—have been found in Ireland and Britain, usually in burials. It used to be thought that these finds were of actual imports from Egypt; now it is more generally thought that they were locally manufactured in imitation of the Egyptian originals.

felsite: a devitrified volcanic glass occasionally used as a substitute for flint, as at Creevykeel, County Sligo.

fire-setting: a technique used by miners to help loosen and break up rocks containing the ore for which they were mining. Essentially it entails lighting fires against the rock containing the ore to loosen it and cause it to fracture.

flint: the most important raw material available to pre-historic people for the manufacture of implements and tools. In Ireland it is abundantly available, but mainly in and around County Antrim, where there are outcrops of cretaceous chalk or limestone almost following the county boundary.

matrices: the actual cavities on moulds that dictate the shape of the object to be cast. By comparing the shapes and sizes of cast bronze articles it is possible to identify those that have been cast in the same matrix and thereby determine if they are *co-matrical*.

megaliths: monuments made of large stones (from the Greek words *megas*, large, and *lithos*, stone).

Neolithic Period: the Late Stone Age (from the Greek words *neos*, late, and *lithos*, stone).

nodule: a lump of flint as it occurs in the parent cretaceous chalk or limestone.

Palaeolithic Period: the Old Stone Age (from the Greek words *palaios*, old, and *lithos*, stone). While a few Palaeolithic implements have been found in Ireland, it is generally considered that they are likely to be recent imports.

passage tombs: the other main group of burial places of the Irish Neolithic Period. Unlike *court tombs*, they prefer round cairns to long cairns and have a tendency to group together in cemeteries. While the classic passage tomb has a long, or fairly long, passage leading to a terminal chamber, often of cruciform plan, others (known as 'undifferentiated') have virtually no passage at all. They are often surrounded by small *satellite tombs*, presumably as their version of subsidiary chambers. Like court tombs, they have a strong tendency to be aligned on the rising sun, to the extent that at Newgrange, County Meath, by dint of a cunningly conceived 'roof-box' the rays of the rising sun penetrate to the back of the chamber at the winter solstice. The other great feature of passage tombs is the art with which many of the constituent stones are decorated.

pits: holes dug into the ground to receive burials of the Earlier Bronze Age; unlike *cists*, they are not lined with stones, though they may be covered with a stone. Between pits and totally encisted graves are many intermediary types, some with a single token stone. Like cists, they are often grouped into cemeteries.

porcellanite: a hard, fine-grained rock, usually speckled dark bluish-grey, particularly suitable for the manufacture of stone axes. It is known to occur at two locations, where there is extensive evidence of exploitation.

portal tombs: commonly believed to be derivatives of *court tombs* and especially of the subsidiary chambers or galleries of court tombs. The majority contain only a single chamber, while others have two. Some have rather vestigial courts. The grave-goods associated with them are similar to those associated with court tombs. Perhaps their most impressive features are the often enormous roof-slabs.

post-glacial: after the Ice Age.

scrapers: the most commonly found form of flint implement. There are many different forms—end scrapers, side scrapers, and hollow scrapers, to name but a few. They are usually believed to have been used mainly for woodworking or leatherworking.

siblings: cast metal objects whose size and shape indicate that they were cast in the same matrix.

tin (symbol Sn): a metallic element whose principal importance in prehistoric times was that, added to copper, it made the harder and stronger alloy known as bronze. It had formerly been assumed that the tin used by the Irish Earlier Bronze Age metalworkers must have been imported from Cornwall; recent research, however, has demonstrated that deposits of tin in County Wicklow would have been quite adequate to satisfy the needs of that industry.

urns: the larger type of pottery vessels of the Earlier Bronze Age in Ireland, normally—but not, apparently, exclusively —used for funerary purposes, which is why they were formerly described as '*cinerary urns*'. Several varieties exist: *collared urns, cordoned urns, encrusted urns,* and *vase urns.*

vases: the other main tradition of Earlier Bronze Age pottery. In contrast with *bowls*, the main lower part of their bodies displays a straight-sided profile.

Sources

General
Cooney, G., and Grogan, E., *Irish Prehistory: A Social Perspective*, Dublin 1994.

Flanagan, Laurence, *Ulster*, London 1970.

Flanagan, Laurence, *A Dictionary of Irish Archaeology*, Dublin 1992.

Herity, Michael, and Eogan, George, *Ireland in Prehistory*, London 1977.

Mallory, J., and McNeill, T., *The Archaeology of Ulster*, Belfast 1991.

Mitchell, Frank, and Ryan, Michael, *Reading the Irish Landscape*, Dublin 1977.

O'Kelly, M. J., *Early Ireland*, Cambridge 1989.

Ryan, Michael (ed.), *The Illustrated Archaeology of Ireland*, Dublin 1991.

Chapter 1
Ryan, Michael, 'An Early Mesolithic site in the Irish midlands', *Antiquity*, vol. 54 (1980).

Woodman, P., 'The post-glacial colonisation of Ireland: the human factors' in Donncha Ó Corráin (ed.), *Irish Antiquity*, Cork 1980.

Chapter 2
Movius, H., *The Irish Stone Age*, Cambridge 1942.

Woodman, P., 'Settlement patterns of the Irish Mesolithic', *Ulster Journal of Archaeology*, vol. 36–37 (1973–74).

Woodman, P., 'Recent excavations at Newferry, Co. Antrim', *Proceedings of the Prehistoric Society*, vol. 43 (1977).

Woodman, P., *The Mesolithic in Ireland*, Oxford 1978.

Woodman, P., *Excavations at Mount Sandel, 1973–77, Co. Londonderry*, Belfast 1985.

Woodman, P., Duggan, M., and McCarthy, A., 'Excavations at Ferriter's Cove: preliminary report', *Journal of the Kerry Archaeological and Historical Society*, vol. 17 (1984).

Chapter 3

Case, H., 'Irish Neolithic pottery: distribution and sequence', *Proceedings of the Prehistoric Society*, vol. 27 (1961).

Case, H., 'Foreign connections in the Irish Neolithic', *Ulster Journal of Archaeology*, vol. 26 (1963).

Case, H., 'Settlement patterns in the North Irish Neolithic', *Ulster Journal of Archaeology*, vol. 32 (1969).

Eogan, George, 'A Neolithic habitation-site and megalithic tomb in Townleyhall townland, Co. Louth', *Journal of the Royal Society of Antiquaries of Ireland*, vol. 93 (1963).

Evans, E. Estyn, *Lyles Hill: A Late Neolithic Site in Co. Antrim*, Belfast 1953.

Flanagan, Laurence, 'An unpublished flint hoard from the Braid Valley, Co. Antrim', *Ulster Journal of Archaeology*, vol. 9 (1966).

Flanagan, Laurence, 'Flint implements from Straleel, Co. Donegal', *Ulster Journal of Archaeology*, vol. 29 (1966).

Flanagan, Laurence, 'An enlarged hollow scraper from north Antrim', *Ulster Journal of Archaeology*, vol. 30 (1967).

Hartnett, P., and Eogan, George, 'Feltrim Hill, Co. Dublin: a Neolithic and Early Christian site', *Journal of the Royal Society of Antiquaries of Ireland*, vol. 94 (1964).

Jope, E., 'Porcellanite axes from factories in north-east Ireland: Tievebulliagh and Rathlin', *Ulster Journal of Archaeology*, vol. 15 (1952).

Waddell, J., 'The Irish Sea in prehistory', *Journal of Irish Archaeology*, vol. 6 (1991–92).

Chapter 4

Case, H., 'Settlement patterns in the Irish Neolithic', *Ulster Journal of Archaeology*, vol. 32 (1969).

Collins, A., 'The excavation of a double horned cairn at Audleystown, Co. Down', *Ulster Journal of Archaeology*, vol. 17 (1954).

Collins, A., 'A horned cairn at Ballynichol, Co. Down', *Ulster Journal of Archaeology*, vol. 19 (1956).

Collins, A., 'Edenmore chambered long cairn, Co. Down', *Ulster Journal of Archaeology*, vol. 22 (1959).

Collins, A., 'Further work at Audleystown long cairn, Co, Down', *Ulster Journal of Archaeology*, vol. 22 (1959).

Collins, A., 'Ballykeel dolmen and cairn', *Ulster Journal of Archaeology*, vol. 28 (1965).

Collins, A., 'Barnes Lower court cairn, Co. Tyrone', *Ulster Journal of Archaeology*, vol. 29 (1966).

Collins, A., 'A court grave at Ballinran, Co. Down', *Ulster Journal of Archaeology*, vol. 39 (1976).

Collins, A., 'Dooey's Cairn, Ballymacaldrack, Co. Antrim', *Ulster Journal of Archaeology*, vol. 39 (1976).

Collins, A., and Wilson, B., 'The excavation of a court cairn at Ballymacdermot, Co. Armagh', *Ulster Journal of Archaeology*, vol. 27 (1964).

Corcoran, J., 'The Carlingford culture', *Proceedings of the Prehistoric Society*, vol. 26 (1960).

Corcoran, J., 'Excavation of two chambered cairns at Kilnagarns Lower, Co. Leitrim', *Journal of the Royal Society of Antiquaries of Ireland*, vol. 94 (1964).

Davies, O., 'Excavations at Ballyrenan, Co. Tyrone', *Journal of the Royal Society of Antiquaries of Ireland*, vol. 67 (1937).

Davies, O., 'Excavation of a horned cairn at Aghanaglack, Co. Fermanagh', *Journal of the Royal Society of Antiquaries of Ireland*, vol. 69 (1939).

Davies, O., 'Excavations at Mourne Park', *Proceedings of the Belfast Natural History and Philosophical Society*, vol. 1 (1939).

Davies, O., 'Excavations at Legland horned cairn', *Proceedings of the Belfast Natural History and Philosophical Society* (1940).

Davies, O., 'Excavations at Ballyreagh, Co. Fermanagh', *Ulster Journal of Archaeology*, vol. 5 (1942).

Davies, O., 'Excavations at a horned cairn at Ballymarlagh, Co. Antrim', *Ulster Journal of Archaeology*, vol. 12 (1949).

Davies, O., and Evans, E. Estyn, 'Excavations at Goward, near Hilltown, Co. Down', *Proceedings of the Belfast Natural History and Philosophical Society* (1933–33).

Davies, O., and Evans, E. Estyn, 'Excavation of a chambered horned cairn at Ballyalton, Co. Down', *Proceedings of the Belfast Natural History and Philosophical Society* (1934).

Davies, O., and Evans, E. Estyn, 'The horned cairns of Ulster', *Ulster Journal of Archaeology*, vol. 6 (1943).

Davies, O., and Radford, C., 'Excavation of the horned cairn of Clady Halliday', *Proceedings of the Belfast Natural History and Philosophical Society* (1935).

de Valera, Ruaidhrí, 'The court cairns of Ireland', *Proceedings of the Royal Irish Academy*, vol. 60C (1960).

de Valera, Ruaidhrí, 'Transeptal court cairns', *Journal of the Royal Society of Antiquaries of Ireland*, vol. 95 (1965).

de Valera, Ruaidhrí, and Ó Nualláin, S., *Survey of the Megalithic Tombs of Ireland, I: Co. Clare*, Dublin 1961.

de Valera, Ruaidhrí, and Ó Nualláin, S., *Survey of the Megalithic Tombs of Ireland, II: Co. Mayo*, Dublin 1964.

de Valera, Ruaidhrí, and Ó Nualláin, S., *Survey of the Megalithic Tombs of Ireland, III: Cos. Galway, Roscommon, Leitrim, Longford, Westmeath, Laoighis, Offaly, Kildare, Cavan*, Dublin 1972.

de Valera, Ruaidhrí, and Ó Nualláin, S., *Survey of the Megalithic Tombs of Ireland, IV: Cos. Cork, Kerry, Limerick, Tipperary*, Dublin 1982.

Evans, E. Estyn, 'Excavations at Aghnaskeagh, Co. Louth: cairn A', *County Louth Archaeological Society Journal*, vol. 9 (1935).

Evans, E. Estyn, 'A chambered cairn in Ballyedmond Park, Co. Down', *Ulster Journal of Archaeology*, vol. 1 (1938).

Evans, E. Estyn, 'Doey's Cairn, Dunloy, Co. Antrim', *Ulster Journal of Archaeology*, vol. 1 (1938).

Evans, E. Estyn, 'Giants' graves', *Ulster Journal of Archaeology*, vol. 1 (1938).

Evans, E. Estyn, 'Excavations at Carnanbane, Co. Londonderry: a double horned cairn', *Proceedings of the Royal Irish Academy*, vol. 45C (1939).

Flanagan, Laurence, 'Court graves and portal graves', *Irish Archaeological Research Forum*, vol. 4 (1977).

Flanagan, Laurence, 'Re-excavations at Knockoneill, Co. Derry', *Ulster Journal of Archaeology*, vol. 43 (1980).

Flanagan, Laurence, and Flanagan, Deirdre, 'The excavation of a court cairn at Bavan, Co. Donegal', *Ulster Journal of Archaeology*, vol. 29 (1966).

Hawkes, J., 'Excavation of a megalithic tomb at Harristown, Co. Waterford', *Journal of the Royal Society of Antiquaries of Ireland*, vol. 71 (1941).

Hencken, H., 'A long cairn at Creevykeel, Co. Sligo', *Journal of the Royal Society of Antiquaries of Ireland*, vol. 69 (1939).

Herity, Michael, 'Irish decorated Neolithic pottery', *Proceedings of the Royal Irish Academy*, vol. 82C (1982).

Herity, Michael, 'The finds from Irish court tombs', *Proceedings of the Royal Irish Academy*, vol. 87C (1987).

Herring, I., 'The forecourt, Hanging Thorn Cairn, McIlwhan's Hill, Ballyutoag, Ligoneil', *Proceedings of the Belfast Natural History and Philosophical Society*, vol. 1 (1937).

Herring, I., 'The Tamnyrankin cairn: west structure', *Journal of the Royal Society of Antiquaries of Ireland*, vol. 71 (1941).

Herring, I., 'Knockoneill excavation, Co. Derry', *Archaeology. Newsletter*, vol. 9 (1949).

Kilbride-Jones, H., 'Double horned cairn at Cohaw, Co. Cavan', *Proceedings of the Royal Irish Academy*, vol. 54C (1951–52).

Kilbride-Jones, H., 'The excavation of a cairn with kennel-hole entrance at Corracloona, Co. Leitrim', *Proceedings of the Royal Irish Academy*, vol. 74C (1974).

O'Kelly, M. J., 'A horned cairn at Shanballyedmond, Co. Tipperary', *Journal of the Cork Historical and Archaeological Society*, vol. 63 (1958).

Ó Nualláin, S., 'A Neolithic house at Ballyglass, near Ballycastle, Co. Mayo', *Journal of the Royal Society of Antiquaries of Ireland*, vol. 102 (1972).

Ó Nualláin, S., 'The central court tombs of the north-west of Ireland', *Journal of the Royal Society of Antiquaries of Ireland*, vol. 106 (1976).

Ó Nualláin, S., 'Irish portal tombs: topography, siting and distribution', *Journal of the Royal Society of Antiquaries of Ireland*, vol. 113 (1983).

Powell, T., 'Excavation of a megalithic tomb at Ballynamona Lower, Co. Waterford', *Journal of the Royal Society of Antiquaries of Ireland*, vol. 68 (1938).

Waterman, D., 'The court cairn at Annaghmare, Co. Armagh', *Ulster Journal of Archaeology*, vol. 28 (1965).

Waterman, D., 'The excavation of a court cairn at Tully, Co. Fermanagh', *Ulster Journal of Archaeology*, vol. 41 (1978).

Chapter 5

Ap Simon, A., 'An Early Neolithic house in Co. Tyrone', *Journal of the Royal Society of Antiquaries of Ireland*, vol. 99 (1969).

Brennan, B., *The Stars and the Stones: Ancient Art and Astronomy in Ireland*, London 1983.

Patrick, J., 'Megalithic exegesis: a comment', *Irish Archaeological Research Forum*, vol. 2 (1975).

Chapter 6

Addyman, P., 'Coney Island, Lough Neagh: prehistoric settlement, Anglo-Norman castle and Elizabethan native fortress', *Ulster Journal of Archaeology*, vol. 28 (1965).

Ap Simon, A., 'The Earlier Bronze Age in the north of Ireland', *Ulster Journal of Archaeology*, vol. 32 (1969).

Case, H., 'Were Beaker People the first metallurgists in Ireland?', *Palaeohistoria*, vol. 12 (1966).

Case, H., 'settlement patterns in the north Irish Neolithic', *Ulster Journal of Archaeology*, vol. 32 (1969).

Chitty, L., 'A beaker-like vessel from Bushmills, Co. Antrim', *Antiquaries' Journal*, vol. 13 (1933).

Clarke, D., *Beaker Pottery in Great Britain and Ireland*, Cambridge 1970.

Coghlan, H., 'A note on Irish copper ores and metals', *Ores and Metals*, London 1963.

Coghlan, H., and Case, H., 'Early metallurgy of copper in Ireland and Britain', *Proceedings of the Prehistorical Society*, vol. 23 (1957).

Davies, O., 'Excavations at the Giant's Grave, Loughash', *Ulster Journal of Archaeology*, vol. 2 (1939).

Davies, O., and Mullin, J., 'The excavation of Cashelbane Cairn, Loughash, Co. Tyrone', *Journal of the Royal Society of Antiquaries of Ireland*, vol. 70 (1940).

Eogan, George, *Excavations at Knowth, I: Smaller Passage Tombs, Neolithic Occupation and Beaker Activity*, Dublin 1984.

Eogan, George, 'Prehistoric and early historic culture change at Brugh na Bóinne', *Proceedings of the Royal Irish Academy*, vol. 91C (1991).

Evans, E. Estyn, *Lyles Hill: A Late Neolithic Site in County Antrim*, Belfast 1953.

Flanagan, Laurence, 'Archaeological acquisitions of Irish origin, 1962', *Ulster Journal of Archaeology*, vol. 27 (1964).

Flanagan, Laurence, 'Court graves and portal graves', *Irish Archaeological Forum*, vol. 4 (1977).

Flanagan, Laurence, 'Re-excavations at Knockoneill, Co. Derry', *Ulster Journal of Archaeology*, vol. 43 (1980).

Flanagan, Laurence, 'Some aspects of the composition of Irish Earlier Bronze Age bronze implements' in Donnchadh Ó Corráin (ed.), *Irish Antiquity*, Cork 1981.

Grogan, Eoin, and Eogan, George, 'Lough Gur excavations by Seán Ó Ríordáin: further Neolithic and Beaker habitations on Knockadoon', *Proceedings of the Royal Irish Academy*, vol. 87 (1987).

Harbison, Peter, 'Mining and metallurgy in Early Bronze Age Ireland', *North Munster Antiquarian Journal*, vol. 10 (1966).

Harbison, Peter, 'Catalogue of Irish Early Bronze Age associated finds containing copper and bronze', *Proceedings of the Royal Irish Academy*, vol. 87C (1968).

Herring, I., 'Cairn excavations at Well Glass Spring, Largantea, Co. Londonderry', *Proceedings of the Belfast Natural History and Philosophical Society*, vol. 1 (1938).

Herring, I. and May, A., 'Cloghnagalla Cairn, Boviel, Co. Londonderry', *Ulster Journal of Archaeology*, vol. 3 (1939).

Liversage, D., 'Excavations at Dalkey Island, Co. Dublin, 1956–1959', *Proceedings of the Royal Irish Academy*, vol. 66C (1968).

Madden, A., 'Beaker pottery in Ireland', *Journal of the Kerry Archaeological and Historical Society*, vol. 1 (1968).

May, A., 'Cornaclery round cairn, Ballydullaghan, Co. Londonderry', *Journal of the Royal Society of Antiquaries of Ireland*, vol. 72 (1942).

May, A., 'Burial mounds, circles and cairn, Gortcorbies, Co. Londonderry', *Journal of the Royal Society of Antiquaries of Ireland*, vol. 77 (1947).

May, A., 'Two Neolithic hearths, Gortcorbies, Co. Londonderry', *Ulster Journal of Archaeology*, vol. 13 (1950).

Ó Ríordáin, Seán P., 'Lough Gur excavations: the great stone circle (B) in Grange townland', *Proceedings of the Royal Irish Academy*, vol. 54C (1951).

Ó Ríordáin, Seán P., 'Lough Gur excavations: Neolithic and Bronze Age houses on Knockadoon', *Proceedings of the Royal Irish Academy*, vol. 56C (1954).

Ó Ríordáin, Seán P., and Ó hÍceadh, G., 'Lough Gur excavations: the megalithic tomb', *Journal of the Royal Society of Antiquaries of Ireland*, vol. 85 (1955).

Pollock, A., and Waterman, D., 'A Bronze Age habitation site at Downpatrick', *Ulster Journal of Archaeology*, vol. 27 (1964).

Scott, B., and Francis, P., 'Native copper in Ulster' in Donnchadh Ó Corráin (ed.), *Irish Antiquity*, Cork 1981.

Simpson, D., 'A stone battle axe from Co. Cork,' *Journal of the Cork Historical and Archaeological Society*, vol. 95 (1990).

Simpson, D., 'The stone battle axes of Ireland', *Journal of the Royal Society of Antiquaries of Ireland*, vol. 120 (1990).

Stout, Geraldine, 'Embanked enclosures of the Boyne Valley', *Proceedings of the Royal Irish Academy*, vol. 92C (1992).

Sweetman, P., 'An earthen enclosure at Monknewtown, Slane, Co. Meath', *Proceedings of the Royal Irish Academy*, vol. 76C (1976).

Chapter 7

Addyman, P., 'Coney Island, Lough Neagh: prehistoric settlement, Anglo-Norman castle and Elizabethan native fortress', *Ulster Journal of Archaeology*, vol. 28 (1965).

Brannon, N., Williams, B., and Williamson, J., 'The salvage excavations of Bronze Age cists, Straid townland, Co. Londonderry' *Ulster Journal of Archaeology*, vol. 53 (1990).

Buckley, Laureen, 'Bronze Age backache', *Archaeology Ireland*, vol. 39 (1997).

Coffey, George, 'The distribution of gold lunulae in Ireland and western Europe', *Proceedings of the Royal Irish Academy*, vol. 27C (1909).

Coffey, George, *The Bronze Age in Ireland*, Dublin 1913.

Coffey, George, and Plunkett, T., 'Report on the excavation of Topped Mountain Cairn', *Proceedings of the Royal Irish Academy*, vol. 20 (1898).

Coghlan, H., and Case, H., 'Early metallurgy of copper in Ireland and Britain', *Proceedings of the Prehistorical Society*, vol. 23 (1957).

Collins, A., 'Excavations in the sandhills at Dundrum, Co. Down, 1950–51', *Ulster Journal of Archaeology*, vol. 15 (1953).

Collins, A., 'Cremation burials from Cos. Armagh and Londonderry', *Ulster Journal of Archaeology*, vol. 28 (1965).

Collins, A., and Evans, E. Estyn, 'A cist burial at Carrickinab, Co. Down', *Ulster Journal of Archaeology*, vol. 31 (1968).

Evans, E. Estyn, *Lyles Hill: A Late Neolithic Site in County Antrim*, Belfast 1953.

Evans, E. Estyn, and Megaw, B., 'The multiple cist cairn at Mount Stewart, Co. Down', *Proceedings of the Prehistorical Society*, vol. 3 (1937).

Flanagan, Laurence, 'Wessex and Ireland in the Early and Middle Bronze Ages', *Berichte des Fünften Internationalen Kongress für Vor und Frühgeschichte* (Hamburg, 1958), 1961.

Flanagan, Laurence, 'The composition of Irish Bronze Age cemeteries', *Irish Archaeological Research Forum*, vol. 3 (1976).

Flanagan, Laurence, 'Industrial resources, production and distribution in Earlier Bronze Age Ireland' in Michael Ryan (ed.), *The Origins of Metallurgy in Atlantic Europe: Proceedings of the Fifth Atlantic Colloquium*, Dublin 1978.

Glover, W., 'A prehistoric bow fragment from Drumwhinny Bog, Kesh, Co. Fermanagh', *Proceedings of the Prehistorical Society*, vol. 45 (1979).

Harbison, Peter, *The Axes of the Early Bronze Age in Ireland*, Munich 1969.

Harbison, Peter, *The Daggers and Halberds of the Earlier Bronze Age in Ireland*, Munich 1969.

Hencken, H., and Movius, H., 'The cemetery-cairn of Knockast', *Proceedings of the Royal Irish Academy*, vol. 41C (1934).

Kavanagh, R., 'The encrusted urn in Ireland', *Proceedings of the Royal Irish Academy*, vol. 73C (1973).

Kavanagh, R., 'Collared and cordoned cinerary urns in Ireland', *Proceedings of the Royal Irish Academy*, vol. 76C (1976).

Kavanagh, R., 'Pygmy cups in Ireland', *Journal of the Royal Society of Antiquaries of Ireland*, vol. 107 (1977).

Magee, R., 'Faience beads of the Irish Bronze Age', *Archaeomaterials*, vol. 7 (1993).

Ó Ríordáin, B., and Waddell, J., *The Funerary Bowls and Vases of the Irish Bronze Age*, Galway 1993.

Ó Ríordáin, Seán P., 'Lough Gur excavations: Neolithic and Bronze Age houses on Knockadoon', *Proceedings of the Royal Irish Academy*, vol. 56C (1954).

Taylor, J., 'The relationship of British Early Bronze Age gold-work to Atlantic Europe' in Michael Ryan (ed.), *The Origins of Metallurgy in Atlantic Europe: Proceedings of the Fifth Atlantic Colloquium*, Dublin 1978.

Waddell, J., 'Irish Bronze Age cists: a survey', *Journal of the Royal Society of Antiquaries of Ireland*, vol. 100 (1970).

Waddell, J., *The Bronze Age Burials of Ireland*, Galway 1990.

Warner, R., 'Irish prehistoric goldwork: a provisional analysis', *Archaeomaterials*, vol. 7 (1993).

Waterman, D., and Waddell, J., 'A Bronze Age cist-cemetery at Stranagalwilly, Co. Tyrone', *Ulster Journal of Archaeology*, vol. 56 (1993).

Williams, B., Wilkinson, J., and Magee, R., 'Bronze Age burials at Kilcroagh, Co. Antrim', *Ulster Journal of Archaeology*, vol. 54–55 (1991–92).

Chapter 8

Boreland, D., 'Late Bronze Age pottery from Haughey's Fort', *Emania*, vol. 14 (1996).

Coles, J., 'European Bronze Age shields', *Proceedings of the Prehistoric Society*, vol. 28 (1962).

Coles, J., 'Irish Bronze Age horns and their relations with north Europe', *Proceedings of the Prehistoric Society*, vol. 29 (1963).

Coles, J., 'Some Irish horns of the Late Bronze Age', *Journal of the Royal Society of Antiquaries of Ireland*, vol. 97 (1967).

Collins, A., and Seaby, W., 'Structures and small finds discovered at Lough Eskragh, Co. Tyrone', *Ulster Journal of Archaeology*, vol. 23 (1960).

Eogan, George, *Catalogue of Irish Bronze Swords*, Dublin 1965.

Eogan, George, *Hoards of the Irish Later Bronze Age*, Dublin 1983.

Eogan, George, 'Pins of the Irish Late Bronze Age', *Journal of the Royal Society of Antiquaries of Ireland*, vol. 104 (1974).

Eogan, George, 'The Later Bronze Age in the light of recent research', *Proceedings of the Prehistoric Society*, vol. 30 (1964).

Hawkes, C., and Smith, M., 'On some buckets and cauldrons of the Bronze and Early Iron Ages', *Antiquaries' Journal*, vol. 37 (1957).

Hawthorne, M., 'A preliminary analysis of wood remains from Haughey's Fort', *Emania*, vol. 8 (1991).

Hodges, H., 'A hunting camp at Cullyhanna Lough near Newtown Hamilton, Co. Armagh', *Ulster Journal of Archaeology*, vol. 21 (1958).

Holmes, P., 'The manufacturing technology of the Irish Bronze Age horns' in Michael Ryan (ed.), *The Origins of Metallurgy in Atlantic Europe*, Dublin 1979.

Lucas, A. T., 'Prehistoric block-wheels from Doogarymore, Co. Roscommon, and Timahoe East, Co. Kildare', *Journal of the Royal Society of Antiquaries of Ireland*, vol. 102 (1972).

Lynn, C., 'Navan Fort: a draft summary of D. M. Waterman's excavations', *Emania*, vol. 1 (1986).

Mallory, J., 'Excavations at Haughey's Fort', *Emania*, vol. 8 (1991).

Mallory, J., 'Haughey's Fort and the Navan Complex in the Late Bronze Age' in J. Waddell and E. Twohig (eds.), *Ireland in the Bronze Age*, Dublin 1995.

Mallory, J., 'Trial excavations at Haughey's Fort', *Emania*, vol. 4 (1988).

Neill, Marie, 'Haughey's Fort excavation, 1991: analysis of wood remains', *Emania*, vol. 14 (1996).

Proudfoot, V., 'A second gold find from Downpatrick', *Ulster Journal of Archaeology*, vol. 20 (1957).

Proudfoot, V., *The Downpatrick Gold Find*, Belfast 1955.

Raftery, B., 'Rathgall, Co. Wicklow: 1970 excavations', *Antiquity*, vol. 45 (1971).

Raftery, B., 'Rathgall: a Late Bronze Age burial in Ireland', *Antiquity*, vol. 47 (1973).

Raftery, B., 'Two recently discovered bronze shields from the Shannon basin', *Journal of the Royal Society of Antiquaries of Ireland*, vol. 112 (1982).

Williams, B., 'Excavations at Lough Eskragh, Co. Tyrone', *Ulster Journal of Archaeology*, vol. 41 (1978).

INDEX TO PLACES IN IRELAND

Index of Objects